Prentice Hall LITERATURE

PENGUIN EDITION

Unit One Resources

Grade Seven

PEARSON

Upper Saddle River, New Jersey
Boston, Massachusetts
Chandler, Arizona
Glenview, Illinois

BQ Tunes Credits
Keith London, Defined Mind, Inc., Executive Producer
Mike Pandolfo, Wonderful, Producer
All songs mixed and mastered by Mike Pandolfo, Wonderful
Vlad Gutkovich, Wonderful, Assistant Engineer
Recorded November 2007 – February 2008 in SoHo, New York City, at
Wonderful, 594 Broadway

ISBN–13: 978-0-13-366435-5
ISBN–10:   0-13-366435-X
8 9 10 V011 12

CC

CONTENTS

Unit 1 Resources: Fiction and Nonfiction

About the Unit Resources

The *Prentice Hall Literature Unit Resources* provide manageable, comprehensive, and easy-to-use teaching materials to support each Student Edition unit. You can use these resources to address your students' different ability levels and learning styles, customize instruction to suit your teaching needs, and diagnose and assess student progress. All of these materials are also available at *PHLitOnline*, a rich, online source of personalized instruction and activities.

Here is a brief description of each element of the *Unit Resources*:

UNIT-LEVEL FEATURES

Big Questions (grades 6–10)

Support for the Big Questions includes complete lyrics to BQ Tunes (engaging songs that incorporate Big Question Vocabulary; available on CD); unit-opener worksheets that practice Big Question Vocabulary, an Applying the Big Question chart, re-rendered from the Student Edition.

Essential Questions (The American Experience; The British Tradition)

Support for the Essential Questions includes unit-opener worksheets that focus on each Essential Question individually and a worksheet to support the end-of-unit Essential Question Workshop.

Skills Concept Maps

Each map presents a graphic look at the relationship between the literature and the skills taught in the unit, with space provided for students' notes.

Vocabulary Workshop, Writing Workshop, and Communications Workshop support

End-of-unit worksheets provide opportunities for students to practice vocabulary, and gather and organize information for their Student Edition assignments.

SELECTION-LEVEL SUPPORT

Vocabulary and Reading Warmups

These exercises and easy reading passages provide selection vocabulary practice for students reading at one or two levels below grade level

Writing About the Big Question (grades 6–10)

These worksheets tie the Big Question to individual selections, while giving students additional practice using the Big Question Vocabulary.

Literary Analysis, Reading, and Vocabulary Builder

A series of worksheets that provide extra practice on each of the main skill strands in the Student Edition. You can find more support for the Literary Analysis and Reading strands in the separate Graphic Organizers Transparencies component.

Integrated Language Skills

The Student Edition Integrated Language Skills features are supported by grammar worksheets and additional pages containing graphic organizers and questions to help students gather and organize information to complete their Student Edition Writing and Listening and Speaking or Research and Technology assignments.

Enrichment

These activities give opportunities for advanced students to focus more closely on topics related to the content or theme of the literature selection.

Unit 1 Resources: Fiction and Nonfiction
ix

ASSESSMENT

Diagnostic Tests

The beginning of each Unit 1 Resources book features a Diagnostic Test. Thereafter, each even-numbered Benchmark Test ends with a 20-question diagnostic component called Vocabulary in Context. Teachers desiring a larger sample for measuring students' reading ability can find an additional 20 questions at *PHLitOnline*.

Benchmark Tests

Twelve Benchmark Tests, spaced evenly throughout the year, assess students' mastery of literary, reading, vocabulary, grammar, and writing skills. A diagnostic Vocabulary in Context, described above, ends each even-numbered Benchmark Test.

Open-Book Tests

For every selection or grouping of selections, there is an Open-Book Test featuring short-answer and extended-response questions and opportunities for oral response. Most Open-Book-Tests also contain a question requiring students to represent information in a graphic organizer. These tests are available as a computer test bank on CD-ROM and at *PHLitOnline*.

Selection Tests

For every selection or grouping of selections, there are two closed-book Selection Tests (A and B) featuring multiple-choice and essay questions. Both tests assess essentially the same material; however Test A is designed for lower-level students, and Test B is designed for students average and above.

ADDITIONAL SUPPORT IN *UNIT ONE RESOURCES*

Pronunciation Guide

A two-page student guide to understanding diacritical marks given in standard dictionary pronunciations; includes practice

Form for Analyzing Primary Source Documents

In support of Primary Sources features in *The American Experience* and *The British Tradition*, a form for analyzing various types of primary sources.

Teaching Guides

To support fluency monitoring, Guide for Assessing Fluency; to support vocabulary instruction through music, a Guide for Teaching with BQ Tunes.

Name _____ Date _____

Guide for Assessing Fluency

The students' *All-in-One Workbooks* feature a series of twelve expository and narrative reading passages to be used to assess reading fluency. The passages have lexiles of increasing difficulty within the grade level range. They are designed to test students' reading accuracy and pace. An optional question is provided to assess comprehension.

The following oral reading rates are recommended goals:

ORAL READING RATES	
Grade	**Words per Minute**
6	115–145 with 90% accuracy
7	147–167 with 90% accuracy
8	156–171 with 90% accuracy
9–10	180–200 with 90% accuracy

Instructional Routine

- Hold reading practice sessions. Choose an appropriate practice passage of about 250 words from the literature students are studying or from another source. You will find a lexile score for each literature selection in your *Teacher's Edition* Time and Resource Managers. You may also use as practice passages the Warm-ups in the *Unit Resources* books and, for grade 6–8, articles in the *Discoveries* series and *Real-Life Readings*.

- Students should read the passage once silently, noting any unfamiliar words. Have them define or explain those words before reading the passage aloud. (Students may add these words to a *Word Wall* later.)

- Then, have students work in pairs to rehearse their oral fluency. (Alternatively, you may lead the class in a choral reading of a single passage.)

- After students have read the passage(s) with understanding, they may time themselves or each other for practice before the formal timed readings are conducted.

Formal Fluency Assessment

- From the students' All-in-One workbook, select a passage at the appropriate lexile level.

- Using an audio recorder, instruct the student to read the passage aloud at a normal pace. Alternatively, you may ask the student to read as you follow along, marking the text. Time the student for one minute.

- Note these types of errors: mispronunciations, omissions, reversals, substitutions, and words with which you have to help the student, after waiting two or three seconds.

- Mark the point in the passage that the student reaches after one minute.

- Use the formula below for determining accuracy and rate.

- Determine the rate by calculating the total number of WCPM (word correct per minute) and comparing the student's results against the goals indicate in the chart above.

- Analyze the results and create a plan for continued student improvement.

Guide for Assessing Fluency

Calculating Fluency

Use this formula to calculate reading fluency:

> Total words read correctly (both correctly read and self-corrected) in one minute *divided by* total words read (words read correctly + errors) × 100 = % accuracy

$$\frac{\text{number of words read correctly}}{\text{number of words read}} \times 100 = \text{WCPM}$$

Example:
$$\frac{137}{145} \times 100 = 94\%$$

Post-reading Comprehension Activity

A short test item allows you quickly to assess student's comprehension. The items include these formats:

- matching
- fill-in-the-blank
- true/false
- short answer

If the student demonstrates difficulty in understanding the passage, you may remediate using selected leveled resources in the *Prentice Hall Literature* program. These components include the Vocabulary and Reading Warm-ups in the *Unit Resources;* the *Reading Kit* Practice and Assess pages, which are aligned with specific skills; and the scaffolded support for comprehension and other ELA skills in the *Reader's Notebooks: Adapted* and *English Learner's Versions.*

Name _____ Date _____

Pronunciation Key Practice—1

Throughout your textbook, you will find vocabulary features that include pronunciation for each new word. In order to pronounce the words correctly, you need to understand the symbols used to indicate different sounds.

Short Vowel Sounds

These sounds are shown with no markings at all:

a   as in at, cap   e   as in end, feather, very
i   as in it, gym, ear   u   as in mud, ton, trouble

Long Vowel Sounds

These sounds are shown with a line over the vowel:

ā   as in ate, rain, break   ē   as in see, steam, piece
ī   as in nice, lie, sky   ō   as in no, oat, low

A. DIRECTIONS: *Read aloud the sounds indicated by the symbols in each item. Then write the word the symbols stand for.*

1. kap _____   6. ker _____
2. kāp _____   7. wird _____
3. tīp _____   8. swet _____
4. klōz _____   9. swēt _____
5. tuf _____   10. nīt _____

Other Vowel Sounds

Notice the special markings used to show the following vowel sounds:

ä   as in father, far, heart   ô   as in all, law, taught
ʊʊ   as in look, would, pull   ōō   as in boot, drew, tune
yōō as in cute, few, use   oi   as in oil, toy, royal
ʊu   as in out, now   ʉ   as in her, sir, word

B. DIRECTIONS: *Read aloud the sounds indicated by the symbols in each item. Then write the word the symbols stand for.*

1. boi _____   6. wʉrk _____
2. kär _____   7. lʉr _____
3. kʊʊd _____   8. kôt _____
4. lōōz _____   9. myōō _____
5. krʊun _____   10. rä _____

Pronunciation Key Practice—2

Some Special Consonant Sounds

These consonant sounds are shown by special two-letter combinations:

hw as in which, white

sh as in shell, mission, fiction

ŋ as in ring, anger, pink

ch as in chew, nature

zh as in vision, treasure

th as in threw, nothing

th as in then, mother

Syllables and Accent Marks

Your textbook will show you how to break a word into syllables, or parts, so that you can pronounce each part correctly. An accent mark (») shows you which syllable to stress when you pronounce a word. Notice the differences in the way you say the following words:

bā´ bē   ō bā´   den´ im   dē nī´

Sounds in Unaccented Syllables

You will often see the following special symbols used in unaccented syllables. The most common is the schwa (ß), which shows an unaccented "uh" sound:

ə as in ago, conceited, category, invisible

'l as in cattle, paddle

'n as in sudden, hidden

Light and Heavy Accents

Some long words have two stressed syllables: a heavy stress on one syllable and a second, lighter stress on another syllable. The lighter stress is shown by an accent mark in lighter type, like this: («)

C. DIRECTIONS: *With a partner, read aloud the sounds indicated by the symbols in each item. Say the words that the symbols stand for.*

1. kôr´əs
2. kən pash´ən
3. brē´ *th*iŋ
4. ig nôrd´

5. mezh´ ər
6. des´ pər ā´ shən
7. im´ə choor´
8. plunj´ iŋ

9. fər bid´ 'n
10. hwim´ pər
11. fun´ də ment´ 'l
12. rek´ əg nīz«

D. DIRECTIONS: *With a partner, read aloud the sounds indicated by the symbols in the following lines. Each group of lines represent the words of a small poem.*

1. ī ēt mī pēz wi*th* hun´ ē.
   īv dun it ôl mī līf.
   it māks *th*ə pēz tāst fun´ ē.
   but it kēps *th*em än *th*ə nīf.

2. dōnt wɹr´ ē if yoor jäb iz smôl
   and yoor ri wôrdz´ är fyoo.
   ri mem´ bər *that* *th*ə mīt´ ē ōk
   wuz wuns ə nut līk yoo.

BQ Tunes Activities

Use **BQ Tunes** to engage students in learning each unit's Big Question vocabulary and introduce the issue that the Big Question raises. You can access **BQ Tunes** recordings and lyrics at *PHLitOnline* or in *Hear It*, the Prentice Hall Audio Program. The lyrics are also provided in your **Unit Resources** books and in the students' **All-in-One Workbooks**. Below are suggested activities for using the songs with your class. Each activity takes 20–25 minutes. Students should have copies of the lyrics available.

Listening Exercise

OBJECTIVE: *To familiarize students with the song vocabulary and initiate discussion of definitions*

1. Instruct students to listen to the selected song, listing words they do not know.
2. Play the selected song.
3. Afterward, ask students to raise their hands if they know the definitions of words they listed, and call on individuals to share their definitions. Write the words on the board as they are called out.
4. Then, ask students to share words for which they did *not* know the definitions, and call on them individually. Write the words on the board as they are called out.
5. Direct students to turn to the selected lyrics and instruct students to infer definitions for the remaining words in the lyrics. If they experience difficulty, encourage them to work in pairs or direct them to a dictionary.
6. Play song again, and instruct students to read the lyrics to reinforce the exercise.

Vocabulary Game Exercise

OBJECTIVE: *To reinforce students' knowledge of Big Question vocabulary in the songs, and to initiate class discussion of definitions.*

1. Divide the students into two teams, each on one side of the room.
2. Play the selected song to the class. Then, play it again as students follow along reading the lyrics.
3. Afterward, read the song's lyrics aloud and, alternating sides, ask each team to define key words as you come upon them. Award a point for each correct definition.
4. Write the words on the board as they are defined, and keep score as the teams win points.
5. Declare the team with the most points the winners.
6. Review vocabulary missed by both teams, and field any questions the students may have.

BQ Tunes Activities

Writing Exercise, Stage 1

OBJECTIVE: *To build students' writing skills, leveraging newly acquired vocabulary*

1. Instruct students to write three contextual sentences, each using a single vocabulary word present in the selected song. The sentences *do not* have to be related to one another.
2. Allow 5 to 7 minutes for students to complete the task.
3. Afterward, ask random students to read what they have composed.
4. Then, ask the class if the sentences satisfied the "contextual" criteria, and discuss the responses.
5. Repeat with as many students as time permits.
6. Field any questions the students may have.

Writing Exercise, Stage 2

OBJECTIVE: *To build students' composition skills, leveraging newly acquired vocabulary*

1. Instruct students to write three contextual sentences, each using a single vocabulary word present in the selected song. The sentences *must* be related to one another, as in a paragraph.
2. Allow 5 to 7 minutes for students to complete the task.
3. Afterward, ask random students to read what they've composed.
4. Then, ask the class if the sentences satisfied the "contextual" criteria and the "relationship" criteria, and discuss the responses.
5. Repeat with as many students as time permits.
6. Field any questions the students may have.

BQ Tunes

Truth, performed by Becca Schack

Awareness is what we need
to know what's going on
Don't leave me in the dark
all common sense gone
What we **perceive**
is not always real
What we understand
not always the deal

Come on and shed some light
Deliver more **insight**
Come on and shed some light
so we can do what's right

Can we find the **truth**
When the answers are hidden
How do we see through
Behind the eyes of deception
Reach deep inside
and you will find
what you're looking for
what you're looking for

We can spend all night
in a heated **debate**
If we don't share our ideas

how can we collaborate
Explain all the reasons why
you do the things you do
So we can **evalulate** the situation
You see it's all about communication

Continued

Factual or **fiction**
Truth or contradiction
Real or fabrication
Aware of your own creation

Can we find the **truth**
When the answers are hidden
How do we see through
Behind the eyes of deception
Reach deep inside
and you will find
what you're looking for
what you're looking for

Child, please don't be confused
Just take my hand and let me show you
It can be simple or it can be hard
The answer often lies within you

Reveal yourself
Come show me who you are
Convince me to believe
No need to go too far
In the end I will **conclude**
a resolution
I'll have made up my mind
and know just what to do
The **evidence** will show
Help us really know
What's **believable** or crazy
Is it a dream or reality

Can we find the **truth**
When the answers are hidden
How do we see through
Behind the eyes of deception
Reach deep inside
and you will find
what you're looking for
what you're looking for

Continued

Song Title: **Truth**

Artist / Performed by Becca Schack

Lyrics by Becca Schack

Music composed by Mike Pandolfo

Produced by Mike Pandolfo, Wonderful

Executive Producer: Keith London, Defined Mind

Name _____   Date _____

Unit 1: Fiction and Nonfiction
Big Question Vocabulary—1

The Big Question: Is there ever truth in fiction?

conclude: *v.* bring something to an end; other form: *conclusion*

convince: *v.* persuade someone to agree; sway someone's thinking; other form: *convincing*

evaluate: *v.* judge how good or successful something is; other forms: *evaluation, evaluating*

perceive: *v.* see or recognize something; discover; identify; other forms: *perception, perceptive*

reveal: *v.* uncover a secret; make something known; other forms: *revealing, revealed*

DIRECTIONS: *Review the vocabulary words and their definitions shown above. Then answer each question.*

1. Mr. Sanchez is a judge for the school talent show. As he watches each act in the show, which of these verbs **best** describes what he must do? Explain your answer. _____
   _____

2. Ms. Chang is directing the weekly meeting of the Teachers' Association. The meeting is almost over. Which verb **best** describes what she should do? Explain your answer. _____
   _____

3. The detective learned the secret identity of the Midnight Thief. He wanted to tell the newspapers the news. Which verb **best** describes what he will do? Explain your answer.
   _____

4. Joanne wants her classmates to be as concerned as she is about global warming. Which verb **best** describes what she should do? Explain your answer. _____
   _____

5. The fog made it difficult for us to see the mountain. Which verb **best** describes what we were trying to do? Explain your answer. _____
   _____

Unit 1: Fiction and Nonfiction
Big Question Vocabulary—2

The Big Question: Is there ever truth in fiction?

awareness: *n.* a person's knowledge or understanding of a situation; other forms: *aware, unaware*

debate: *n.* a discussion between people with opposite views

      v. discuss different views on a subject; other form: *debatable*

evidence: *n.* facts, objects, or signs that prove that something is true; other form: *evident*

fiction: *n.* stories about imaginary people and events; other forms: *fictitious, fictional*

reality: *n.* what actually happens or is true; real life; other forms: *real, realism*

A. DIRECTIONS: *Review the vocabulary words listed above. On the line that precedes each question, write **Yes** or **No** to answer it. Then explain your response on the line that follows it.*

_____**1.** Would a book of *fiction* be the best source for facts about George Washington?

_____

_____**2.** Would photographs and eyewitness reports serve as reliable *evidence* regarding what happened at a sporting event?

_____

_____**3.** At a *debate*, are all participants expected to share the same opinion?

_____

B. DIRECTIONS: *Follow each of the directions.*

1. Explain the difference between **fiction** and **reality**. Give an example of each.

_____

_____

_____

2. Give three pieces of **evidence** that would raise someone's **awareness** of a fire. _____

_____

_____

_____

Unit 1: Fiction and Nonfiction
Big Question Vocabulary—3

The Big Question: Is there ever truth in fiction?

believable: *adj.* able to be believed; other forms: *belief, believe, believer, believably, disbelief*

explain: *v.* describe or demonstrate something in a way that makes it clear and understandable; other form: *explanation*

factual: *adj.* based on facts; truthful; other form: *fact*

insight: *n.* personal understanding or wisdom on a subject; other form: *insightful*

truth: *n.* what can be proved, based on facts; other forms: *true, truly*

A. DIRECTIONS: *For each vocabulary word, list three things or reasons as instructed. Then, use the vocabulary word in a sentence about one of the things or reasons.*

Example: List three things that are examples of **fiction.**

a story about elves   a story about talking horses   a story about flying cats

Sentence: *In the story, the cats built an airplane and flew to a planet ruled by mice.*

---

1. List three things about cats that are *believable.*

_____   _____   _____

Sentence: _____

2. List three things about your school that are *factual.*

_____   _____   _____

Sentence: _____

3. Give three reasons for *explaining* safety rules to young children.

_____   _____   _____

Sentence: _____

4. List three *insights* you have about the importance of friendship.

_____   _____   _____

Sentence: _____

5. List three *truths* about trees.

_____   _____   _____

Sentence: _____

Name _____ Date _____

Unit 1: Fiction and Nonfiction
Applying the Big Question

Is there ever truth in fiction?

DIRECTIONS: *Complete the chart below to apply what you have learned about finding truth in fiction. One row has been completed for you.*

Example	Facts	Where facts are found	How the facts are revealed	How facts connect to fiction	What I learned
From Literature	Jewish families were killed and all Jews had to wear stars.	These facts were in the story "Suzy and Leah".	Suzy read Leah's journal, and Suzy's mother explained the treatment of the Jews.	The characters Suzy and Leah are fictional characters.	Some fictional stories include historical facts that can be proven.
From Literature					
From Science					
From Social Studies					
From Real Life					

Name _____ Date _____

Diagnostic Test

Identify the answer choice that best completes the statement.

1. We sat around the fire and _____ hot dogs.
   A. released
   B. ripped
   C. roasted
   D. relaxed

2. He was not pleased with her actions and gave her a _____ look.
   A. failing
   B. muffling
   C. awakening
   D. withering

3. Parents want their children to study hard and get a good _____ .
   A. situation
   B. education
   C. concentration
   D. college

4. Since Maria moved across town, I _____ see her.
   A. seldom
   B. merely
   C. generally
   D. naturally

5. I gave my niece a quarter, and she _____ it in her hand.
   A. pecked
   B. tagged
   C. clutched
   D. formed

6. They went to the park and _____ slowly along the paths.
   A. lurched
   B. swayed
   C. perched
   D. strolled

7. Come and sit down next to me on this nice soft _____ .
   A. staircase
   B. sofa
   C. balcony
   D. dam

8. This book was written by my favorite_____ .
   A. waiter
   B. author
   C. narrator
   D. boarder

9. When I sent her the invitation, she_____ very quickly.
   A. reassured
   B. resigned
   C. responded
   D. referred

10. Mom arranged her vacation pictures in this_____ .
    A. photograph
    B. film
    C. diary
    D. album

11. The_____ of ducks marched down the road to the pond.
    A. covey
    B. grove
    C. gallery
    D. bulk

12. His favorite shirt is colorful and_____ .
    A. prickly
    B. tame
    C. striped
    D. cuffs

13. After the players lost the championship game, they were_____ .
    A. discouraged
    B. deceived
    C. discovered
    D. drenched

14. In spite of the storm, the boat was safe because it was_____ .
    A. anchored
    B. slackened
    C. erected
    D. groped

15. Our country is a_____ of fifty states.
    A. federal
    B. standard
    C. union
    D. civilization

16. The landscapers of the new golf course used a special _____ .
    A. tee
    B. hedge
    C. backyard
    D. turf

17. When Alan received his check, he _____ took it to the bank.
    A. promptly
    B. ordinarily
    C. apparently
    D. absolutely

18. Study all the facts, and then form a _____ .
    A. confusion
    B. conclusion
    C. constitution
    D. consciousness

19. He was a famous musician best known for his _____ .
    A. operas
    B. documents
    C. essays
    D. announcements

20. The fearful skier froze as he heard the noise of the _____ .
    A. rut
    B. tremor
    C. avalanche
    D. tornado

21. This important meeting will start _____ at nine o'clock.
    A. frequently
    B. incredibly
    C. powerfully
    D. precisely

22. Before she can serve as president, she must take the _____ of office.
    A. republic
    B. oath
    C. democracy
    D. disposition

23. She is always happy, and I like that kind of _____ .
    A. activity
    B. affair
    C. ado
    D. attitude

24. There was so much food to choose from that I just took a _____ of each.
   A. sampling
   B. connection
   C. session
   D. prospect

25. All the seats at the concert were _____ .
   A. occupied
   B. acquainted
   C. approved
   D. occurred

26. Candles, flowers, and soft music are so _____ .
   A. handy
   B. ignorant
   C. romantic
   D. normal

27. She loves life and is _____ it to the fullest.
   A. informing
   B. escorting
   C. experiencing
   D. assuming

28. You will find the glossary in the _____ .
   A. influenza
   B. homesickness
   C. internal
   D. appendix

29. At three o'clock, the rock star _____ in our town in his special bus.
   A. maneuvered
   B. arrived
   C. clustered
   D. improvised

30. The black rock in the valley is a form of _____ rock.
   A. hilltop
   B. crevice
   C. barrier
   D. volcanic

31. The elephant pushed against the cage _____ .
   A. mightily
   B. originally
   C. conveniently
   D. admittedly

32. Sherlock Holmes _____ many clues before he discovered the identity of the criminal.
   A. reeked
   B. detected
   C. scoffed
   D. compounded

33. At our first rehearsal, the play was explained by the _____ .
   A. granddaughter
   B. director
   C. captor
   D. interpreter

34. To please everyone's tastes, we have a wide _____ of food.
   A. apprehension
   B. remembrance
   C. assortment
   D. recitation

35. Here is a picture of the college where he is _____ .
   A. enrolled
   B. compelled
   C. inserted
   D. detached

36. After he was found guilty, the robber was _____ .
   A. pursued
   B. donated
   C. imprisoned
   D. confirmed

37. I couldn't see my hand in front of my face because the night was so _____ .
   A. ominous
   B. unique
   C. vital
   D. foggy

38. Because she was prepared for the meeting, she was able to _____ her ideas.
- **A.** commit
- **B.** predict
- **C.** convey
- **D.** speculate

39. If you try hard enough, you may be able to _____ your habit of biting your nails.
- **A.** heave
- **B.** depart
- **C.** regain
- **D.** overcome

40. Her job was to save animals, and she worked very _____ at it.
- **A.** passionately
- **B.** simultaneously
- **C.** impossibly
- **D.** pungently

Name _____

Starting Date _____ Ending Date _____

Unit 1: Fiction and Nonfiction Skills Concept Map—1
What is the best way to find the truth?

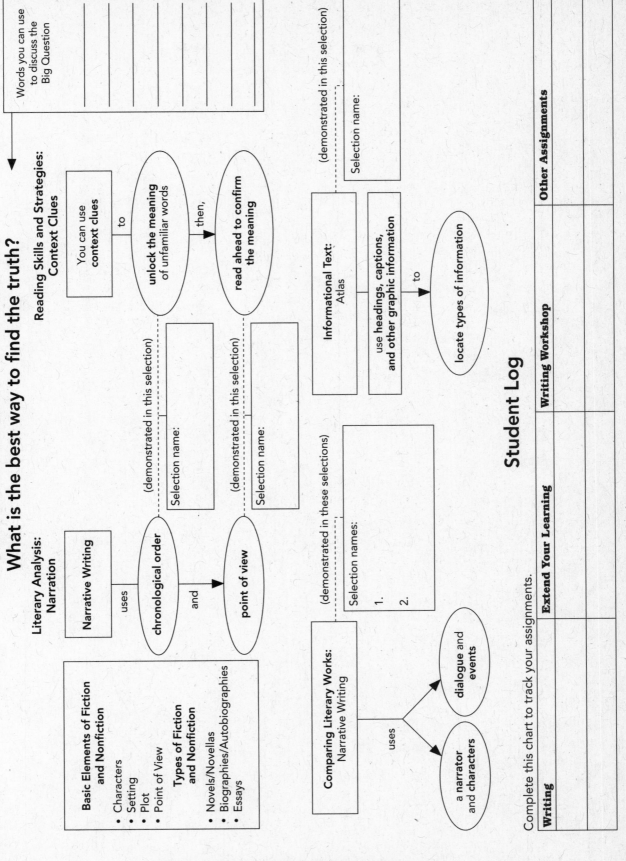

Words you can use
to discuss the
Big Question

**Reading Skills and Strategies:
Context Clues**

You can use
context clues — to → **unlock the meaning** of unfamiliar words — then, → **read ahead to confirm the meaning**

(demonstrated in this selection)

Selection name:

Informational Text:
Atlas

use headings, captions,
and other graphic information — to → locate types of information

**Literary Analysis:
Narration**

Narrative Writing — uses → chronological order — and → **point of view**

(demonstrated in this selection)

Selection name:

(demonstrated in this selection)

Selection name:

**Basic Elements of Fiction
and Nonfiction**

• Characters
• Setting
• Plot
• Point of View

**Types of Fiction
and Nonfiction**

• Novels/Novellas
• Biographies/Autobiographies
• Essays

Comparing Literary Works:
Narrative Writing — uses →

dialogue and
events

a narrator
and characters

(demonstrated in these selections)

Selection names:

1.

2.

Student Log

Complete this chart to track your assignments.

Writing	Extend Your Learning	Writing Workshop	Other Assignments

Vocabulary Warm-up Word Lists

Study these words from the selections. Then, complete the activities that follow.

Word List A

achievement [uh CHEEV muhnt] *n.* something accomplished; a feat
Everyone applauded Erin's <u>achievement</u> in gymnastics.

anchor [ANG ker] *n.* a person who coordinates a news broadcast
The <u>anchor</u> led the evening news with a story about medicine.

angle [ANG guhl] *n.* a point of view; standpoint
The commentator's <u>angle</u> is that the policy benefits everyone.

broadcasting [BRAWD kast ing] *adj.* of, or having to do with, radio or television
Hunter has always wanted to have a <u>broadcasting</u> career.

interview [IN tuhr vyoo] *v.* to ask a person questions, as for a newspaper report
The reporter plans to <u>interview</u> each witness.

photographer [fuh TAHG ruh fer] *n.* a person who takes pictures
My sister hired a professional <u>photographer</u> for her wedding.

reputation [rep yoo TAY shuhn] *n.* how a person is seen or thought of
The scandal ruined the senator's <u>reputation</u>.

technology [tek NAHL uh jee] *n.* methods or machines of applied science
Julia is studying automotive <u>technology</u> at a technical school.

Word List B

approximately [uh PRAHK suh mit lee] *adj.* about; around
We had <u>approximately</u> an inch of rain yesterday.

complaints [kuhm PLAYNTS] *n.* expressions of dissatisfaction or discomfort
The dissatisfied diners voiced <u>complaints</u> about the poor food.

fantastic [fan TAS tik] *adj.* amazing; unbelievable
The roller coaster is a <u>fantastic</u> ride.

foul [FOWL] *adj.* unpleasant; disagreeable
The terrible weather put Andrea in a <u>foul</u> mood.

humanity [hyoo MAN uh tee] *n.* the human race
All of <u>humanity</u> should be concerned about the environment.

majestic [muh JES tik] *adj.* having or showing great dignity, beauty, and grandeur
Conducting herself with dignity and grandeur, the woman was nothing short of <u>majestic</u>.

pondered [PAHN derd] *v.* considered carefully; puzzled over
Caleb <u>pondered</u> the wisdom of going hiking in the rain.

wavering [WAY vuhr ing] *v.* swaying; fluttering; being uncertain
On election day, Miranda was still <u>wavering</u> between the two candidates.

"Three-Century Woman" by Richard Peck
"The Fall of the Hindenburg" by Michael Morrison
Vocabulary Warm-up Exercises

Exercise A *Fill in each blank in the paragraph below with an appropriate word from Word List A. Use each word only once.*

The [1] _____ who coordinates our local news program is especially informative. Everyone agrees that her [2] _____ has gotten better every year. In her brief [3] _____ career she has acquired many loyal fans. We appreciate her [4] _____, the point of view from which she presents a story. We are impressed with the way she uses communications [5] _____ to [6] _____ officials and eyewitnesses in distant locations. One recent [7] _____ was her exclusive talk with the [8] _____ who took the pictures of a firefighter rescuing a child.

Exercise B *Decide whether each statement below is true or false. Circle T or F. Then, explain your answer.*

1. If your voice is <u>wavering</u>, you are speaking loudly and clearly.
   T / F _____

2. It is probably best to avoid someone who is in a <u>foul</u> mood.
   T / F _____

3. Dogs and cats are members of <u>humanity</u>.
   T / F _____

4. It would be appropriate to feel sorry for a <u>majestic</u> person.
   T / F _____

5. If you had a <u>fantastic</u> time at the beach, you would want to go back again.
   T / F _____

6. If you <u>pondered</u> a decision, you made a snap judgment.
   T / F _____

7. If you know the exact number of CDs in your collection, you know <u>approximately</u> how many CDs you have.
   T / F _____

8. If you have many <u>complaints</u> about your health, you should see a doctor.
   T / F _____

"Three-Century Woman" by Richard Peck
"The Fall of the Hindenburg" by Michael Morrison
Reading Warm-up A

Read the following passage. Pay special attention to the underlined words. Then, read it again, and complete the activities. Use a separate sheet of paper for your written answers.

Do you have good communication skills? If so, you might want to consider a career in journalism. A job as a news <u>anchor</u>, local reporter, or foreign correspondent can be exciting. To earn a good <u>reputation</u> in any of these jobs, you must be able to write and speak clearly and effectively.

Because it takes a great deal of training and preparation, becoming a news anchor is considered an <u>achievement</u>. News anchors, also called newscasters or news analysts, play an important role in society. Their job begins with the gathering of information from various sources. They prepare stories. Then they make broadcasts on radio or television. Their stories might be on local, state, national, or international events. They also prepare introductions to videotaped news stories. Finally, they introduce transmissions of stories in progress. They must be familiar with satellite <u>technology</u>, which allows for the instantaneous transmission of news from around the world.

Reporters and correspondents must do a great deal of background work. They investigate leads and tips. They <u>interview</u> witnesses and experts. Often, they must act as a <u>photographer</u> as well, taking pictures at the scene of a breaking story. Later, in an office, they organize the information. They determine the <u>angle</u>, or slant, from which they will tell the story. Then they write the report. If they are in a remote location, they send the story electronically to their home office.

One way to prepare for a career in journalism is to get a degree in journalism or mass communication. About 400 colleges and universities in the United States offer programs that lead to those degrees. For a <u>broadcasting</u> career, take courses in radio and television news and production. For a career with a newspaper or magazine, take courses in editorial journalism.

1. Circle the words in the second paragraph that give other names for an <u>anchor</u>. What does a news *anchor* do?

2. Underline the words that tell what you must be able to do to earn a good <u>reputation</u> in journalism. Use *reputation* in a sentence.

3. Underline the words that tell why it is an <u>achievement</u> to become a news anchor. Name an *achievement* that you are proud of.

4. Circle the word that tells what kind of <u>technology</u> a news anchor should be familiar with. What is *technology*?

5. Circle the words that tell who reporters <u>interview</u>. If you were to *interview* a news anchor, what would you ask?

6. Underline the words that tell what a news <u>photographer</u> does. If you were a *photographer*, what kinds of pictures would you enjoy taking?

7. Circle the word that means about the same as <u>angle</u>. What *angle* would you use for a story about a lost dog?

8. Underline the words that tell how to prepare for a <u>broadcasting</u> career. Define *broadcasting*.

Unit 1 Resources: Fiction and Nonfiction
15

"Three-Century Woman" by Richard Peck
"The Fall of the Hindenburg" by Michael Morrison

Reading Warm-up B

Read the following passage. Pay special attention to the underlined words. Then, read it again, and complete the activities. Use a separate sheet of paper for your written answers.

When spending time with older people, have you ever <u>pondered</u> what it will be like to grow old? Old age is something most of <u>humanity</u> faces sooner or later. Therefore, it is important to know what to expect.

As we age, we undergo certain physical and mental changes. One obvious change is in the condition of the skin. The <u>fantastic</u> skin that you have now may not always look so wonderful. As we age, our skin loses some of its elastic quality. As a result, it sags and wrinkles. Those effects may be worse in people who spend a great deal of time in the sun. So it is a good idea to avoid excess exposure to the sun when you are young.

During the aging process, the senses may become less sharp. Vision may blur or dim. The senses of hearing, smell, and taste may also fade. Again, there are things you can do now to lessen the effects of aging. For example, if you avoid overexposure to loud noise, you will lessen the risk of experiencing a hearing loss. If you avoid smoking, you may not experience a decreased sense of smell or taste.

Another <u>complaint</u> voiced by older people is weakened lung function. Air pollution, smoking, and lack of exercise can make this condition worse. It is important, therefore, to get into the habit of exercising. Walk, ride a bicycle, or jog regularly. Exercise is good for your muscles, and it is good for your lungs, too.

Thoughts about the aging process do not have to put you in a <u>foul</u>, unpleasant mood. Consider the sixty-year-old who has always exercised regularly. You will not see that person <u>wavering</u> uncertainly as he or she walks down the street. No, indeed! That sixty-year-old will have a <u>majestic</u> bearing, with <u>approximately</u> 80 percent of the strength he or she had at age twenty-five.

The best advice one can follow is to enjoy a healthy lifestyle. If you do, the effects of aging can be minimized.

1. Underline the words that tell what you might have <u>pondered</u> after spending time with older people. What is another way of saying *pondered*?

2. Circle the words that tell what most of <u>humanity</u> will have to face sooner or later. What is the root word of *humanity*?

3. Underline the word that means about the same as <u>fantastic</u>. Write a sentence about something *fantastic*.

4. Circle the words that name one of the other <u>complaints</u> of older people. What are two *complaints* about old age that you have heard?

5. Circle the word that means about the same as <u>foul</u>. What might put you in a *foul* mood?

6. Circle the word that describes <u>wavering</u>. Use *wavering* in a sentence.

7. Circle the words that explain why the sixty-year-old has a <u>majestic</u> bearing. What does *majestic* mean?

8. Underline the words that tell <u>approximately</u> how much strength the person with a majestic bearing has. Define *approximately*.

Richard Peck
Listening and Viewing

Segment 1: Meet Richard Peck
- From where does Richard Peck draw his inspiration to write stories about young people?
- If you were writing a story, where might you get ideas for writing?

_____

_____

_____

_____

Segment 2: Fiction and Nonfiction
- Do you agree with Richard Peck that fiction can be "truer than fact"?
- How might a work of fiction be more convincing than a work of nonfiction, such as a newspaper article?

_____

_____

_____

_____

Segment 3: The Writing Process
- Why does Richard Peck throw out the first chapter of a book once he has written the ending?
- Which one of Richard Peck's writing methods would you use? Why?

_____

_____

_____

_____

Segment 4: The Rewards of Writing
- Why does Richard Peck believe readers "have an advantage" over people who do not read?
- How has reading helped you better understand another person, a situation, or yourself? Explain.

_____

_____

_____

_____

Learning About Fiction and Nonfiction

This chart compares and contrasts **fiction** and **nonfiction**:

Fiction	Nonfiction
tells about *made-up* people or animals, called **characters**: The characters experience a series of made-up events, called the **plot**; the plot takes place at a certain real or imagined time in a certain real or imagined location, which is the **setting**; the plot also contains a problem, or **conflict**, that characters must solve	tells about *real* people, animals, places, things, events, and ideas; presents facts and discusses ideas; may reflect the **historical context** of its time by making references to current events, society, and culture
may be told from the perspective of a character in the story (**first-person point of view**) or a narrator outside the story (**third-person point of view**)	is told from the **perspective** of the author
takes the form of short stories, novellas, novels	takes the form of biographies, autobiographies, memoirs, letters, journals, diaries, essays, articles, textbooks, and documents, such as application forms and instructions
to explain, inform, persuade, or entertain	to explain, inform, persuade, or entertain

A. DIRECTIONS: *Using clues in each title,* write fiction *or* nonfiction *on the line.*

_____ 1. "My Family Came From Mars"

_____ 2. "Historic Landings on the Moon"

_____ 3. *The Life of Thomas Jefferson*

_____ 4. *Jackie Rabbit, King of the Meadow*

_____ 5. "How to Make Oatmeal Bread"

B. DIRECTIONS: *Read this paragraph carefully, and decide whether it is fiction or nonfiction. Indicate your choice. Then, explain what hints led you to make your choice.*

The Ramirez family set off on their summer vacation yesterday. Luis was excited. It was the first trip that his family had taken since coming to the United States last year. Luis had brought along two books to read during the trip. He'd have plenty of time to read. After all, flying to a distant galaxy would take at least a week.

Fiction / Nonfiction: _____

Explanation: _____

Name _____ Date _____

"The Three-Century Woman" by Richard Peck
Model Selection: Fiction

Every work of **fiction** includes made-up people or animals, called **characters,** and a made-up series of events, called the **plot.** The plot may seem realistic. For example, it may be a story about students like you. On the other hand, the plot may be a fantasy. It might, for example, feature talking cats.

The plot takes place at a certain time and in a certain location, called the **setting.** The setting may or may not be real. Every plot contains a problem, or **conflict,** that one or more characters must solve.

A speaker, called the **narrator,** tells the story from a certain perspective, or **point of view.** If the narrator is a character in the story, he or she tells it from the **first-person point of view.** If the narrator is outside the story, he or she tells it from the **third-person point of view.**

Examples of fiction include novels, novellas, and short stories.

A. DIRECTIONS: *"The Three-Century Woman" is a work of fiction. Complete the following items to provide details about its characters, narrator, setting, and plot.*

1. The **characters:** _____

   _____

2. Is the **narrator** inside or outside the story? _____

3. Is the story told from the **first-person** or **third-person** point of view? _____

   _____

4. Clues that indicate the point of view: _____

   _____

5. When does the story take place? _____

   _____

6. Where does the story take place? _____

   _____

7. Is the **setting** realistic or imaginary? Explain. _____

   _____

8. Is the **plot** realistic or fantastic? _____

9. Examples of real or fantastic **plot** elements: _____

   _____

10. What **conflict,** or problem, do the characters face?

    _____

    _____

Name _____ Date _____

Model Selection: Nonfiction

Nonfiction deals with *real* people, animals, places, things, events, and ideas. It may present facts or discuss ideas.

A work of nonfiction is narrated from the **point of view,** or perspective, of the author. Often nonfiction reflects the **historical context** of its time by including references to current events, society, or culture. For example, an article about the American Revolution would contain social and cultural information about the East Coast of North America in the mid-1700s.

Works of nonfiction include biographies, autobiographies, memoirs, letters, journals, diaries, essays, articles, textbooks, and various documents, such as application forms and instructions.

A. DIRECTIONS: *Answer these questions about "The Fall of the* Hindenburg.*"*

1. What real event does the article discuss?

_____

2. On what date, and in what location, did the event take place?

_____

3. List three facts that the author presents.

_____

_____

_____

4. What conclusions can you draw about the topic, based on your reading of the article?

_____

_____

5. Give an example of a detail that sets a historical context for the article.

_____

B. DIRECTIONS: *Authors have one or more purposes for writing a piece of nonfiction. For example, an author might write to explain how to do something, to tell the story of a person's life, to inform readers about a topic, to persuade readers to share an opinion, or to share a personal experience. In your opinion, what was Michael Morrison's purpose for writing "The Fall of the Hindenburg"? Support your answer by citing facts, reasons, and examples from the article.*

_____

_____

_____

"The Three-Century Woman" by Richard Peck
"The Fall of the Hindenburg" by Michael Morrison
Open-Book Test

Short Answer *Write your responses to the questions in this section on the lines provided.*

1. You are writing a short story. Two characters experience a conflict about which one of them will pilot the new spaceship to Jupiter. Is this story fiction or nonfiction? Explain.

   _____

   _____

2. Is an eyewitness's journal account of Lincoln's assassination fiction or nonfiction? Explain your answer.

   _____

   _____

3. A friend recommends a book about two neighbors who have an argument. What other information do you need to determine whether the book is fiction or nonfiction? Explain your answer, using what you know about these two forms of writing.

   _____

   _____

   _____

4. Near the beginning of "The Three-Century Woman," the narrator's mother drives quickly through an intersection. Explain why that action might make Megan nervous. Use the definiton of *intersection*.

   _____

   _____

5. In the middle of "The Three-Century Woman," Mom reacts negatively to Great-grandma's appearance. Tell what she says and explain why she is annoyed by how Great-grandma looks.

   _____

   _____

   _____

6. In the middle of "The Three-Century Woman," the narrator says Great-grandma "pondered for the camera" as she told about the Hindenburg. Why might Great-grandma have pondered? Use the definition of *pondered* in your answer. Consider whether she is telling the truth.

   _____

   _____

   _____

Unit 1 Resources: Fiction and Nonfiction

7. In "The Three-Century Woman," Great-grandma uses factual information to support her description of some of the "amazing times" she has lived through. How do you know that the story is fiction, even though it contains historical facts? Explain your answer.

_____

_____

_____

_____

8. The reporter in "The Three-Century Woman" describes Great-grandma as "venerable." Do you agree with his description? Use an example from the story to support your response.

_____

_____

_____

_____

9. As he watched the Hindenburg fall, one reporter cried, "Oh, the Humanity!" What did he mean? Use details from the selection to support your answer.

_____

_____

_____

_____

10. In the chart below, list facts about the Hindenburg that Great-grandma tells the reporters in "The Three-Century Woman." Then, list details that she makes up to add to the story. On the line, explain why Great-grandma added the details.

Facts	Fiction

_____

Essay

Write an extended response to the question of your choice or to the question or questions your teacher assigns you.

11. What elements of "The Fall of the Hindenburg" help you recognize that it is nonfiction? Use details from the essay to support your response.

12. The fictional element of setting plays an important role in "The Three-Century Woman." Use details from the story to show how at least one of the characters is affected by where the action takes place.

13. Imagine you are the TV reporter who interviewed Great-grandma in "The Three-Century Woman." You have discovered that she was not in fact on the Hindenburg. Write your report about Great-grandma. Do you still think she is a "venerable lady"?

14. **Thinking About the Big Question: What is the best way to find the truth?** In an essay, write about the idea of truth as seen through the eyes of Great-grandma in "The Three-Century Woman." Consider whether her stories to the reporters are in fact true and whether she recognizes that. Use details from the selection for support.

Oral Response

15. Go back to question 4, 5, or 9 or to the question your teacher assigns you. Take a few minutes to expand your answer and prepare an oral response. Find additional details in "The Three-Century Woman" or "The Fall of the Hindenburg" that support your points. If necessary, make notes to guide your oral response.

Name _____ Date _____

Selection Test A

Learning About Fiction and Nonfiction *Identify the letter of the choice that best answers the question.*

_____ 1. Which statement about <u>fiction</u> is true?
    A. All fiction is based on facts.
    B. All fiction contains a made-up series of events.
    C. All fiction is told from the first-person point of view.
    D. All fiction involves animal characters.

_____ 2. Which statement is true about <u>nonfiction</u>?
    A. One or more characters solve a problem.
    B. Animals often do "human" things, like talk and wear clothing.
    C. It deals with real people rather than made-up characters.
    D. The setting may or may not be real.

_____ 3. What is the series of events called in a work of <u>fiction</u>?
    A. conflict
    B. plot
    C. setting
    D. point of view

_____ 4. Many works of <u>fiction</u> contain a message about life. What is this element called?
    A. conflict
    B. tone
    C. novella
    D. theme

_____ 5. Which of the following is an example of <u>nonfiction</u>?
    A. essay
    B. novel
    C. short story
    D. novella

Critical Reading

_____ 6. Who is the narrator of "The Three-Century Woman"?
    A. Megan
    B. Mom
    C. Aunt Gloria
    D. Mrs. Breckenridge

_____ 7. What is the setting of "The Three-Century Woman"?
   A. the Northbrook Mall
   B. a hotel room in San Francisco
   C. the Lakehurst Naval Air Station
   D. a room at Whispering Oaks

_____ 8. Why is Mrs. Breckenridge a "three-century woman"?
   A. She has lived for three hundred years.
   B. She has lived in three centuries.
   C. She is famous.
   D. She is a great-grandmother.

_____ 9. Which event does Mrs. Breckenridge claim to remember?
   A. the crash of the *Hindenburg*
   B. the sinking of the *Titanic*
   C. the Vietnam War
   D. a meeting with Abraham Lincoln

_____ 10. Why does Mrs. Breckenridge recall untrue "memories" in her interview with the news anchor?
   A. She has always wanted to be famous, and she sees this as her last chance.
   B. She is angry because the anchor is interested in her memories, not in her as a person.
   C. She is annoyed with the anchor because he dyes his hair and wears an expensive suit.
   D. She wants Megan to think that she has had an eventful, fascinating life.

_____ 11. What is the main event in "The Fall of the *Hindenburg*"?
   A. The *Hindenburg* crashes into the Atlantic Ocean.
   B. The *Hindenburg* crash-lands during a hurricane.
   C. The *Hindenburg* explodes and burns while landing.
   D. The *Hindenburg* is shot down during a naval battle.

_____ 12. According to Michael Morrison, which statement about "The Fall of the *Hindenburg*" is true?
   A. The crash was most likely caused by a bolt of lightning.
   B. The crash was most likely caused by enemies of Germany.
   C. The crash was most likely caused when hydrogen caught fire.
   D. The crash was most likely caused when varnish caught fire.

_____ **13.** Which of the following is a fact that is stated in "The Fall of the *Hindenburg*"?
   A. After catching fire, the *Hindenburg* sank off the Atlantic coast.
   B. Many on board the *Hindenburg* did not die when it caught fire.
   C. The library was the only part of the *Hindenburg* that did not burn.
   D. Scientists at NASA blame the explosion on the Nazi government.

_____ **14.** A reporter cried out "Oh, the Humanity!" when he witnessed the burning of the *Hindenburg*. What do his words suggest about his feelings?
   A. He was annoyed.
   B. He was angry.
   C. He was surprised but relieved.
   D. He was shocked and saddened.

_____ **15.** What do "The Three-Century Woman" and "The Fall of the *Hindenburg*" have in common?
   A. Both refer to the San Francisco earthquake.
   B. Both refer to the explosion of the *Hindenburg*.
   C. Both center on the memories of Mrs. Breckenridge.
   D. Both are told from the first-person point of view.

Essay

16. At the end of "The Three-Century Woman," Mrs. Breckenridge points to Megan and says, "Once upon a time, I was your age. How scary is that?" In an essay, explain the meaning of Mrs. Breckenridge's statement.

17. Imagine that you were an eyewitness to the explosion and burning of the *Hindenburg*. In an essay, report on the incident. Be sure to include a summary of the main events.

18. Thinking About the Big Question: What is the best way to find the truth? In an essay, write about the idea of truth as seen through the eyes of Great-grandma in "The Three-Century Woman." Consider whether her stories to the reporters are in fact true and whether she knows whether or not they are true. Use details from the selection for support.

"The Three-Century Woman" by Richard Peck
"The Fall of the *Hindenburg*" by Michael Morrison
Selection Test B

Learning About Fiction and Nonfiction *Identify the letter of the choice that best completes the statement or answers the question.*

_____ 1. Which statement is true of all works of <u>fiction</u>?
   A. They involve real people or real animals.
   B. They are told from the first-person point of view.
   C. They are told by a speaker, who is called the narrator.
   D. They take place at a particular time and have a realistic setting.

_____ 2. Which statement is true of <u>nonfiction</u>?
   A. It contains a plot, or a series of events.
   B. It may deal with imaginary characters.
   C. It is narrated from a character's point of view.
   D. It is narrated from the author's point of view.

_____ 3. The <u>setting</u> of a work of fiction may best be defined as
   A. the conflict or problem in the story.
   B. the time and location of the story.
   C. the point of view of the story.
   D. the series of events in the story.

_____ 4. Which statement is true about works of fiction in which the <u>narrator</u> is a character in the story?
   A. They are told from the first-person point of view.
   B. They are told from the third-person point of view.
   C. They are told from the point of view of the author.
   D. They are told from the point of view of a real person.

_____ 5. Which of the following is an example of <u>fiction</u>?
   A. a speech
   B. an essay
   C. a novella
   D. a biography

_____ 6. Which of the following is *not* an example of <u>nonfiction</u>?
   A. an explanation of how wolves hunt
   B. someone's observations of a wolf
   C. an essay comparing wolves with dogs
   D. a journal entry written by a wolf

Critical Reading

_____ 7. Which statement is true of "The Three-Century Woman"?
   A. Its narrator is a fourteen-year-old girl.
   B. Its narrator is an elderly woman.
   C. Its narrator is called Aunt Gloria.
   D. Its narrator is not a character in the story.

___ 8. Which statement best describes the characters in "The Three-Century Woman"?
   A. They are not at all realistic.
   B. They have many realistic qualities.
   C. They are real people.
   D. They are entirely fantastic.

___ 9. According to Mrs. Breckenridge, which historical event did she experience?
   A. the San Francisco earthquake
   B. the sinking of the *Titanic*
   C. the Battle of Gettysburg
   D. the discovery of uranium

___ 10. Which statement is true about the stories that Mrs. Breckenridge tells the news anchor?
   A. They are based on true events that she experienced many years before.
   B. They are based on imaginary events that she has read about in works of fiction.
   C. They are based on true events that she never experienced firsthand.
   D. They are based on imaginary events that she has written about in works of fiction.

___ 11. Which of the following statements best describes Mrs. Breckenridge?
   A. She has a poor memory.
   B. She is imaginative and clever.
   C. She has led an eventful life.
   D. She always tells the truth.

___ 12. Mrs. Breckenridge says that the TV anchor "put my nose out of joint." What does she mean?
   A. He made her angry.
   B. He made her comfortable.
   C. He wasted her time.
   D. He hurt her nose.

___ 13. At the end of the story, the narrator tells Mrs. Breckenridge, "I'll come and see you more often." She says this because
   A. she knows that her great-grandmother is lonely.
   B. she wants to hear more about the *Hindenburg*.
   C. she realizes that she has enjoyed the visit.
   D. she admires her great-grandmother's fame.

___ 14. Which statement best describes the theme of "The Three-Century Woman"?
   A. Old people have much to teach about the events that happened in their lifetime.
   B. Old people must be protected from people who want to take advantage of them.
   C. Although they may be frail, old people may be as clever as they always were.
   D. Many old people prefer to relive the past rather than live their life in the present.

____ 15. The *Hindenburg* may best be described as
   A. a giant airship kept aloft by hydrogen.
   B. a huge airplane fueled by hydrogen.
   C. a giant ship that could travel underwater.
   D. a huge submarine fueled by hydrogen.

____ 16. Which statement is true about the setting of "The Fall of the *Hindenburg*"?
   A. It takes place in Germany in 1937.
   B. It takes place in New Jersey in 1937.
   C. It takes place over the Atlantic in 1937.
   D. It takes place in New Jersey in 2001.

____ 17. Which fact provides historical context for the period in which "The Fall of the *Hindenburg*" takes place?
   A. The ship turns into a ball of flames in only thirty-four seconds.
   B. NASA completed scientific research on the cause of the crash.
   C. Germany was governed by the Nazis at the time of the crash.
   D. People still believe the crash was caused by a hydrogen explosion.

____ 18. Which of the following is a fact that is stated in "The Fall of the *Hindenburg*"?
   A. Some passengers survived by jumping from the burning ship.
   B. Everyone on board the ship at the time of the fire was killed.
   C. Germany was well-known for producing giant zeppelins.
   D. The ship was struck by lightning just before it exploded.

____ 19. The radio reporter Herb Morrison cried out, "Oh, the Humanity!" because
   A. he had never seen such a huge airship before.
   B. his parents were passengers on the airship.
   C. he was shocked and dismayed by the tragedy.
   D. he knew that what he said would be remembered.

____ 20. "The Fall of the *Hindenburg*" is an example of
   A. realistic fiction.   C. a biography.
   B. an article.   D. a memoir.

Essay

21. At the beginning of "The Three-Century Woman," Megan does not look forward to visiting her great-grandmother. In an essay, discuss how her feelings have changed by the end of the story. Support your response with references to her actions and words at the end of the story.

22. "The Fall of the *Hindenburg*" contains many facts and details about the *Hindenburg*. In an essay, use those facts and details to compare and contrast the *Hindenburg* with a modern type of carrier, such as a large passenger ship or a jet plane.

23. **Thinking About the Big Question: What is the best way to find the truth?** In an essay, write about the idea of truth as seen through the eyes of Great-grandma in "The Three-Century Woman." Consider whether her stories to the reporters are in fact true and whether she recognizes that. Use details from the selection for support.

Vocabulary Warm-up Word Lists

Study these words from "Papa's Parrot." Then, complete the activities that follow.

Word List A

bins [BINZ] *n.* large containers for storing things
Jordan filled the <u>bins</u> with toys as he cleaned the playroom.

furnace [FER nis] *n.* a machine that burns fuel to produce heat
The <u>furnace</u> kept the house warm and cozy on cold winter days.

maple [MAY puhl] *adj.* flavored with syrup made from the sap of the sugar maple tree
The <u>maple</u> fudge is very sweet.

merely [MEER lee] *adv.* only or simply; no more than
The student <u>merely</u> glanced at the instructions and so misunderstood them.

roasted [ROHST id] *adj.* cooked over an open fire
The <u>roasted</u> marshmallows, cooked over hot coals, turned brown.

stroll [STROHL] *v.* to walk in a slow, relaxed way
We often <u>stroll</u> along the streets on cool summer evenings.

sample [SAM puhl] *v.* to try one of something to find out what it is like
At the store, Maria will <u>sample</u> the cheeses to find one she likes.

twilight [TWY lyt] *adj.* like the dim light between sunset and night time
In the <u>twilight</u> glow, it was hard to read the newspaper.

Word List B

ambulance [AM byoo luhns] *n.* a vehicle used to rush sick or injured people to a hospital
When my brother broke his leg, we called an <u>ambulance</u>.

arriving [uh RYV ing] *v.* coming to a place
Laura's mother was <u>arriving</u> on the evening train.

batch [BACH] *n.* a number of things produced or taken as a group
The <u>batch</u> of oatmeal cookies smelled good.

embarrassed [em BAR uhst] *adj.* felt ashamed or uncomfortable
The child was <u>embarrassed</u> by his foolish mistake.

operas [AHP er uhz] *n.* plays in which most of the words are sung; **soap operas** are dramatic daytime television programs featuring a continuing story
Aaron listened to Mozart's <u>operas</u>, while his brother followed the stories of several <u>soap operas</u>.

romantic [roh MAN tik] *adj.* having a spirit or mood of adventure, love, or excitement
Couples danced to the <u>romantic</u> music.

smelly [SMEL ee] *adj.* having an unpleasant odor
The <u>smelly</u> garbage was taken to the dump.

strawberry [STRAW ber ee] *adj.* having the flavor or color of a strawberry
Sam's favorite drink is a <u>strawberry</u> milkshake.

"Papa's Parrot" by Cynthia Rylant
Vocabulary Warm-up Exercises

Exercise A *Fill in each blank in the paragraph below with an appropriate word from Word List A. Use each word only once.*

Eric loved going camping with his family. Maybe it was because he liked to

[1] _____ along the lake each afternoon. Maybe it was because of the

[2] _____ calm that spread over the campsite just after sunset. Then it

would be time to get logs and kindling from the storage [3] _____ and

build a fire. Eric's parents cooked over the fire. They might make [4] _____

chicken or [5] _____ flavored cornbread. The fire was as warm as a

blazing [6] _____. After dinner, they might [7] _____ the

berries Eric had picked. At those times, Eric imagined how the pioneers might have felt

when they cooked and ate outdoors. For him camping was [8] _____ an

adventure. For them it was necessary.

Exercise B *Answer the questions with complete explanations.*

Example: If you were very <u>quiet</u>, would your neighbors be likely to complain that you were making too much noise?

    No, they would not, because a <u>quiet</u> person is someone who does not make noise.

1. If you were transported in an <u>ambulance</u>, would you be on your way home?

    _____

2. If someone has made a <u>batch</u> of cookies, has he or she made just two of them?

    _____

3. When you listen to <u>operas</u>, do you hear much music?

    _____

4. Are <u>strawberry</u> milkshakes flavored with bananas?

    _____

5. Might someone feel <u>embarrassed</u> if his or her diary was published on the Internet?

    _____

6. Might a <u>romantic</u> novel tell the story of ordinary people doing everyday things?

    _____

7. Would a table near a <u>smelly</u> garbage can be a good place for a picnic?

    _____

8. If you were <u>arriving</u> somewhere, would you have just left home?

    _____

"Papa's Parrot" by Cynthia Rylant
Reading Warm-up A

Read the following passage. Pay special attention to the underlined words. Then, read it again, and complete the activities. Use a separate sheet of paper for your written answers.

The Ojibwe are an American Indian people from the area around the Great Lakes. In the past the Ojibwe moved from place to place depending on the season of the year. They moved in that way because each season posed a different challenge to their survival.

Different locations gave the Ojibwe the food and shelter they needed at different times of the year. In March, for example, the dim <u>twilight</u> days of winter drew to an end. There was more daylight, and spring was coming. The Ojibwe packed their tools and clothing. They headed to the forests to make <u>maple</u> syrup.

After cutting a gash in a maple tree, workers collected the sap in a bucket. They heated the sap over hot stones or an open fire. At last the fire would get hot enough to boil the sap. The fire boiled the sap in much the same way that a <u>furnace</u> heats fuel to warm a house.

Throughout the year the Ojibwe used the maple syrup to season <u>roasted</u> meats and vegetables. They also used it to make candies, which they stored in <u>bins</u>. Throughout the year, children would <u>sample</u> those sweets.

Maple sugaring was more than <u>merely</u> a time for work. It was also a time to be together. After all, the Ojibwe had spent the long winter in small groups. Now people would gather in larger groups. They would <u>stroll</u> among the maple trees and exchange news and stories. Today many Ojibwe wish to continue the tradition of maple sugaring. They turn the sap into syrup in the old way. By doing that, they honor an important part of their culture.

1. Circle the word that describes the <u>twilight</u> days of winter. How were days in March different from the days earlier in the winter?

2. Underline the sentences that tell how the Ojibwe made <u>maple</u> syrup. What *maple* flavored food might you eat?

3. Underline the words that tell what a <u>furnace</u> does. Then tell what a *furnace* is.

4. Circle the words that describe the kinds of <u>roasted</u> foods the Ojibwe ate. What *roasted* food do you eat?

5. Circle the word that tells what was stored in <u>bins</u>. What is another word for *bins*?

6. Circle the word that tells what the children liked to <u>sample</u>. What does *sample* mean?

7. Circle the words that tell what was more than <u>merely</u> a time for work. Define *merely*.

8. Underline the words that tell where the Ojibwe would <u>stroll</u>. Use *stroll* in a sentence.

"Papa's Parrot" by Cynthia Rylant
Reading Warm-up B

Read the following passage. Pay special attention to the underlined words. Then, read it again, and complete the activities. Use a separate sheet of paper for your written answers.

The summer was over, and Kaitlin was on a train. Soon she would be <u>arriving</u> in her hometown, where her mother would meet her. The thirteen-year-old had spent the last eight weeks with her great-grandmother, helping her garden and shop and do housework.

At first, Kaitlin had not liked the idea of spending her summer that way. She had wanted to be with her friends. That plan changed, however, when her mother had to go out of town on business.

So Kaitlin had packed her bags. Her great-grandmother met her at the train station with a smile and a hug, but Kaitlin felt <u>embarrassed</u>. She did not know the woman well, and she thought that her perfume was <u>smelly</u>. Getting along was difficult in the beginning, but soon the old woman and the girl began to talk about many things. Kaitlin's great-grandmother talked a great deal about World War II. She had been a nurse overseas during the war. It was a <u>romantic</u> story. She had ridden in an <u>ambulance</u> and saved soldiers' lives. She had had many adventures.

On many evenings, Kaitlin's great-grandmother would show Kaitlin photographs. Kaitlin's favorite was a photograph of her own mother as a young girl. In the picture Kaitlin's mother is picking flowers in the same garden where Kaitlin was now spending so much time.

As the summer wore on, Kaitlin and her great-grandmother fell into an easy routine. They gardened in the morning. Every afternoon they took a break to watch Kaitlin's great-grandmother's favorite <u>soap-operas</u>. Often, as they followed the stories on daytime television, they would snack on a <u>batch</u> of homemade cookies or a dish of <u>strawberry</u> ice cream.

As Kaitlin looked out the train window, she realized that she would never forget this summer. She had made a new friend and had learned many things about her family and the world.

1. Underline the words that tell where Kaitlin will be <u>arriving</u>. Use *arriving* in a sentence.

2. Underline the words that explain why Kaitlin felt <u>embarrassed</u>. What does *embarrassed* mean?

3. Circle the words that tell what Kaitlin found <u>smelly</u>. What does *smelly* mean?

4. Underline the words that tell why Kaitlin's great-grandmother's story was <u>romantic</u>. Define *romantic*.

5. Why might a nurse ride in an <u>ambulance</u>? Use *ambulance* in a sentence.

6. What is the difference between <u>soap operas</u> and musical *operas*?

7. Circle the words that tell what was in a <u>batch</u>. What does *batch* mean?

8. Circle the words that describe what is <u>strawberry</u> flavored.

"Papa's Parrot" by Cynthia Rylant

Writing About the Big Question

What is the best way to find the truth?

Big Question Vocabulary

awareness	believable	conclude	convince	debate
evaluate	evidence	explain	factual	fiction
insight	perceive	reality	reveal	truth

A. *Use one or more words from the list above to complete each sentence.*

1. When a person has _____, he or she may know things that were not told to him or her.

2. It is sometimes difficult for someone to _____ strong feelings.

3. When someone acts indifferent toward me, I _____ that he or she does not like me.

4. When someone is very friendly and warm toward me, I _____ that he or she likes me.

B. *Answer the questions. Use at least one of the vocabulary words in each answer:*

1. Have you ever been unsure about how someone feels about you? Explain.

_____

_____

_____

2. Was the truth about the person's feelings ever revealed? If so, how? If not, what can you do to gain insight into how the person feels about you?

_____

_____

_____

C. *Complete the first sentence below. Then, answer the question to write a short paragraph connecting the sentence to the Big Question.*

One time I learned the truth about _____ when

_____

How could you use that truth in a fictional story?

_____

_____

_____

_____

"Papa's Parrot" by Cynthia Rylant

Reading: Use Context Clues to Unlock the Meaning

Context, the words and phrases surrounding a word, can help you understand a word you do not know. When you come across an unfamiliar word, **use context clues to unlock the meaning.** Look for a word or words that might mean the same thing or have the opposite meaning of the unfamiliar word. In addition, you may find definitions, examples, or descriptions of the unfamiliar word. For example, in this passage from "Papa's Parrot," the italicized words are clues to the meaning of *unpack*:

New shipments of candy and nuts would be arriving. . . .

...Harry told his father that he would go to the store every day after school and <u>unpack</u> boxes. He would *sort out all the candy and nuts.*

As you read, use context clues to find possible meanings for unfamiliar words. Check the words in a dictionary after you read.

DIRECTIONS: *Read each of the following sentences or short passages from "Papa's Parrot." Look at the underlined word. Then, find other words in the passage that can be used as context clues to help you figure out the meaning of the underlined word. Write the context clue or clues on the first line. Write the meaning of the underlined word on the second line. Then, check your answer by looking up the underlined word in a dictionary.*

Hint: Sometimes the context clues appear a distance away from the unfamiliar word. For item 3, below, the context clue appears in the first paragraph of the story.

1. Harry stopped liking candy and nuts when he was around seven, but, in spite of this, he and Mr. Tillian had <u>remained</u> friends and were still friends the year Harry turned twelve.

   Context clues: _____

   Meaning of word: _____

2. At home things were different. Harry and his father joked with each other at the dinner table as they always had—Mr. Tillian <u>teasing</u> Harry about his smelly socks; Harry teasing Mr. Tillian about his blubbery stomach.

   Context clues: _____

   Meaning of word: _____

3. Though his father was fat and merely owned a candy and nut shop, Harry Tillian liked his papa. . . . Harry and his father joked with each other at the dinner table as they always had—Mr. Tillian teasing Harry about his smelly socks; Harry teasing Mr. Tillian about his <u>blubbery</u> stomach.

   Context clues: _____

   Meaning of word: _____

"Papa's Parrot" by Cynthia Rylant
Literary Analysis: Narrative Writing

Narrative writing is any type of writing that tells a story. The act or process of telling a story is also called **narration.**

- A narrative is usually told in chronological order—the order in which events occur in time.
- A narrative may be fiction, nonfiction, or poetry.

When you look at events in chronological order, you see that events that occur later in a narrative often depend on events that occurred earlier. For example, in "Papa's Parrot," the part of the story in which Harry walks by his father's store and hears him talking to Rocky must follow the part in which Mr. Tillian buys Rocky in the first place.

DIRECTIONS: *Below is a list of events from "Papa's Parrot." Put the events in chronological order by writing a number from 1 to 10 on the line before the event. Remember that each event has to make sense in terms of what has already occurred in the story.*

____ A. Harry stops going to the candy and nut shop when he sees his father talking to Rocky.

____ B. Harry goes to the candy and nut shop to unpack boxes and feed Rocky.

____ C. Harry yells at Rocky and throws peppermints at him.

____ D. Mr. Tillian buys a parrot, spending more money than he can afford.

____ E. Harry understands what Rocky means and goes to visit his father in the hospital.

____ F. Mr. Tillian falls ill and is taken to the hospital.

____ G. When they were young, Harry and his friends stopped by his father's candy and nut shop after school to buy penny candy or roasted peanuts.

____ H. Mr. Tillian talks to Rocky, and the two watch television together.

____ I. After Harry enters junior high school, he and his friends stop going to the candy and nut shop and spend more time playing video games and shopping for records.

____ J. The parrot says, "Hello, Rocky!" and "Where's Harry?" over and over.

Name _____ Date _____

"Papa's Parrot" by Cynthia Rylant
Vocabulary Builder

Word List

clusters   ignored   merely   perch   resumed   shipments

A. DIRECTIONS: *Think about the meaning of the italicized Word List word in each item below. Then, answer the question, and explain your answer.*

1. After his hospital stay, Mr. Tillian *resumed* his place in the candy and nut shop. Were his customers pleased?

    _____

2. While Mr. Tillian was in the hospital, Harry *ignored* his friends. Were his friends pleased?

    _____

3. When Harry threw a cluster of peppermints at the cage, Rocky clung to his *perch*. Was Rocky scared?

    _____

4. Mr. Tillian worried about the new *shipments* of candy and nuts arriving at his shop. Who would handle them?

    _____

5. In Harry's eyes, Mr. Tillian *merely* owned a candy and nut shop. Was Harry ashamed of his father's occupation?

    _____

6. Rocky's cage was next to the sign for the maple *clusters*. What other similar items does Mr. Tillian have in his store?

    _____

B. WORD STUDY The prefix *re-* means "back" or "again." Use the context of the sentences and the meaning of the prefix to explain your answer to each question.

1. If you program a song for constant *replay*, does that mean that you like it or dislike it?

    _____

2. When a football coach *repositions* the players on the field, what is he doing?

    _____

3. If you *rethink* a decision, are you happy with the choice you made?

    _____

"Papa's Parrot" by Cynthia Rylant
Enrichment: Science

Wild parrots live in tropical forests in South America, Australia, and Asia. They live where the weather is always warm and wet. The birds are brightly colored in shades of blue, red, green, and yellow. The people who live in these tropical lands, as well as tourists who visit, enjoy the birds. They like to watch the flashes of color as the parrots fly through the forest.

Many parrots have been captured and sold as pets. In addition, many parrots have lost their habitats. Parrots lose their habitats when forests are cleared for farming and housing. When too many parrots of the same kind, or *species*, are captured or lose their habitats, the species dies out. The species does not survive.

A group of people formed the Wildlife Conservation Society to study and protect wildlife—including parrots. They have come up with a number of solutions. For example, they have set aside parcels of land, or *reserves*, where birds and animals are protected. They have also looked for ways to protect parrots and other birds that have lost their nesting places. Scientists have made imitation hollow trees in which the parrots build their nests. In addition, scientists raise parrot chicks in captivity and then release them in the wild.

Many people now realize that saving endangered species is good for tourism and good for the earth.

DIRECTIONS: *Use the information in the passage above to answer these questions.*

1. What are two reasons for the decrease in the number of parrots in their natural habitat?

   _____

   _____

   _____

   _____

2. What are three things people are doing to protect parrots and help them survive?

   _____

   _____

   _____

   _____

3. Which two groups of people enjoy the sight of wild parrots?

   _____

   _____

Name _____ Date _____

"**Papa's Parrot**" by Cynthia Rylant
Open-Book Test

Short Answer *Write your responses to the questions in this section on the lines provided.*

1. In the first sentence of "Papa's Parrot," we learn that Mr. Tillian *merely* owned a small shop. Which word or words in the sentence help you understand the meaning of the word *merely*? Explain your answer.

   _____

   _____

   _____

2. In "Papa's Parrot," as Harry starts to become a teenager, his relationship with his father changes. How does Harry change? Use details from the story to support your answer.

   _____

   _____

   _____

   _____

3. In "Papa's Parrot," Mr. Tillian decides to get a pet. Why does he get a pet, and why does he choose a parrot? Use information from the story to support your response.

   _____

   _____

   _____

   _____

4. Mr. Tillian *ignored* Harry's shocked response to his purchase of a parrot. What is one way in which Mr. Tillian might have *ignored* Harry's remarks? Use the definition of *ignored* to explain your answer.

   _____

   _____

   _____

5. In the middle of "Papa's Parrot," Harry experiences a second change in how he feels about his father's store. Use story details to explain what the change is and why the change occurs.

   _____

   _____

   _____

6. After Harry fixed up Rocky's cage in "Papa's Parrot," he *resumed* organizing the candy. Suppose he was unable to *resume* his work. What would happen? Explain your answer. Include the definition of *resume* in your response.

_____

_____

7. Toward the end of "Papa's Parrot," Harry and the parrot have a conversation. After their conversation, Harry throws some peppermints and explodes in tears. Why does Harry have such a powerful reaction? Use details from the story to support your response.

_____

_____

_____

8. Read the last paragraph of "Papa's Parrot." What word or words suggest the meaning of the word *furnace*? Include the meaning of the word *furnace* in your answer.

_____

_____

_____

9. Use the graphic organizer to list important events in the beginning, middle, and end of "Papa's Parrot." Then, tell over what period of time the events happen.

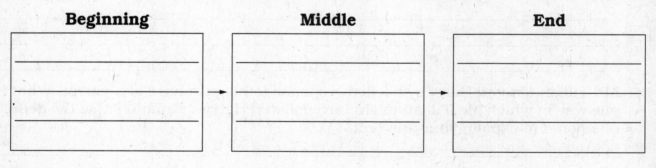

| Beginning | Middle | End |

_____

10. "Papa's Parrot" is an example of *narration*, or *narrative writing*. Explain one way the author lets you know that "Papa's Parrot" is narrative writing.

_____

_____

_____

Essay

Write an extended response to the question of your choice or to the question or questions your teacher assigns you.

11. Harry goes through several changes in the course of "Papa's Parrot." How would you describe these changes in the beginning, middle, and end of the story? Write a brief description of Harry in each part of the story. Use details from the story to support your impressions.

12. The parrot, Rocky, repeats many different remarks he has heard throughout "Papa's Parrot." What do you think is the most important thing that Rocky says? Explain your answer in an essay, using details from the story to support your opinion.

13. Do you think Mr. Tillian is mostly angry at Harry, or do you think he understands his son's behavior? Write a brief essay that explains Mr. Tillian's overall opinion of his son in "Papa's Parrot." Use examples from the story to justify your point of view.

14. **Thinking About the Big Question: What is the best way to find the truth?** In the story of "Papa's Parrot," how does Harry find the truth? In an essay, explain whether this is the best way for Harry to hear the truth. Use details from the story as support for your ideas.

Oral Response

15. Go back to question 2, 5, 7, or 9 or to the question your teacher assigns you. Take a few minutes to expand your answer and prepare an oral response. Find additional details in "Papa's Parrot" that support your points. If necessary, make notes to guide your oral response.

"Papa's Parrot" by Cynthia Rylant
Selection Test A

Critical Reading *Identify the letter of the choice that best answers the question.*

____ 1. In "Papa's Parrot," Harry and his friends often stop by the candy and nut shop when they are young. What about those visits does Mr. Tillian enjoy most?
   A. He enjoys their interest in his store.
   B. He enjoys showing off his parrot.
   C. He enjoys having company.
   D. He enjoys the money they spend.

____ 2. In "Papa's Parrot," what is a major change in the lives of Harry and his friends when they enter junior high school?
   A. They like burgers better than candy.
   B. They have more spending money.
   C. They do not like Mr. Tillian's parrot.
   D. They do not have time after school.

____ 3. In "Papa's Parrot," when does Mr. Tillian buy Rocky?
   A. when Harry is in elementary school
   B. when Harry is about seven
   C. after he comes home from the hospital
   D. after Harry stops coming to the shop

____ 4. In "Papa's Parrot," why does Mr. Tillian choose a parrot as a pet?
   A. Parrots are colorful.
   B. Parrots are easy to care for.
   C. Parrots attract customers to a store.
   D. Parrots can talk.

____ 5. Use context clues in this passage from "Papa's Parrot" to choose the correct meaning of the underlined word.

   > Harry would <u>stroll</u> past the shop, on his way somewhere else, and he'd take a quick look inside to see what his dad was doing. Mr. Tillian was always talking to the bird. So Harry kept walking.

   A. look
   B. run
   C. walk
   D. bike

Unit 1 Resources: Fiction and Nonfiction

___ 6. In "Papa's Parrot," why does Harry come to feel embarrassed by his father?
   A. His father owns a candy shop.
   B. His father talks to a parrot.
   C. His father is fat.
   D. His father dislikes his friends.

___ 7. Use context clues in this passage from "Papa's Parrot" to find the correct meaning of the underlined word.

   Harry and his father joked with each other at the dinner table as they always had—Mr. Tillian teasing Harry about his smelly socks; Harry teasing Mr. Tillian about his blubbery stomach.

   A. joking
   B. criticizing
   C. lecturing
   D. teaching

___ 8. In "Papa's Parrot," Harry begins to avoid his father at the shop but still jokes with him at home. Why is their relationship different at home?
   A. Mr. Tillian does not talk to the parrot at home.
   B. Mr. Tillian does not worry about the shop at home.
   C. There are no shipments of candy and nuts to unpack at home.
   D. There is no television for Mr. Tillian to watch at home.

___ 9. Use context clues in this passage from "Papa's Parrot" to choose the correct meaning of the underlined word.

   Harry opened the new boxes his father hadn't gotten to. Peppermints. Jawbreakers. Toffee creams. Strawberry kisses. Harry traveled from bin to bin, putting the candies where they belonged.

   A. store
   B. counter
   C. container
   D. floor

___ 10. In "Papa's Parrot," when does Harry realize how much his father has missed him?
   A. when he passes the shop each day
   B. when Rocky says, "Where's Harry?"
   C. when he sees the candy all over the floor
   D. when he visits his father in the hospital

____ **11.** In "Papa's Parrot," what is Harry feeling when he throws peppermints at Rocky?
A. joy
B. amusement
C. guilt
D. fear

Vocabulary and Grammar

____ **12.** In which sentence about "Papa's Parrot" is the word *ignored* used correctly?
A. Harry ignored the parrot by feeding it and cleaning its cage.
B. The parrot ignored Harry by chattering constantly.
C. Mr. Tillian ignored the symptoms of his illness until they became unavoidable.
D. The children ignored the candy shop because they liked seeing the parrot.

____ **13.** In which sentence about "Papa's Parrot" is the word *resumed* used correctly?
A. After taking a short break, Harry resumed the task of sorting the candies.
B. When Mr. Tillian fell ill, he resumed that he would be sent to the hospital.
C. The children who came into the shop resumed the bag of nuts in no time flat.
D. When he applied for an after-school job, Harry resumed his experience.

____ **14.** How many common nouns are in this sentence from "Papa's Parrot"?
For years, after school, Harry had always stopped in to see his father at work.
A. 2   B. 3   C. 4   D. 5

Essay

15. In an essay, compare and contrast Mr. Tillian's treatment of Rocky with Harry's treatment of the parrot. Does either character change his behavior toward the parrot? Refer to events in "Papa's Parrot" to support your statements.

16. In an essay, show how Harry's feelings about his father change as the events of "Papa's Parrot" unfold. Begin by considering Harry's feelings about his father at the beginning of the story. Then, follow Harry as he enters junior high school and deals with his father's illness. Cite examples from each part of the story to illustrate your statements.

17. Thinking About the Big Question: What is the best way to find the truth? In the story of "Papa's Parrot," Harry finds out the truth about his father's feelings in an unexpected way. In an essay, explain whether this is the best way for Harry to hear the truth. Use details from the story as support for your ideas.

Name _____ Date _____

"Papa's Parrot" by Cynthia Rylant
Selection Test B

Critical Reading *Identify the letter of the choice that best completes the statement or answers the question.*

____ 1. In "Papa's Parrot," when are Harry and his father the best of friends?
   A. during Harry's early childhood
   B. when Harry is a teenager
   C. before Harry enters junior high school
   D. after Harry finishes junior high school

____ 2. In "Papa's Parrot," why do Harry and his friends begin to go to Mr. Tillian's shop less often?
   A. They have new interests.
   B. They get after-school jobs.
   C. Mr. Tillian prefers the company of his parrot.
   D. Tension develops between Harry and his father.

____ 3. What do you learn about Mr. Tillian in the following passage from "Papa's Parrot"?
   A new group of children came to Mr. Tillian's shop now. But not Harry Tillian and his friends.
   A. He has affection for children of all ages.
   B. His favorite young person is his son, Harry.
   C. He is familiar with neighborhood routines.
   D. He is capable of running a profitable store.

____ 4. Which aspect of Mr. Tillian's character in "Papa's Parrot" is revealed by the fact that he buys the parrot "for more money than he could really afford"?
   A. He is not always practical.
   B. He understands tropical birds.
   C. He is a good businessman.
   D. He is self-sufficient and reliable.

____ 5. In this passage, which of the following choices is a context clue that could help you figure out that *romantic* means "having to do with stories or feelings about love"?
   When business was slow, Mr. Tillian would turn on a small color television he had sitting in a corner, and he and Rocky would watch the soap operas. Rocky liked to scream when the <u>romantic</u> music came on, and Mr. Tillian would yell at him to shut up.
   A. "a small color television"
   B. "would watch the soap operas"
   C. "Rocky liked to scream"
   D. "Mr. Tillian would yell at him"

____ 6. In "Papa's Parrot," when Harry and his father tease each other and joke together at the dinner table, their behavior could be described as
   A. surly and rude.
   B. comfortable and quiet.
   C. distant and somber.
   D. relaxed and affectionate.

Name _____ **Date** _____

____ **7.** In these passages from "Papa's Parrot," which of the following choices is a context clue that could help you figure out that *blubbery* means "flabby"?

> Though his father was fat and merely owned a candy and nut shop, Harry Tillian liked his father . . .

> Harry and his father joked . . . —Mr. Tillian teasing Harry about his smelly socks; Harry teasing Mr. Tillian about his blubbery stomach.

   A. "fat"
   B. "candy"
   C. "joked"
   D. "smelly"

____ **8.** Which of the following choices is a context clue that could help you figure out that *shipments* means "goods sent to a person or a company"?

> He worried about his shop. New shipments of candy and nuts would be arriving. Rocky would be hungry. Who would take care of things?

   A. "worried about his shop"
   B. "candy and nuts would be arriving"
   C. "Rocky would be hungry."
   D. "Who would take care of things?"

____ **9.** In "Papa's Parrot," when does Harry go to the candy and nut shop to unpack the candy and feed Rocky?
   A. before he begins junior high school
   B. after he begins junior high school
   C. the day his father is taken to the hospital
   D. after he visits his father in the hospital

____ **10.** In "Papa's Parrot," why is Harry surprised by the sight of the "Closed" sign at the candy and nut shop?
   A. Harry has never seen the shop closed before.
   B. Harry has never seen the shop closed at that time of day.
   C. Harry had not known that the shop had gone out of business.
   D. Harry had not known that his father had a "Closed" sign.

____ **11.** In "Papa's Parrot," when does Harry learn that his father has missed Harry's visits to the shop?
   A. when Rocky keeps saying, "Where's Harry?"
   B. when Harry visits his father in the hospital
   C. when Rocky screams and clings to his perch
   D. when Harry walks past the shop after school

____ **12.** In the course of "Papa's Parrot," which of the following choices describes the basic relationship between Harry and his father?
   A. They are always fond of each other and close to each other.
   B. There is always a tenseness and a distance between them.
   C. They are always fond of each other, but they grow more distant.
   D. There is always a tenseness between them, but they grow closer.

____ 13. At the end of "Papa's Parrot," how does Harry feel about Rocky?
   A. Harry is still embarrassed by his father's interest in the parrot.
   B. Harry thinks that the parrot is a good if argumentative companion.
   C. Harry is concerned about the parrot and feels protective of it.
   D. Harry is angry with the parrot for coming between him and his father.

____ 14. What does the following passage from "Papa's Parrot" add to the story?
   Harry sobbed, "I'm here." The tears were coming.
   A. It shows the shock of realization.   C. It shows Harry's embarrassment.
   B. It provides a touch of humor.   D. It presents a fact about Harry.

Vocabulary and Grammar

____ 15. In which sentence about "Papa's Parrot" is the word *ignored* used correctly?
   A. The children ignored the candy, examining every piece.
   B. The parrot ignored Mr. Tillian, screaming at him all day long.
   C. Mr. Tillian ignored the signs of his illness until he collapsed.
   D. Harry ignored his father at home, joking with him as he always had.

____ 16. In which sentence about "Papa's Parrot" is the word *resumed* used correctly?
   A. After a pause, Harry resumed the task of sorting the candies.
   B. The children purchased and resumed two bags of nuts every day.
   C. The parrot resumed its perch after squawking and flying around the room.
   D. When customers saw the "Closed" sign, they resumed Mr. Tillian was ill.

____ 17. Which words in this sentence from "Papa's Parrot" are common nouns?
   Though his father was fat and merely owned a . . . shop, Harry Tillian liked his papa.
   A. father, shop, papa   C. father, shop, Harry Tillian, papa
   B. father, fat, shop, papa   D. father, fat, shop, Harry Tillian, papa

____ 18. Which words in this passage from "Papa's Parrot" are proper nouns?
   Rocky was good company for Mr. Tillian. When business was slow, Mr. Tillian would turn on the small color television. . . . So Harry kept walking.

   A. company, business, television
   B. Rocky, Mr. Tillian, Mr. Tillian, Harry
   C. Mr. Tillian, Mr. Tillian, Harry
   D. Rocky, company, Mr. Tillian, business, Mr. Tillian, television, Harry

Essay

19. In an essay, consider the relationship between Harry and his father in "Papa's Parrot." Might one or both characters have acted differently? Do you think that Mr. Tillian should have told his son that he missed the boy and was lonely? Do you think that Harry should have paid more attention to his father?

20. **Thinking About the Big Question: What is the best way to find the truth?** In the story of "Papa's Parrot," how does Harry find the truth? In an essay, explain whether this is the best way for Harry to hear the truth. Use details from the story as support for your ideas.

Vocabulary Warm-up Word Lists

Study these words from "MK." Then, apply your knowledge to the activities that follow.

Word List A

deceive [di SEEV] *v.* to make someone believe what is not true
  Zach will <u>deceive</u> his friends if he tells them a lie.

difficulty [DIF i kuhl tee] *n.* the condition of being hard to do or hard to deal with
  Lauren had <u>difficulty</u> doing the complicated math problem.

education [ej oo KAY shun] *n.* the process of getting training or knowledge
  The doctor went to school for a long time to get a medical <u>education</u>.

emergency [ee MER juhn see] *adj.* urgent and unexpected; needing attention right away
  The babysitter kept <u>emergency</u> phone numbers handy in case he needed help in a hurry.

fake [FAYK] *adj.* false; not genuine
  The <u>fake</u> diamonds did not fool the jeweler.

generally [JEN er uh lee] *adv.* usually; in most instances
  Alexis <u>generally</u> walks her dog twice a day.

immediate [i MEE dee it] *adj.* happening or done at once
  The patient's heart condition required <u>immediate</u> care.

verge [VERJ] *n.* the edge or border of something
  The unhappy employees were on the <u>verge</u> of leaving their jobs.

Word List B

Bible [BY bul] *n.* the sacred book of Christianity
  The minister opened the <u>Bible</u> to the Book of Acts.

commit [kuh MIT] *v.* to agree to something by making a promise
  David will <u>commit</u> himself to two hours of volunteer work a week.

historians [his TAW ree uhnz] *n.* people who study and write about the past
  <u>Historians</u> have written a great deal about the battles of the Civil War.

ignorant [IG nawr uhnt] *adj.* having little knowledge
  Daniel has not studied geology, so when it comes to identifying rocks, he is <u>ignorant</u>.

informed [in FOHRMD] *v.* told someone something
  Rachel <u>informed</u> Jason that she would meet him at the airport.

normal [NAWR muhl] *adj.* being or feeling the usual way
  Taylor felt <u>normal</u> once she got over the flu.

oath [OHTH] *n.* a serious, formal promise
  The president takes an <u>oath</u> to serve the country.

sessions [SESH uhnz] *n.* the meetings of a group
  The class had two <u>sessions</u> a week, meeting every Monday and Friday.

Name _____   Date _____

"MK" by Jean Fritz
Vocabulary Warm-up Exercises

Exerise A *Fill in each blank in the paragraph below with an appropriate word from Word List A. Use each word only once.*

It is important never to use the [1] _____ phone number 911 for a

[2] _____ situation. It is against the law to [3] _____ peo-

ple who are dealing with real emergencies. Think of the [4] _____ there

would be if someone needed [5] _____ attention and all the lines were

busy. [6] _____, people who respond to emergencies have received the

[7] _____ that teaches them to help quickly in serious situations and

gently guide people through their distress. So, if you find yourself on the

[8] _____ of making such a call, think again. Be a solid citizen! Do not

fool those workers and interrupt their important efforts.

Exercise B *Revise each sentence so that the underlined vocabulary word is used in a logical way. Be sure to keep the vocabulary word in your revision.*

Example: Because our plan was <u>practical</u>, it made no sense.
Because our plan was <u>practical</u>, it made a lot of sense.

1. The minister opened her <u>Bible</u> and read the story of America's settlers.
   _____

2. Hannah will <u>commit</u> herself to the project, so she will not be involved in it.
   _____

3. <u>Historians</u> are likely to talk about topics that have to do with science.
   _____

4. Being <u>ignorant</u> of the schedule, Andrew was always on time.
   _____

5. Because Megan was not <u>informed</u> of the date, she marked it on her calendar.
   _____

6. The <u>normal</u> time to eat dessert is before the main dish is served.
   _____

7. The president's <u>oath</u> was not a serious promise to serve the country.
   _____

8. Gym class has three <u>sessions</u> a week, so students meet for gym every day.
   _____

Name _____ Date _____

"MK" by Jean Fritz
Reading Warm-up A

Read the following passage. Pay special attention to the underlined words. Then, read it again, and complete the activities. Use a separate sheet of paper for your written answers.

Dear Mom and Dad,

Here I am, writing to you from Camp Hope. I am enjoying my job as a camp counselor very much. The children are respectful. They may get wild at times, but they generally listen to me when I ask them to calm down.

It has surprised me how much I enjoy being away from home (for a while, at least). As you know, I was nervous before I left. It was only with great difficulty that I got on the bus two weeks ago to come here. In fact, before I left, I thought I might have to deceive you. That's right! I thought about coming down with a fake attack of the flu the night before camp started, but I knew that would not be right.

When we talked about how I was feeling, you gave me good advice. You told me this experience would be an education for me. You were right, because I feel as if I have learned a great deal about working with people. The job has given me confidence and has shown me how well I can get along with others. You also told me that I would be able to handle emergency situations. You said that if I could not handle them myself, I would know how to get help. In fact, this afternoon at the pool one of the children got a cramp while swimming. He needed immediate attention. At once, I followed the procedures. First I sounded the siren. Then I jumped into the water and pulled him out. The little guy was fine. I was on the verge of tears—I felt both joy and relief because I had saved a little boy.

Well, that's all for now. Hope everything is going well at home. I'll see you in a few weeks.

Love,

Brittany

1. Circle the words that tell what the children at camp generally do. Provide a synonym for *generally*.

2. Underline a clue that shows that Brittany had difficulty before she left for camp. Define *difficulty*.

3. Underline Brittany's plan to deceive her parents. Why did she plan to *deceive* them?

4. Describe what a fake attack of the flu might be like. Tell what *fake* means.

5. Underline a sentence that tells one way in which Brittany is getting an education at camp. Use *education* in a sentence.

6. What did Brittany do that shows she can handle emergency situations? Define *emergency*.

7. Circle the phrase that means immediate. Write about something that requires *immediate* attention.

8. Underline the reasons Brittany was on the verge of tears. What might put you on the verge of tears?

"**MK**" by Jean Fritz
Reading Warm-up B

Read the following passage. Pay special attention to the underlined words. Then, read it again, and complete the activities. Use a separate sheet of paper for your written answers.

The Supreme Court is one of three branches of the United States government. <u>Historians</u>, people who study the events of the past, say that when the Court was first created, its judges did not know what their duties would be. They had not been <u>informed</u> by the framers of the Constitution.

The framers knew only that they wanted three branches of government: the executive, the legislative, and the judicial. In that way, the president, Congress, and the Supreme Court would ensure that no one branch of government had too much power.

It was left to Congress and the Supreme Court itself to determine the Court's duties. In 1790, the first group of judges met in the first of many <u>sessions</u>. <u>Ignorant</u> of their powers, the judges proposed what their duties ought to be. After all, the judges had taken an <u>oath</u> on the <u>Bible</u> to serve their country faithfully.

Still, the early Supreme Courts lacked direction. The judges did not <u>commit</u> themselves to judging controversial cases. That changed in 1801, when John Marshall was appointed head of the Court by President John Adams. Chief Justice Marshall took steps to shape the power of the court. An important case was *Marbury vs. Madison.* In it Marshall made sure that the Supreme Court had the power to interpret the Constitution. That meant that the court could decide whether the laws made by Congress and the states were allowable.

Since then the <u>normal</u> business of the Court has been to decide only the most important issues.

1. Underline the phrase that tells what <u>historians</u> are. Use *historians* in a sentence.

2. Circle the words in the first paragraph whose meaning is similar to "not <u>informed</u>." What were the judges not *informed* of?

3. Underline the words that help explain what <u>sessions</u> are. What *sessions* might you attend?

4. What were the judges <u>ignorant</u> of? Define *ignorant*.

5. What is the <u>Bible</u>? Use *Bible* in a sentence.

6. What is another word for <u>oath</u>? Who else might take an *oath*?

7. Did the early court <u>commit</u> itself to judging serious cases? Why or why not?

8. Underline the words that tell what the <u>normal</u> business of the court is today. What does *normal* mean?

"MK" by Jean Fritz
Writing About the Big Question

What is the best way to find the truth?

Big Question Vocabulary

awareness	believable	conclude	convince	debate
evaluate	evidence	explain	factual	fiction
insight	perceive	reality	reveal	truth

A. *Use one or more words from the list above to complete each sentence*

1. In _____, an author may mix in some truth.

2. A reader can often determine which parts of a fictional story have elements of _____.

3. A _____ fictional story is not always true.

B. *Answer the questions.*

1. Name a fictional book, movie, or television show that was so believable, you were convinced that at least part of it was based on truth.

   _____

   _____

2. Explain what elements of the fictional work were realistic.

   _____

   _____

   _____

   _____

C. *Complete the sentence below. Then, answer the question by writing a short paragraph connecting the sentence to the Big Question.*

A story from my childhood that I would like to tell is _____

_____

If you made the story into a work of fiction, what would you change, and what would stay the same?

_____

_____

_____

_____

Unit 1 Resources: Fiction and Nonfiction

"**MK**" by Jean Fritz

Reading: Use Context Clues to Unlock the Meaning

Context, the words and phrases surrounding a word, can help you understand a word you do not know. When you come across an unfamiliar word, **use context clues to unlock the meaning.** Look for a word or words that might mean the same thing or have the opposite meaning of the unfamiliar word. In addition, you may find definitions, examples, or descriptions of the unfamiliar word. For example, in this passage from "MK," the italicized words are clues to the meaning of *protected:*

> The women and children going to Shanghai would be <u>protected</u> *from bullets by steel barriers erected around the deck.*

As you read, use context clues to find possible meanings for unfamiliar words. Check the words in a dictionary after you read.

DIRECTIONS: *Read each of the following sentences or short passages from "MK." Look at the underlined word. Then, find other words in the passage that can be used as context clues to help you figure out the meaning of the underlined word. Write the context clue or clues on the first line. Write the meaning of the underlined word on the second line. Then, check your answer by looking up the underlined word in a dictionary.*

1. I couldn't let on how I really felt. . . . "I'll be okay," I said, sniffing back fake tears. Sometimes it's necessary to <u>deceive</u> your parents if you love them, and I did love mine.

   Context clues: _____

   Meaning of word: _____

2. The girls were given what looked like dance cards and the boys were supposed to sign up for the talk sessions they wanted. Of course a girl could feel like a <u>wallflower</u> if her card wasn't filled up, but mine usually was.

   Context clues: _____

   Meaning of word: _____

3. It was a three-day trip across most of the <u>continent</u>, but it didn't seem long. Every minute America was under us and rushing past our windows—the Rocky Mountains, the Mississippi River, flat ranch land, small towns, forests, boys dragging school bags over dusty roads.

   Context clues: _____

   Meaning of word: _____

4. I decided that American children were <u>ignorant</u>. Didn't their teachers teach them anything?

   Context clues: _____

   Meaning of word: _____

"**MK**" by Jean Fritz
Literary Analysis: Narrative

Narrative writing is any type of writing that tells a story. The act or process of telling a story is also called **narration.**

- A narrative is usually told in chronological order—the order in which events occur in time.
- A narrative may be fiction, nonfiction, or poetry.

When you look at events in chronological order, you see that events that occur later in a narrative often depend on events that occurred earlier. In "MK," for example, the part of the story in which Jean takes her first steps on American soil must follow the part in which Jean and her family cross the Pacific Ocean to reach America.

DIRECTIONS: *Below is a list of ten events from "MK." Put the events in chronological order by writing a number from 1 to 10 on the line before the event. Remember that each event has to make sense in terms of what has already occurred in the story.*

——— **A.** Paula, Jean's roommate at the Shanghai American School, cuts Jean's hair in a bob, the latest American style.

——— **B.** Jean and most of the other passengers are seasick as they cross the Pacific Ocean on a steamer.

——— **C.** Fletcher Barrett tells Jean that he is in love with her.

——— **D.** In America, Jean wonders why her classmates are ignorant.

——— **E.** Jean's mother enrolls Jean in the Shanghai American School.

——— **F.** When Jean is almost ready to fall in love, her parents appear and tell her that the family is leaving China for America.

——— **G.** When Jean meets her aunts and uncles and grandmother, she is thrilled to be part of a real family.

——— **H.** Jean's mother learns that all of the American women and children in Wuhan must leave for Shanghai.

——— **I.** In college, Jean reads about "real" Americans and makes a decision to write about them someday.

——— **J.** When Jean first enters the Shanghai American School, she wonders why people make a fuss about football.

Name _____ Date _____

Vocabulary Builder

Word List

adequate   deceive   ignorant   quest   relation   transformation

A. DIRECTIONS: *Read the incomplete paragraph below. On each line, write one of the words from the Word List. Think about the meaning of each word in the context of the paragraph.*

I was watching a quiz show one night. I tried to answer a series of questions about China. I realized I didn't know as much as I thought I did. In fact, I was (1) _____ about the country and its people. I decided to begin a search for information. My (2) _____ began at the library, where I found many books on China. Some of them were (3) _____, but others did not provide enough information to suit my purposes. Next, I checked out the Internet. There I learned about the country's topography and its rivers. A month later, I had read ten books, consulted a dozen Web sites, and watched three documentaries. I had undergone a (4) _____. I had changed from someone who knew little about China to someone who knew a great deal. I had truly learned who I was in (5) _____ to the Chinese people. I would not try to (6) _____ myself again by thinking that I was educated when I was, in fact, uneducated.

B. DIRECTIONS: *On each line, write the letter of the word whose meaning is the same as that of the Word List word.*

____ **1.** quest
    A. trial   **B.** story   **C.** search   **D.** query

____ **2.** adequate
    A. absent   **B.** enough   **C.** insufficient   **D.** compassionate

____ **3.** deceive
    A. promise   **B.** yell   **C.** educate   **D.** mislead

C. WORD STUDY The prefix *in-* means "not." Use the context of the sentences and the meaning of the prefix to answer each question.

1. Why might an *indecisive* person take a long time in the candy aisle of a store?

_____

2. Why would it be a good idea to have safety education for *inexperienced* drivers?

_____

"MK" by Jean Fritz
Enrichment: Making History Live

"MK" is from a book called *Homesick: My Own Story*. The author, Jean Fritz, was homesick for America. She knew America only from books and from stories her parents had told her. Her home then was China. She had friends, but she was often lonely. She escaped from her loneliness by writing in a journal. There she described what she felt about life and the people she knew.

In America, Jean began learning about the people who had helped make the country work. She began to write stories for children, but at first none of them were published. She worked in a children's library and got to know what children like to read. Then, she tried to sell her stories again, and that time she succeeded.

Jean Fritz has published more than 25 books for young readers. The books are about Americans and American history. Because she looks for unusual facts about her subjects, most of her books have interesting titles. Some of them are *Why Don't You Get a Horse, Sam Adams? Can't You Make Them Behave, King George? And Then What Happened, Paul Revere?* and *What's the Big Idea, Ben Franklin?*

Before Jean Fritz writes about a person or a period in history, she reads a great deal. She travels to the places where the person lived or the event took place. She never makes up dialogue for real people. She uses only their own words from journals, diaries, and letters.

In an interview, Fritz said:

Why do I write so much about history? Sometimes I think it is because I spent my childhood in China, hearing about America from my parents and having to wait until I was thirteen to get here. So I felt a need to make up for lost time. . . . Sometimes I think it is because I like stories, and of course history is packed jam-full of stories. Every person has his or her own stories, and I like to find out about them. It's a little like eavesdropping, and I'm pretty good at that!

DIRECTIONS: *Use the information in the passage above to answer these questions.*

1. What activity did Jean Fritz begin early in her life that may have helped her become a writer? Why did she engage in this activity?

   _____

2. What made Jean Fritz want to learn about and write about American history?

   _____

   _____

   _____

3. Why do many of Jean Fritz's books have unusual titles?

   _____

4. What rule does Jean Fritz have about writing dialogue for characters from history?

   _____

   _____

"**Papa's Parrot**" by Cynthia Rylant
"**MK**" by Jean Fritz

Integrated Language Skills: Grammar

Common and Proper Nouns

All nouns can be classified as either **common nouns** or **proper nouns**. A **common noun** names a person, place, or thing—such as a feeling or an idea. Common nouns are not capitalized unless they begin a sentence or are an important word in a title. In the following sentence, the common nouns are underlined.

Harry had always stopped in to see his <u>father</u> at <u>work</u>.

In that sentence, the words *father* and *work* are general names for a person and a place.

A **proper noun** names a specific person, place, or thing. Proper nouns are always capitalized. In the following sentence, the proper noun is underlined.

<u>Harry Tillian</u> liked his papa.

Harry Tillian is a proper noun because it names a specific person.

A. PRACTICE: *The following sentences are from or based on "Papa's Parrot" or "MK." Circle each proper noun, and underline each common noun.*

1. "Rocky was good company for Mr. Tillian."
2. "New shipments of candy and nuts would be arriving. Rocky would be hungry."
3. "Harry told his father that he would go to the store every day after school and unpack boxes."
4. Jean had just finished sixth grade at the British School in Wuhan.
5. "All American women and children had to catch the . . . boat to Shanghai."
6. "Mr. Barrett met us in Shanghai and drove us to their home, where his wife was on the front porch."

B. Writing Application: *Rewrite each of the following sentences. Replace as many of the common nouns as you can with a proper noun to make the information more specific.*

1. The author lived in another country when she was young.

   _____

2. The boy was disappointed when his father bought a parrot.

   _____

3. The author moved to another country.

   _____

4. The parrot showed by his speech that the father missed his son.

   _____

Name _____ Date _____

"Papa's Parrot" by Cynthia Rylant
"MK" by Jean Fritz

Integrated Language Skills: Support for Writing a Brief Essay

"Papa's Parrot": Use the graphic organizer below to record details that show what Harry was like before he entered junior high school and after he entered junior high school.

Before Entering Junior High

_____
_____
_____
_____
_____
_____
_____

After Entering Junior High

_____
_____
_____
_____
_____
_____
_____

"MK": Use this graphic organizer to record details that show Jean's feelings about America before and after she arrives in the United States.

Before Arriving in the U.S.

_____
_____
_____
_____
_____
_____

After Arriving in the U.S.

_____
_____
_____
_____
_____
_____

Now, use your notes to draft a brief compare-and-contrast essay.

Name _____ Date _____

Integrated Language Skills: Support for Extend Your Learning

Listening and Speaking: "Papa's Parrot"

With your partner, decide who will read the narration, who will read Harry's lines, and who will read Rocky's lines. (Perhaps you will decide to divide the narration, with each of you taking turns reading a paragraph.) Then, answer the following questions about the parts you will be reading.

When should I stand, and when should I sit? When should I speak loudly and when softly?

_____

_____

_____

At what parts should I show strong emotion? How should I read those parts?

_____

_____

_____

Which words should I stress for effect?

_____

_____

Listening and Speaking: "MK"

After you have decided which passage from "MK" you would like to present to the class in a dramatic reading, answer the following questions.

When should I stand and when should I sit? When should I speak loudly and when should I speak softly?

_____

_____

_____

At what parts should I show strong emotion? How should I read those parts?

_____

_____

_____

Which words should I stress for effect?

_____

_____

_____

"MK" by Jean Fritz
Open-Book Test

Short Answer *Write your responses to the questions in this section on the lines provided.*

1. How did being an MK make the author different from other children in China? Use details from the beginning of "MK" to support your response.

   _____

   _____

   _____

2. The author of "MK" observes that "we wouldn't be MKs or even Ks forever." What feelings does the author show with that statement? Use details from the beginning of "MK" to explain your answer.

   _____

   _____

3. Soon after "MK" begins, the author describes being sent to Shanghai with her mother. What were they fleeing, and why? Use details from the narrative to support your answer.

   _____

   _____

4. In "MK," the author says that the travelers to Shanghai were "protected from bullets by steel *barriers* erected around the deck." Which nearby word or words suggest the meaning of the word *barriers*? Explain your answer.

   _____

   _____

5. In the middle of "MK," Mrs. Barrett is surprised by the narrator's less than adequate greeting. What might have been a more *adequate* greeting, according to Mrs. Barrett? Demonstrate an understanding of the word *adequate* as you explain your answer.

   _____

   _____

   _____

6. Jean Fritz writes in "MK" that she loved reading about the Pilgrims on the *Mayflower*. Why might she have enjoyed reading about the early arrivals in the New World? Justify your answer with details from the middle of "MK."

   _____

   _____

   _____

7. How did outside events play a role in the personal life of the author of "MK"? Use details from the middle of the narrative to show the level of control she had over her own life.

_____

_____

_____

_____

8. In "MK," the author's life changed in many ways when she started attending the American School. Use the graphic organizer to list two events she experienced there and her reactions to them. Then, on the lines, explain how her reactions were or were not surprising to her.

Events at American School	Reaction

_____

_____

9. Toward the end of "MK," the author writes about students in America who asked her questions that she considered *ignorant*. Give an example of why she thought the children were *ignorant*.

_____

_____

_____

_____

10. At the end of "MK," the author writes that George Washington was *persuaded* to run for the presidency for a second term. Which phrases or sentences in the same paragraph suggest the meaning of *persuaded*? Use information from "MK" to support your response.

_____

_____

_____

_____

_____

Essay

Write an extended response to the question of your choice or to the question or questions your teacher assigns you.

11. Based on your reading, is the author glad to have been a Missionary Kid, or did she mostly dislike the experience? In a brief essay, explore this question. Use details from "MK" to support your point of view.

12. Do you think the author of "MK" had good reasons for reacting against Fletcher Barrett so strongly? Give your answer in a brief essay with supporting examples from the narrative. Consider whether her reaction to him was justified.

13. As a child, the author of "MK" identified strongly with the experience of the Pilgrims. In the later part of her narrative, she makes another mental connection to early American history. In an essay, describe some of the connections she makes with historical figures, and explore their meaning to her.

14. **Thinking About the Big Question: What is the best way to find the truth?** The author of "MK" had very definite ideas about what was true about America and being an American. In an essay, explain how she found those truths and how her ideas changed when she finally lived in America. Consider what she eventually came to believe about herself. Use examples from the essay in your writing.

Oral Response

15. Go back to question 1, 4, 6, or 7 or to the question your teacher assigns you. Take a few minutes to expand your answer and prepare an oral response. Find additional details in "MK" that support your points. If necessary, make notes to guide your oral response.

"**MK**" by Jean Fritz
Selection Test A

Critical Reading *Identify the letter of the choice that best answers the question.*

____ 1. What does the narrator of "MK" mean when she says, "we wouldn't be MKs or even Ks forever"?

   A. Their parents would not be missionaries forever.

   B. The missionaries would not be in China forever.

   C. They would not always be missionaries' children or even children.

   D. They would not be missionaries' children once they were in America.

____ 2. When she is living in Wuhan, the narrator of "MK" suggests that she does not identify with China or its people. Which statement expresses that suggestion?

   A. Her family depends on a German family for phone calls.

   B. All American women and children have to leave Wuhan for Shanghai.

   C. Her family will return to America after she finishes seventh grade.

   D. The fighting Chinese warlords have nothing to do with her.

____ 3. Use context clues in this sentence from "MK" to choose the correct meaning of *emergency*.

   Since we had no phone, we depended on our German neighbors for <u>emergency</u> messages.

   A. coded

   B. unexpected

   C. social

   D. foreign

____ 4. Why does the narrator of "MK" turn to her book about Priscilla Alden so often?

   A. She likes to read about another newcomer to America.

   B. Priscilla Alden was also the daughter of missionaries.

   C. It is her father's favorite book.

   D. Priscilla Alden also lived in China.

____ 5. What happens in "MK" just after the narrator's mother learns that the British school in Wuhan has closed?

   A. Her family makes plans to return to America.

   B. She and her mother remain with the Barretts.

   C. Her mother enrolls her in the Shanghai American School.

   D. Fletcher Barrett enrolls in the British school in Wuhan.

____ 6. What does the narrator of "MK" realize when she first enters the grounds of the Shanghai American School?

A. The British school in Wuhan is more American than the Shanghai school.

B. The Shanghai American School is just like the British school in Wuhan.

C. She does not feel any more like an American than she had in Wuhan.

D. She will never feel like an American as long as she is in China.

____ 7. In "MK," what do the students at the Shanghai American School do at their dances?

A. They dance with one another.

B. They talk to their teachers.

C. They talk to one another.

D. They cut one another's hair.

____ 8. What happens in "MK" just before the narrator's parents tell her they are going to America?

A. She learns to dance.

B. She decides to fall in love.

C. She decides to become a writer.

D. She realizes she is a wallflower.

____ 9. Use context clues in this passage from "MK" to choose the symptom that is characteristic of seasickness.

> Passengers spent most of their time in their cabins. If they came out for a meal, they were lucky if they could get it down before it came back up again. I had my share of <u>seasickness</u>, so of course I was glad to reach San Francisco.

A. headaches

B. tiredness

C. hunger

D. vomiting

____ 10. What do the context clues in this passage from "MK" suggest about the meaning of *lurched*?

> I couldn't wait to take my first steps on American soil, but I expected the American soil to hold still for me. Instead, it swayed as if we were all still at sea, and I <u>lurched</u> about as I had been doing for the last three weeks.

A. ran quickly

B. walked unsteadily

C. stopped suddenly

D. turned slowly

____ 11. In "MK," what is the narrator's major disappointment in her new school in America?

    A. The other students seem ignorant.

    B. The other students seem curious.

    C. She dislikes her teachers.

    D. She misses her Chinese friends.

Vocabulary and Grammar

____ 12. In which sentence about "MK" is the word *quest* used correctly?

    A. Jean watched a quest from her deck chair.

    B. Jean was on a quest to be a true American.

    C. Jean and Fletcher ate a quest at midday.

    D. Fletcher asked a quest about Jean's love life.

____ 13. What would someone do if he or she wanted to *deceive*?

    A. He or she would check the mailbox.

    B. He or she would tell the truth.

    C. He or she would tell a lie.

    D. He or she would dance.

____ 14. How many proper nouns are in this sentence about "MK"?

When Jean was walking along a beach in Maine, she saw a bluebell that reminded her of her summers at Kuling in China.

    A. 3   B. 4   C. 7   D. 8

Essay

15. How does the narrator feel about her country of birth at the beginning of "MK," and then at the end? Do her feelings change? If so, in what ways? In an essay, discuss Jean's feelings about China and her relationship to it. Refer to events in the text to support your points.

16. Although "MK" is a narrative, the events in the story are not told in chronological order. In an essay, outline the order of events in the story. Where is the narrator at the beginning? Where is she next? Where is she at the end? Then, tell why the writer might have chosen to narrate the events in that order.

17. **Thinking About the Big Question: What is the best way to find the truth?** The author of "MK" had very definite ideas about what was true about America and being an American. In an essay, explain how her ideas changed after she lived in America for a while. Use examples from the essay in your writing.

"**MK**" by Jean Fritz
Selection Test B

Critical Reading *Identify the letter of the choice that best completes the statement or answers the question.*

____ 1. As an adult, what does the narrator of "MK" think that she has gained by spending her youth as an MK?
  A. a love of wild bluebells
  B. an appreciation of American heroes
  C. a sharp sense of time and place
  D. a fear of armies on the move

____ 2. Use context clues in this sentence to choose the correct meaning of *commit*.
  I have noticed, that those MKs who were born in China and stayed there through their high school years were more likely to <u>commit</u> their lives in some way to China.

  A. expose
  B. return
  C. travel
  D. give

____ 3. Use context clues in this passage to choose the correct description of a ricksha.
  My mother and I had been in a ricksha on the way to the racecourse. . . .The ricksha-pullers were fast runners.

  A. a racehorse
  B. a race track
  C. a vehicle
  D. a gunboat

____ 4. When the narrator of "MK" is living in Wuhan, the American women and children flee because the Chinese army is near. What does that information suggest?
  A. The country's internal conflicts may affect foreigners.
  B. They would be safe because they were traveling together.
  C. Civil wars take many lives on both sides of the conflict.
  D. Living near a river is always a good idea during wartime.

____ 5. In "MK," what division does the swinging door in the dormitory provide?
  A. It separates the boys from the girls.
  B. It separates students from teachers.
  C. It separates junior high students from high school students.
  D. It separates Americans from other foreign students.

____ 6. In "MK," what does Paula, the narrator's roommate at the Shanghai American School, mean to suggest by the following remark?
  "I happen to know you're an MK, . . . but you don't have to look like one."

  A. Jean does not look stylish.
  B. Jean is dressed like an American.
  C. Jean is wearing a school uniform.
  D. Jean is wearing traditional Chinese clothing.

____ 7. Use context clues in this passage to choose the correct meaning of *wallflower*.

Of course a girl could feel like a <u>wallflower</u> if her card wasn't filled up, but mine usually was.

    A. a kind of climbing ivy

    B. a flowered wallpaper

    C. an unpopular person

    D. a skilled dancer

____ 8. For the narrator of "MK," what is the *major* difference between traveling on the Yangtze River and crossing the Pacific Ocean?

    A. "Beef tea" is not served on the Yangtze River trip.

    B. There are no deck chairs on the Yangtze River trip.

    C. Only women and children travel on the Yangtze River.

    D. The ocean crossing is rough and the passengers are seasick.

____ 9. How is the narrator of "MK" like Priscilla Alden?

    A. Both are writers.

    B. Both are new to America.

    C. Both are in love with John Alden.

    D. Both are disappointed in America.

____ 10. Why does the narrator of "MK" think that the American students are ignorant?

    A. They do not know anything about MKs.

    B. They do not know the name of her hometown in China.

    C. They do not know anything about the Pilgrims.

    D. They do not know anything about life in China.

____ 11. Why does the narrator of "MK" come to think so highly of George Washington?

    A. He served two terms as president.

    B. He worked on the Constitution.

    C. He did what the country needed instead of what he wanted.

    D. He led the American army during the Revolutionary War.

____ 12. In "MK," the narrator tells about events in her life in which general order?

    A. first as an adult, then as a child, and finally as an adult

    B. first as a child, then as a teenager, and finally as an adult

    C. first as an adult, then as a child, and finally as a teenager

    D. first as a child, then as a teenager, and finally as an adult

____ 13. Which of the following sentences describes the order of events in "MK"?

    A. Jean attends school in Wuhan, visits the Barretts, and sees bluebells in Maine.

    B. Jean attends the Shanghai American School, comes to America, and notices bluebells in Maine.

    C. Jean notices bluebells in Maine, attends the Shanghai American School, and travels in a ricksha to the racecourse.

    D. Jean notices bluebells in Maine, decides that American children are ignorant, and realizes that she wants to be a writer someday.

Vocabulary and Grammar

____ 14. Someone who is *ignorant* is most likely
   A. unattentive.
   B. unprepared.
   C. uninformed.
   D. unrelated.

____ 15. In which sentence is the word *adequate* used correctly?
   A. Because the food supply was adequate, we had enough to eat.
   B. The adequate carried water from the mountains to the city.
   C. The supply of rice was adequate to the supply of wheat.
   D. The child was well liked because her behavior was adequate.

____ 16. Which words in the following passage from "MK" are proper nouns?
   I had just finished sixth grade at the British School in Wuhan. . . . I knew that there was fighting up and down the Yangtze River, but the Chinese were always fighting.
   A. British School, Wuhan, Yangtze River, Chinese
   B. sixth grade, fighting, fighting
   C. I, British School, Wuhan, I, Yangtze River, Chinese
   D. I, sixth grade, fighting, up, down, fighting

____ 17. Which words in the following sentences from "MK" are common nouns?
   I told myself this was like Stephen in the Bible who was stoned to death. He just didn't have a ricksha handy.
   A. I, myself, this, who, he
   B. Stephen, Bible
   C. I, myself, death, ricksha
   D. death, ricksha

Essay

18. Although "MK" is a narrative, the events in the story are not told in strict chronological order. In an essay, outline the sequence of events in "MK." Where is the narrator at the beginning? Where is she next? Where is she at the end? Then, consider the effect of that sequence of events. Why might the writer have chosen to relate the events out of order?

19. In an essay, describe what the narrator of "MK" tells the reader about Priscilla Alden. Then, explain how Alden and the narrator are alike and how they are different. Finally, consider why Priscilla Alden was important to the narrator. Cite events and details from "MK" to support your points.

20. **Thinking About the Big Question: What is the best way to find the truth?** The author of "MK" had very definite ideas about what was true about America and being an American. In an essay, explain how she found those truths and how her ideas changed when she finally lived in America. Consider what she eventually came to believe about herself. Use examples from the essay in your writing.

Vocabulary Warm-up Word Lists

Study these words from An American Childhood. *Then, complete the activities.*

Word List A

bordered [BAWR derd] *v.* surrounded
Several low hedges <u>bordered</u> our vegetable garden but did not keep out small animals.

compare [kuhm PAYR] *v.* to notice similarities and differences between things
Buyers should <u>compare</u> prices before they buy a car.

considered [kuhn SID erd] *v.* regarded something in a particular way
Mike <u>considered</u> his older brother's room off limits.

flung [FLUHNG] *v.* threw something forcefully
Christopher <u>flung</u> the wet towel into the dryer.

glory [GLAWR ee] *n.* something that creates feelings of wonder or joy; honor or fame
The athlete felt the <u>glory</u> of winning the race.

immense [im MENS] *adj.* huge or enormous
The <u>immense</u> roller coaster has steep, scary drops.

seldom [SEL duhm] *adv.* not very often; rarely
Emily <u>seldom</u> goes to bed before ten o'clock.

strategy [STRAT uh jee] *n.* a smart plan for getting something done
John's <u>strategy</u> for passing the test earned him an A.

Word List B

adult [uh DULT] *n.* a fully grown person
One <u>adult</u> accompanied each group of children on the hiking trip.

apparently [uh PAR uhnt lee] *adv.* obviously or clearly
<u>Apparently</u>, Joe was too busy rushing to class to stop and say hello.

approved [uh PROOVD] *v.* thought something was acceptable or good
Much to Samantha's relief, her mother <u>approved</u> of her new outfit.

childhood [CHYLD hood] *n.* the time when someone is a child
<u>Childhood</u> is a time for playing with friends and going to school.

complex [kahm PLEKS] *adj.* very complicated
Tyler could not follow the <u>complex</u> instructions in the computer manual.

incredibly [in KRED uh blee] *adv.* in a way that is hard to believe
The squirrel ran into the busy road and, <u>incredibly</u>, made it safely across.

precisely [pree SYS lee] *adv.* exactly or very accurately
Sarah knew <u>precisely</u> where she was in the city.

skilled [SKILD] *adj.* able to do something well
James, a <u>skilled</u> musician, teaches piano and guitar.

from **An American Childhood** by Annie Dillard
Vocabulary Warm-up Exercises

Exercise A *Fill in each blank in the paragraph below with an appropriate word from Word List A. Use each word only once.*

When he was a child, Juan [1] _____ reading a waste of time. It was an [2] _____ task for him to begin a book, and he [3] _____ finished one. Then one day during an argument, his brother [4] _____ a book at him. Its cover was [5] _____ with photographs of Olympic athletes. The goal of the book was to [6] _____ the [7] _____ that each athlete used to succeed. That book introduced Juan to the [8] _____ of reading.

Exercise B *Answer the questions with complete explanations.*

Example: If Nicole <u>never</u> goes swimming, does she swim all the time?
No; never means "not at all," so if Nicole never goes swimming, she would not go swimming at any time.

1. Is a <u>complex</u> question easy to answer?
   _____

2. If a witness was <u>apparently</u> dishonest, would a jury believe him or her?
   _____

3. If a horse ran <u>incredibly</u> fast, would it be likely to win a race?
   _____

4. If you arrive for a movie <u>precisely</u> on time, are you a minute or two late?
   _____

5. Is someone who plays the piano perfectly a <u>skilled</u> musician?
   _____

6. If your teacher <u>approved</u> of a topic for a science project, would you do your project on that topic?
   _____

7. If only <u>adults</u> are allowed to join a club, would you be allowed to join?
   _____

8. Is <u>childhood</u> a time for having a career?
   _____

Name _____ Date _____

from **An American Childhood** by Annie Dillard
Reading Warm-up A

Read the following passage. Pay special attention to the underlined words. Then, read it again, and complete the activities. Use a separate sheet of paper for your written answers.

When I was young, there were two places in the neighborhood where children could play: in a back yard and in an empty lot.

Most of my friends <u>considered</u> back yards boring. They were too safe and familiar. Yet it was there that we enjoyed the simple games of dodge ball and tag. In the bushes that <u>bordered</u> our yards, we had endless chances to observe birds and insects. In one yard we pitched a tent every summer. We would hide out in it and read comic books while eating peanut-butter sandwiches. Another back yard had an <u>immense</u> brick barbecue beside a neat patio with tables and chairs. You could roast a whole cow in that barbecue. Usually, we just roasted hot dogs.

Yes, back yards were safe. When we wanted adventure, however, a back yard could not <u>compare</u> to an empty lot. There were three empty lots on our block, one on the east side of the street and two on the west side. Among the rows of houses, they stood out like missing teeth. Of course the lots were not really empty. Every inch was covered with prickly weeds. We had a <u>strategy</u> for trampling down the weeds to make a hiding place. First we pulled up our socks to protect our legs. Then, very carefully, we would walk in a circle, around and around, until we had tramped down the space.

The lots contained a great amount of trash, too, that drivers and playful winds had <u>flung</u> there: candy wrappers, potato-chip bags, soda cans—you name it. In other words, the lots were great places for finding stuff. We <u>seldom</u> found objects of value, but we did not mind that. It was the hunt that mattered. We needed only to find something unexpected, however small, to experience the <u>glory</u> of discovery.

Ah, yes. When I was young, back yards were safe, and a child could get lost in an empty lot.

1. Underline the sentence that tells why the children <u>considered</u> the back yard boring. Do you agree or disagree? Why or why not?

2. Circle the word that tells what <u>bordered</u> the yards. Then, tell what *bordered* means.

3. Underline the sentence that describes how <u>immense</u> the barbecue was. Do you believe that description? Why or why not?

4. Underline the phrase that tells when a back yard could not <u>compare</u> to an empty lot. In what way can you *compare* the two?

5. Underline the sentences that explain the children's <u>strategy</u> for making a hiding place. Tell what *strategy* means.

6. Circle the word that tells what was <u>flung</u> into the lots. Describe the action of having *flung* something.

7. Why did the children not mind that they <u>seldom</u> found valuable objects? What does *seldom* mean?

8. What gave the children their moment of <u>glory</u>? Describe a moment of *glory* in your life.

from **An American Childhood** by Annie Dillard
Reading Warm-up B

Read the following passage. Pay special attention to the underlined words. Then, read it again, and complete the activities. Use a separate sheet of paper for your written answers.

The little house on Tampa Street in New Orleans was as neat as a postcard. That is how Lila Jackson Brown liked it, and that is how she kept it. The only thing she loved more than her house was her son, Kevin.

Kevin spent his early <u>childhood</u> with his mother, but when he turned fourteen, he went to live with his father in San Francisco. His mother <u>approved</u> of the move because she believed that a teenage boy needed his father's guidance.

Kevin's father, Thomas Brown, was a <u>skilled</u> carpenter. Building contractors all over the city admired his work and gave him plenty of jobs. Thomas hoped that his son would become a carpenter, too. Kevin, however, wanted a career in communications technology. That, Kevin argued, was where the *big* money was.

"Work is a <u>complex</u> undertaking," Thomas told him. "Making money is only one part of job satisfaction. When you are an <u>adult</u>, you will understand that."

Shortly after Kevin graduated from high school, his mother became ill. Kevin postponed tech school and returned to New Orleans. His father went with him.

When they arrived, they noticed how the little house had changed. "The place is rundown," Kevin remarked. "<u>Apparently</u>, Mom has been too sick to keep it up."

"We can fix it," his father said, "if you are willing."

Kevin was willing. While his father rebuilt the back porch, Kevin refinished cupboards, sanded floors, and repaired windows. By the time his mother was feeling better, the house looked <u>precisely</u> as it had before he went away.

"So, what do you think?" Thomas asked his son.

Kevin looked at the house. It had been a hard job, harder than he had ever imagined it would be. Yet, <u>incredibly</u>, he had enjoyed the work and had never felt more satisfaction.

"I think," Kevin answered, "that I'm now an adult."

1. With whom did Kevin spend his early <u>childhood</u>? Use *childhood* in a sentence.

2. Explain why Kevin's mother <u>approved</u> of his move. What does *approved* mean?

3. Underline the sentence that shows that Thomas was <u>skilled</u>. Name something at which you are *skilled*.

4. Circle the word that tells what Thomas thinks is <u>complex</u>. Write a sentence, using the word *complex*.

5. Rewrite the sentence that includes the word <u>adult</u>, using a synonym for *adult*.

6. Underline the sentence that explains why the house was <u>apparently</u> run down. What does *apparently* mean?

7. Describe how the house looked, using a word that means the same thing as <u>precisely</u>.

8. <u>Incredibly</u>, Kevin enjoyed the work. What does that sentence mean? What is a synonym for *incredibly*?

from **An American Childhood** by Annie Dillard
Writing About the Big Question

What is the best way to find the truth?

Big Question Vocabulary

awareness	believable	conclude	convince	debate
evaluate	evidence	explain	factual	fiction
insight	perceive	reality	reveal	truth

A. *Use one or more words from the list above to complete each sentence.*

1. The details in a story can make a story _____ .

2. Even when writing a work of fiction, it helps if there is _____ in the details.

3. Authors must have a(n) _____ of details in order to make people believe the story they are telling.

B. *Answer the questions.*

1. Add details to this sentence to make it more believable: *As I walked home, I was cold.*

   _____

   _____

   _____

2. Now, add details to the same sentence to reveal that you are writing a sentence that is fantastic and not realistic.

   _____

   _____

C. *Complete the sentence below. Then, write a short paragraph connecting the sentence to the Big Question.*

The details in a story help _____

Write a short fictional paragraph with realistic details.

   _____

   _____

   _____

   _____

   _____

Unit 1 Resources: Fiction and Nonfiction

Name _____ Date _____

from **An American Childhood** by Annie Dillard
Reading: Reread and Read Ahead to Confirm Meaning

Context clues are the examples, descriptions, and other details in the text around an unfamiliar or unusual word or expression. Sometimes these clues can help you figure out what the word or expression means. When you come across an unfamiliar word, use the context clues to figure out what the word probably means. **Reread and read ahead to confirm the meaning.**

Read this example from *An American Childhood:*

But if you flung yourself <u>wholeheartedly</u> at the back of his knees—if you gathered and joined body and soul and pointed them diving fearlessly . . .

Which context clues tell you what *wholeheartedly* means? If you look for clues before and after the word, you find the phrases "flung yourself," "joined body and soul," and "pointed them diving fearlessly." These suggest that *wholeheartedly* probably means something like "completely" or "fully"—which it does.

DIRECTIONS: *Read each quotation from* An American Childhood. *Figure out the meaning of the underlined word by looking for context clues. Write the context clue or clues on the first line. Write the meaning of the word on the second line. Then, check your definitions in a dictionary.*

1. I started making an iceball—a perfect iceball, from perfectly white snow, perfectly spherical, . . . I had just <u>embarked</u> on the iceball project when we heard tire chains come clanking from afar.

   Context clues: _____

   Meaning of word: _____

2. Wordless, we split up. We were on our turf; we could lose ourselves in the neighborhood backyards, everyone for himself. I paused and considered. Everyone had <u>vanished</u> except Mikey Fahey, who was just rounding the corner of a yellow brick house.

   Context clues: _____

   _____

   Meaning of word: _____

3. You have to <u>fling</u> yourself at what you're doing, you have to point yourself, forget yourself, aim, dive.

   Context clues: _____

   Meaning of word: _____

4. Mikey and I unzipped our jackets. I pulled off my <u>sopping</u> mittens. . . . The man's lower pants legs were wet, his cuffs were full of snow.

   Context clues: _____

   Meaning of word: _____

from **An American Childhood** by Annie Dillard
Literary Analysis: Point of View

Point of view is the perspective from which a narrative is told. Point of view affects the kinds of details that are revealed to the reader.

- **First-person point of view:** The narrator is a character who participates in the action of the story and tells the story using the words *I* and *me*. The narrator can reveal only his or her own observations, thoughts, and feelings.
- **Third-person point of view:** The narrator is not a character in the story and uses third-person pronouns such as *he, she,* and *they* to refer to the characters. The narrator may know and reveal the observations, thoughts, and feelings of more than one person or character in the narrative.

Read this example from *An American Childhood:*

It was a long time before he could speak. I had some difficulty at first recalling why we were there. My lips felt swollen; I couldn't see out of the sides of my eyes; I kept coughing.

You can see from the pronouns *I, we,* and *my* that the event is being told from the first-person point of view. The speaker is there—her lips are swollen; her eyes are clouded; she is coughing.

DIRECTIONS: *Read each quotation from* An American Childhood. *Underline each pronoun that shows that the event is told from the first-person point of view. Then, on the lines that follow, briefly describe what you learned from or about the speaker.*

1. Boys welcomed me at baseball, too, for I had, through enthusiastic practice, what was weirdly known as a boy's arm.

   What I learned: _____

   _____

2. He ran after us, and we ran away from him, up the snowy Reynolds sidewalk. At the corner, I looked back; incredibly, he was still after us. . . . All of a sudden, we were running for our lives.

   What I learned: _____

   _____

3. He chased us silently over picket fences, through thorny hedges, between houses, around garbage cans, and across streets. Every time I glanced back, choking for breath, I expected he would have quit. He must have been as breathless as we were.

   What I learned: _____

   _____

Name _____ Date _____

from **An American Childhood** by Annie Dillard
Vocabulary Builder

Word List

compelled   improvising   perfunctorily   righteous   strategy   translucent

A. DIRECTIONS: *Think about the meaning of the underlined Word List word in each sentence. Then, answer the question.*

1. The children came up with a <u>strategy</u> for throwing snowballs at passing vehicles. Did the children have a plan? How do you know?

   _____

2. The man <u>compelled</u> Dillard to run through the neighborhood. Did she have a choice? How do you know?

   _____

3. Dillard and Mikey were <u>improvising</u> their escape route as they went along. Had they planned an escape route? How do you know?

   _____

4. When the man finally caught the kids, he said his words <u>perfunctorily</u>. Did his words hold unique meaning? How do you know?

   _____

5. Dillard describes the man's anger as <u>righteous</u>. Did he believe he was correct to be angry? How do you know?

   _____

6. Dillard's iceball was completely <u>translucent</u>. Could you see light through it? How do you know?

   _____

B. WORD STUDY: The Latin prefix *trans-* means "over," "across," or "through." Words containing the prefix *trans-* include *transfer* ("to move from one place to another") and *translator* ("someone who converts one language to another"). Consider these meanings as you answer each question.

1. Why might you need to *transfer* your records if you change schools?

   _____

2. Why might you need a *translator* in a foreign country?

   _____

Name _____ Date _____

from An American Childhood by Annie Dillard
Enrichment: Documentary Films

The excerpt from *An American Childhood* is a work of nonfiction. By definition, nonfiction presents true, factual information about an event, an era, a place, or a life story, as in this selection. Similar to written works of nonfiction, documentary films also present factual information. Documentary filmmakers can show real-life events by combining a variety of resources. They might use photographs, newspaper clippings, videotaped interviews, or news footage (such as videotape of a city during a major snowstorm). Documentaries focus on people, places, events, or a combination of the three.

DIRECTIONS: *Imagine that you have been hired to make a documentary film based on the excerpt you read from* An American Childhood. *First, think about when the events in the selection take place. (When was Annie Dillard born? How old is she when the events that she describes take place? What year was it?) Then, think about what photographs and newspaper clippings you might find. Consider whom you might interview and videotape. Complete the following chart by describing an item for each resource that is listed.*

Type of Resource	An American Childhood: The Snowball Episode
Photographs	
Interviews	
Film/Video	
Newspaper clippings	

from **An American Childhood** by Annie Dillard
Open-Book Test

Short Answer *Write your responses to the questions in this section on the lines provided.*

1. This excerpt from *An American Childhood* begins with a description of football. What elements of the chase later in the selection are similar to this opening description? Use information from the beginning of the selection to support your response.

   _____

   _____

   _____

2. In the beginning of the excerpt from *An American Childhood*, the author explains that football involves having a *strategy* for each play. Give an example of what might happen if the players did not have a *strategy*.

   _____

   _____

3. Choose a sentence from the excerpt from *American Childhood* that shows that the selection is written from the first-person point of view. Underline the word or words that indicate the point of view.

   _____

   _____

4. In *An American Childhood*, a man in a Buick stops his car and chases Annie and the boys. Why does he take this action? Use details from the selection to support your answer. Include your opinion about whether he means to cause real harm.

   _____

   _____

5. Reread the middle of the chase in *An American Childhood*. The author writes, "Every time I glanced back, choking for breath, I expected he would have quit." Which words help you understand the meaning of *glanced*? In your response, explain why the author glanced back.

   _____

   _____

6. At the end of the chase in *An American Childhood*, the author says that the man and the two children were *staggering*. Which words in the sentence suggest the meaning of *staggering*? Include in your response a reason that they are *staggering*.

   _____

   _____

   _____

7. In the middle of the excerpt from *An American Childhood*, the reader begins to get a sense that the author admires the driver of the Buick. Why do you think Dillard grows to admire him? Use details from the selection to help you respond.

_____

_____

_____

8. In the middle of the excerpt from *An American Childhood*, the author describes how the children ran away from the driver, *improvising* as they ran. Give an example from the selection that shows one of the ways in which the children *improvised*. In your answer, include an explanation of the meaning of *improvised*.

_____

_____

_____

9. Reread the final sentence of the excerpt from *An American Childhood*. If the narrative had been written from the third-person point of view, how might the ending be different? Write two sentences to end the narrative in the third person.

_____

_____

_____

_____

10. Because the excerpt from *An American Childhood* is told from the first-person point of view, the reader knows only what the narrator feels and thinks. Use the organizer to list two things the reader can know from the narrator and two things the reader cannot know. Then, on the lines, explain whether you think the narrative would be better in the third person.

Known	Unknown

_____

_____

Essay

Write an extended response to the question of your choice or to the question or questions your teacher assigns you.

11. Annie Dillard writes in *An American Childhood* about playing football. Why does she like football so much? Write a brief essay in which you explore her feelings. Use details from the rest of the selection to support your opinion.

12. When the driver of the Buick finally catches up with the children in the excerpt from *An American Childhood*, the author seems surprisingly disappointed. In a brief essay, explore her feelings at that moment. Which statement shows her disappointment, and how can her feelings best be explained?

13. Reread the last sentence of the excerpt from *An American Childhood*. In an essay, explore the connection between this sentence and Annie's philosophy of life. Think about how long the chase has gone on and why she is so impressed with the young man. Use details from the selection to support your interpretation.

14. **Thinking About the Big Question: What is the best way to find the truth?** Because the excerpt from *An American Childhood* is written in the first-person point of view, the reader learns the author's version of the truth of what happened to her and her friends. However, there is also the driver's version of the truth of the episode. Whose truth is the real one? In an essay, explore this question. Use details from the selection to support your points.

Oral Response

15. Go back to question 1, 4, 7, or 10 or a question your teacher assigns you. Take a few minutes to expand your answer and prepare an oral response. Find additional details in the excerpt from *An American Childhood* that support your points. If necessary, make notes to guide your oral response.

Name _____ Date _____

from **An American Childhood** by Annie Dillard
Selection Test A

Critical Reading *Identify the letter of the choice that best answers the question.*

____ 1. At the beginning of the excerpt from *An American Childhood,* what important thing do you learn about Annie Dillard when she talks about playing football?
   A. She thinks football is a difficult game.
   B. She has never fooled the other team.
   C. She values concentration and courage.
   D. She realizes how hard it is to get hurt.

____ 2. In *An American Childhood,* why are the children throwing snowballs at cars?
   A. They are already bored with winter.
   B. They want the drivers to chase them.
   C. The cars are getting in the way of their street game.
   D. The cars are moving slowly and make good targets.

____ 3. Use context clues in the following passage from *An American Childhood* to choose the correct meaning of the underlined word.

   > He chased us silently over picket fences, through thorny hedges, between houses, around garbage cans, and across streets. Every time I <u>glanced</u> back, choking for breath, I expected he would have quit.

   A. fell   C. gasped loudly
   B. looked quickly   D. shoved

____ 4. Use context clues in the following passage from *An American Childhood* to choose the correct meaning of the underlined word.

   > Mikey and I had nowhere to go, in our own neighborhood or out of it, but away from this man who was chasing us. He <u>impelled</u> us forward.

   A. caught   C. helped
   B. pushed   D. called

____ 5. In *An American Childhood,* after the man catches her and Mikey, Dillard says:

   > He had released our jackets; . . . he knew we weren't going anywhere. We all played by the rules.

   What does she mean?
   A. The children will have to unzip their jackets so they do not catch cold.
   B. The children will have to help the man find his way back to his car.
   C. The children will not try to run away once they have been fairly caught.
   D. The children will wait for the man to catch his breath so he can scold them.

____ **6.** Why does the man chase the children in *An American Childhood*?
   A. to have some fun
   B. to get some exercise
   C. to get their names and call the police
   D. to teach them a lesson

____ **7.** Dillard writes from the first-person point of view in *An American Childhood*. Which of the following statements is always true of a first-person narrative?
   A. It is about a childhood memory.
   B. It is told by one of the characters.
   C. It describes characters' thoughts and actions.
   D. It includes conversations among characters.

____ **8.** *An American Childhood* is told from the first-person point of view. What information must therefore be left out of the story?
   A. how the man feels as he chases the two children
   B. how Dillard feels when she plays football
   C. how Dillard feels when she is chased by the man
   D. how the neighborhood looks as Dillard runs through it

____ **9.** Which word best describes the young Annie Dillard in *An American Childhood*?
   A. troublesome
   B. funny
   C. adventurous
   D. lonely

____ **10.** Why does Dillard admire the driver of the Buick in *An American Childhood*?
   A. He eventually outruns her and Mikey.
   B. He throws himself into the chase.
   C. He is braver than other drivers.
   D. He scolds them after he has caught them.

____ **11.** What lesson does Annie Dillard share in *An American Childhood*?
   A. the importance of telling the truth
   B. the joy of flinging oneself into life's events
   C. the danger of throwing snowballs at cars
   D. the importance of not talking to strangers

Vocabulary and Grammar

____ 12. In which sentence is the word *strategy* used correctly?

  A. When children throw snowballs at cars, they are wise to plan a strategy for escape.

  B. When traffic slows to a strategy, it is a good time for children to aim their snowballs.

  C. When the man catches the two children, he scolds them with his strategy.

  D. When Dillard looks back on her childhood, she remembers the strategy of winter.

____ 13. Which of the following phrases from *An American Childhood* contains a plural possessive noun?

  A. your team's score   C. the man's lower pants legs

  B. the cars' tires   D. the backyard's new snow

____ 14. In which sentence about *An American Childhood* is an apostrophe used correctly to form a plural possessive noun?

  A. The narrator appears to be proud of having a boys' arm.

  B. The childrens' snowball hit the windshield of the black Buick.

  C. All the car's tires made tracks in the newly fallen snow.

  D. Dillard and Mikey ran through all the neighbors' front yards.

Essay

15. In an essay, explain why Annie Dillard might have chosen to write *An American Childhood* from the first-person point of view. How would her comments about playing football and her description of being chased through the snow have been different if they had been written from the third-person point of view? Cite examples from the story to support your points.

16. This selection from *An American Childhood* creates a picture of Annie Dillard as a girl. In an essay, describe what she was like. Then, consider whether you would have liked her. Refer to Dillard's thoughts and adventures to support your points.

17. **Thinking About the Big Question: What is the best way to find the truth?** In *An American Childhood*, the reader learns the author's version of the truth of what happened to her and her friends while they are out throwing snowballs at passing cars. What would be the driver's version of what happened? Which version would you trust more? In an essay, explore this question. Use details from the selection to support your points.

from **An American Childhood** by Annie Dillard
Selection Test B

Critical Reading *Identify the letter of the choice that best completes the statement or answers the question.*

_____ 1. In the excerpt from *An American Childhood*, what is the author's purpose in writing about football?
   A. to show that football is a fine sport
   B. to show how to plan football strategy
   C. to show that she values concentration and courage
   D. to show that hesitation might lead to an injury

_____ 2. Use context clues in the following passage from *An American Childhood* to choose the correct meaning of the underlined word.

   But if you flung yourself <u>wholeheartedly</u> at the back of his knees—if you gathered and joined body and soul and pointed them diving fearlessly—then you likely wouldn't get hurt.

   A. incompletely
   B. lovingly
   C. dangerously
   D. enthusiastically

_____ 3. The narrator of *An American Childhood* says that she developed "a boy's arm" after practicing baseball enthusiastically. What does this information reveal about her?
   A. She is naturally athletic.
   B. She works hard at what she does.
   C. She prefers boys' sports.
   D. She thinks physical skill is unimportant.

_____ 4. Why do the children throw snowballs at the cars in the excerpt from *An American Childhood*?
   A. They are practicing their aim.
   B. They want to cause an accident.
   C. The drivers go too fast and splatter snow in all the yards.
   D. The drivers go slowly and make their cars natural targets.

_____ 5. Use context clues in the following passage from *An American Childhood* to choose the correct meaning of the underlined word.

   He ran after us, and we ran away from him, up the snowy Reynolds sidewalk. At the corner, I looked back; <u>incredibly</u>, he was still after us. He was in city clothes: a suit and tie, street shoes. Any normal adult would have quit.

   A. certainly
   B. unbelievably
   C. hopefully
   D. sickeningly

_____ 6. In *An American Childhood,* what is so unusual about the man in the black Buick?
   A. He is driving fast despite the snow.
   B. He chases the children through the neighborhood.
   C. He closes the car door when he gets out of the car.
   D. He runs like a professional athlete.

_____ 7. Use context clues in this passage from *An American Childhood* to choose the correct meaning of the underlined word.

   We were on our <u>turf</u>; we could lose ourselves in the neighborhood backyards, everyone for himself.

   A. frozen pond
   B. familiar territory
   C. best behavior
   D. guard

_____ 8. Why does the author of *An American Childhood* describe the path of the chase in such detail?
   A. to show what a good memory she has
   B. to show that adults can run as fast as children
   C. to show that the man does not know the neighborhood well
   D. to show how determined the man is to catch the children

_____ 9. Use context clues in this passage from *An American Childhood* to choose the correct meaning of the underlined word.

   But how could the glory have lasted forever? We could have run through every backyard in North America until we got to Panama. But when he trapped us at the lip of the Panama Canal, what precisely could he have done to <u>prolong</u> the drama of the chase and cap its glory?

   A. explain
   B. lengthen
   C. act out
   D. reveal

_____ 10. Which statement from *An American Childhood* explains what Dillard finds disappointing about being captured by the man?
   A. "The point was that he had chased us passionately without giving up."
   B. "Now he came down to earth. I wanted the glory to last forever."
   C. "He could only have fried Mikey Fahey and me in boiling oil, say."
   D. "We could have run through every backyard . . . until we got to Panama."

_____ 11. At the end of the excerpt from *An American Childhood,* what understanding does Dillard reach about her experience?
   A. It eventually caused her to give up playing football with the boys.
   B. It required more of her than any other experience she has had.
   C. It has taught her the value of keeping in good physical shape.
   D. It has made her want to travel through North America to Panama.

_____ **12.** What lesson does Dillard share in this selection from *An American Childhood*?
   A. the importance of telling the truth
   B. the joy of doing things passionately
   C. the danger of throwing snowballs
   D. the importance of being physically fit

_____ **13.** Dillard wrote *An American Childhood* in the first person. Which of the following accurately describes every first-person narrative?
   A. It relates an incident from childhood.
   B. It is told by one of the characters in the story.
   C. It reveals the thoughts of all the characters.
   D. It is told from several points of view.

_____ **14.** If Dillard had *not* written *An American Childhood* from the first-person point of view, we might have learned
   A. why Dillard thought football was such a fine game.
   B. what Dillard and her friends did on snowy mornings.
   C. what the man was thinking as he chased the children.
   D. what the man said when he caught Dillard and Mikey.

Vocabulary and Grammar

_____ **15.** Which sentence about *An American Childhood* uses the word *compelled* correctly?
   A. After much practice, Dillard compelled "a boy's arm."
   B. The children compelled to throw snowballs at the cars.
   C. The snowball compelled against the Buick's windshield.
   D. The cold compelled the children to wear mittens and jackets.

_____ **16.** Which of the following phrases from *An American Childhood* contains a plural possessive noun?
   A. boy's arm   C. the grocery store's delivery driveway
   B. the cars' tires   D. the man's lower pants legs

Essay

17. An author's purpose is his or her reason for writing. Writers of autobiographies have many different reasons for telling their life story. In an essay, explain what Annie Dillard's purpose might have been for writing about this incident from her childhood. Support your explanation with details from the excerpt from *An American Childhood*.

18. In an essay, consider what the driver of the black Buick in *An American Childhood* might have to say about the snowball incident and the chase. What might he think of the children? How might he explain his continuing the chase long after "any normal adult would have quit"? In your essay, explain what information the man would reveal that Dillard, as a first-person narrator, does not reveal.

19. Thinking About the Big Question: What is the best way to find the truth? Because the excerpt from *An American Childhood* is written in the first-person point of view, the reader learns the author's version of the truth of what happened to her and her friends. However, there is also the driver's version of the truth of the episode. Whose truth is the real one? In an essay, explore this question. Use details from the selection to support your points.

Study these words from "The Luckiest Time of All." Then, complete the activities.

Word List A

cutest [KYOOT ist] *adj.* prettiest or most attractive
Babies are attractive because they have the <u>cutest</u> faces, especially when they laugh.

exactly [eg ZAKT lee] *adv.* precisely; just how
The map led the travelers to <u>exactly</u> the right spot, so they found the hotel without a problem.

hind [HYND] *adj.* back or rear
The angry horse reared up on its <u>hind</u> legs.

luck [LUK] *n.* something that happens to someone by chance
Some games are a matter of <u>luck</u>, not skill.

noticed [NOHT ist] *v.* saw or became aware of something
Kayla read the message on the bulletin board as soon as she <u>noticed</u> it.

pennies [PEN eez] *n.* coins that are the smallest unit of U.S. money
Ben exchanged five hundred <u>pennies</u> for five dollar bills.

reminds [ri MYNDZ] *v.* causes someone to remember something
That picture of the beach <u>reminds</u> me of summer vacation.

shined [SHYND] *v.* gave off a bright light
The light from the lighthouse <u>shined</u> far out to sea.

Word List B

acquainted [uh KWAYN tid] *v.* became familiar; got to know someone, but not well
Joshua became <u>acquainted</u> with Jessica at a party they both went to.

blooms [BLOOMZ] *n.* flowers
Ashley picked pretty white <u>blooms</u> off the lilac bush.

granddaughter [GRAN dawt er] *n.* the daughter of someone's son or daughter
The picture showed a mother, her daughter, and the daughter's daughter—the <u>granddaughter</u>.

length [LENGKTH] *n.* the amount from beginning to end
Cody cut a <u>length</u> of string long enough to go around the box.

porch [PAWRCH] *n.* a roofed structure attached to the outside of a house
We sat outside the house on the front <u>porch</u> and watched the fireflies.

spied [SPYD] *v.* caught sight of something or somebody
Jennifer <u>spied</u> her reflection in the store window as she walked by.

twine [TWYN] *n.* a very strong string made of two or more strands twisted together
When we moved, Uncle Larry used <u>twine</u> to tie cartons together.

twirl [TWERL] *v.* to turn or spin around quickly
The skater could <u>twirl</u> like a toy top.

"The Luckiest Time of All" by Lucille Clifton
Vocabulary Warm-up Exercises

Exercise A *Fill in each blank in the paragraph below with an appropriate word from Word List A. Use each word only once.*

The charms on Alyssa's bracelet [1] _____ like drops of sunlight when she moved. The bracelet had many charms, but the [2] _____ was a tiny unicorn rearing up on its [3] _____ legs. Alyssa believed that it brought her good [4] _____. "It [5] _____ me of a charm I once had," her mother said. "It looked [6] _____ like yours." One day her mother [7] _____ that the clasp was broken. "I can fix that," she said. "What will it cost me?" Cynthia asked, making a joke. "Only [8] _____," her mother answered, "but a lot of them." Alyssa said, "It's a deal!"

Exercise B *Decide whether each statement below is true or false. Circle T or F. Then, explain your answer.*

1. If someone has <u>spied</u> an object, it is well hidden.
   T / F _____

2. If you are <u>acquainted</u> with someone, you know him or her well.
   T / F _____

3. A <u>granddaughter</u> is the daughter of someone's grandmother.
   T / F _____

4. The <u>length</u> of a snake is measured from its middle to the tip of its tail.
   T / F _____

5. You would most likely see <u>blooms</u> underground.
   T / F _____

6. A <u>porch</u> is a good place to sit if you enjoy the outdoors but like to stay close to home.
   T / F _____

7. <u>Twine</u> is stronger than string.
   T / F _____

8. If you <u>twirl</u> around fast, you will become dizzy.
   T / F _____

"The Luckiest Time of All" by Lucille Clifton
Reading Warm-up A

Read the following passage. Pay special attention to the underlined words. Then, read it again, and complete the activities. Use a separate sheet of paper for your written answers.

Early circuses were small by today's standards, but they brought big excitement to the prairie during the 1800s. Every summer, when the sun <u>shined</u> its brightest, people waited for the circus to come to town. They knew the wait was over when they heard jolly music fill the air. Children ran along the road, trailing after the colorful wagons and shouting, "The circus! The circus is here!"

Oh, yes, the summer circus was a big deal.

The reason for all the excitement was simple: entertainment was scarce on the prairie. Once the circus arrived, for a few days anyway, there was a great deal of it. It was cheap, too. For a few <u>pennies</u>, a family could see a troop of acrobats, a high-wire act, and maybe a magic show. The trapeze artist flying through the air never failed to astonish the crowd. When the man on the high wire put one foot <u>exactly</u> in front of the other and then wobbled a bit, everyone gasped. Animal acts were always popular, too, because the animals performed the <u>cutest</u> tricks: They jumped through hoops and danced on their <u>hind</u> legs. Most circuses had at least one wild animal to thrill the audiences.

A separate ticket got you into the side show, a tent filled with curiosities. With any <u>luck</u> you could see a two-headed chicken, a bearded lady, and a tattooed man. Some side shows advertised unbelievable sights. "Come see the amazing Gonzo!" the announcer shouted. "He <u>reminds</u> me of my brother-in-law, half-man, half-beast! You decide which half is which!" Just about everyone <u>noticed</u> that the "beast" half was a fake, but nobody cared. It was fun, and that is why everyone was there: to have fun and to be amazed.

1. Circle the words that tell what happened when the sun <u>shined</u> brightest. Write about a summer event, using the word *shined*.

2. Circle the words that tell what a family could see for a few <u>pennies</u>. What can you buy with a few *pennies* today?

3. Tell what the man on the high wire did <u>exactly</u>. Explain why he had to do it *exactly*.

4. Circle the word that tells who or what did the <u>cutest</u> tricks. Explain why their tricks were the *cutest* ones.

5. Circle the word that tells what the animals did on their <u>hind</u> legs. Name an animal that can stand on its *hind* legs.

6. Circle some things people could see with any <u>luck</u>. Explain why it was a matter of *luck*.

7. Circle what it is that <u>reminds</u> the announcer of his brother-in-law. Do you believe him? Why or why not?

8. Circle what it was that people <u>noticed</u> about Gonzo. What in particular might they have *noticed*?

"The Luckiest Time of All" by Lucille Clifton
Reading Warm-up B

Read the following passage. Pay special attention to the underlined words. Then, read it again, and complete the activities. Use a separate sheet of paper for your written answers.

"Come here, child. Come on now. I won't bite!"

The young girl standing outside the house obeyed reluctantly. Her mother gave her a slight push. Then, slowly, she stepped onto the porch. The man who had spoken to her sat in a rocker near the front door. He looked fierce.

"That's better," he said. "You're Olivia, and you know who I am."

The girl nodded. "Yes, you're my grandfather."

"Right, I'm your granddad Bill. I think it's time we got acquainted, don't you?"

The girl nodded again. Although her mother returned home frequently, this was Olivia's first visit to the United States. She felt awkward, especially in front of this stern man. She stiffly held out a bouquet of daisy blooms and softly said, "These are for you."

Olivia's mother stepped onto the porch. "Sorry we're late, Dad." She kissed her father's cheek and whispered, "Olivia is shy, but she'll come around."

The man accepted the flowers from his granddaughter. "Thank you, Olivia—and this is for you." He presented the girl with a white box tied with twine.

While her mother and grandfather watched, Olivia undid the knot and the length of twine fell away. Cautiously, Olivia lifted the lid. She spied a delicate object beneath a layer of tissue and eagerly pushed the thin paper aside.

"Ohhhh!" she gasped, "it's lovely!"

"It's a music box. It was my grandmother's," her grandfather said.

Olivia wound the key, and a tinkling waltz filled the air. She began to twirl around, forgetting her awkwardness. Her grandfather said, "My granny gave it to me because she knew I appreciated beautiful music."

Olivia stopped spinning. "Do you? I do, too!"

She watched a smile slowly warm her grandfather's face, and all at once Olivia felt at home.

1. Circle the words that indicate where the porch is. What is a *porch*?

2. Rewrite the sentence that contains the word acquainted. Use your own words to replace *acquainted*.

3. Circle the words that help explain what blooms are. What are your favorite wildflower *blooms*?

4. Explain how Olivia and her mother are related to Granddad Bill.

5. Circle the words that tell what was tied with twine. Name something you might tie with *twine*.

6. Explain how you would measure a *length* of twine.

7. Describe what Olivia spied in the box. Use *spied* in a sentence.

8. When did Olivia begin to twirl around? Where would you be likely to see someone *twirl*?

Unit 1 Resources: Fiction and Nonfiction

"The Luckiest Time of All" by Lucille Clifton
Writing About the Big Question

What is the best way to find the truth?

Big Question Vocabulary

awareness	believable	conclude	convince	debate
evaluate	evidence	explain	factual	fiction
insight	perceive	reality	reveal	truth

A. *Use one or more words from the list above to complete each sentence.*

1. When somebody shares his or her beliefs, we must _____ whether those beliefs are consistent with our own beliefs.

2. If we _____ that our own beliefs are different, it is okay to disagree.

3. Beliefs may not be based in _____.

B. *Answer the questions. Use at least one of the vocabulary words in each answer.*

1. Name two objects that people believe bring them good or bad luck.

   _____   _____

2. Do you believe that an object can bring you luck? Explain.

   _____

   _____

   _____

C. *Complete the sentence below. Then, answer the question to write a short paragraph connecting the sentence to the Big Question:*

In order to be believable, character's behavior' must be _____.

In a work of fiction, what makes a character's behaviors believable? What is the advantage of having believable characters in a story?

_____

_____

_____

_____

"The Luckiest Time of All" by Lucille Clifton
Reading: Reread and Read Ahead to Confirm Meaning

Context clues are the examples, descriptions, and other details in the text around an unfamiliar or unusual word or expression. Sometimes these clues can help you figure out what the word or expression means. When you come across an unfamiliar word or expression, use the context clues to figure out what the word probably means. **Reread and read ahead to confirm the meaning.**

In "The Luckiest Time of All," the writer sometimes uses words and phrases that may mean something different from the meanings of the individual words. Look at this example:

"Somethin like the circus. Me and Ovella wanted to join that thing and see the world. Nothin wrong at home or nothin, we just wanted to travel and see new things and have <u>high</u> times."

In another context, you would probably decide that *high* means "tall" or "rising above." In this context, notice the words and phrases around the word *high:* "somethin like the circus," "see the world," and "wanted to travel and see new things." These context clues tell you that in this selection, *high* means "exciting."

DIRECTIONS: *Read each quotation from "The Luckiest Time of All." Figure out the meaning of the underlined word or expression by looking for context clues. Write the context clue or clues on the first two lines. Write the meaning of the word or expression on the next line.*

1. We got there after a good little walk and it was the <u>world</u>, Baby, such music and wonders as we never had seen! They had everything there, or seemed like it.

    Context clues: _____

    _____

    Meaning of word: _____

2. But the stone was gone from my hand and Lord, it hit that dancin dog right on his nose! Well, he <u>lit out</u> after me, poor thing. He <u>lit out</u> after me and I flew! Round and round the Silas Greene we run.

    Context clues: _____

    _____

    Meaning of word: _____

3. I stopped then and walked slow and shy to where he had picked up that poor dog to see if he was hurt, <u>cradlin</u> him and talkin to him soft and sweet.

    Context clues: _____

    Meaning of word: _____

4. He . . . helped me find my stone. . . . We search and searched and at last he <u>spied</u> it!

    Context clues: _____

    _____

    Meaning of word: _____

"The Luckiest Time of All" by Lucille Clifton
Literary Analysis: Point of View

Point of view is the perspective from which a narrative is told. Point of view affects the kinds of details that are revealed to the reader.

- **First-person point of view:** The narrator is a character who participates in the action of the story and tells the story using the words *I* and *me*. The narrator can reveal only his or her own observations, thoughts, and feelings.
- **Third-person point of view:** The narrator is not a character in the story and uses third-person pronouns such as *he, she*, and *they* to refer to the characters. The narrator may know and reveal the observations, thoughts, and feelings of more than one person or character in the narrative.

Read this example from the beginning of "The Luckiest Time of All":

Mrs. Elzie F. Pickens was rocking slowly on the porch one afternoon when her Great-granddaughter, Tee, brought her a big bunch of dogwood blooms, and that was the beginning of a story.

"Ahh, now that dogwood reminds me of the day I met your Great-granddaddy, Mr. Pickens, Sweet Tee."

The story begins by introducing two characters, Mrs. Elzie F. Pickens and her great-granddaughter, Tee. The pronoun *her* tells you that the narrative is told from the third-person point of view. In the first paragraph of dialogue, Elzie is telling her story using the pronoun *I*, but that does not mean the story is a first-person account. It is not a first-person account because Elzie is not the narrator. The narrator is quoting Elzie as she tells her story to Tee.

DIRECTIONS: *Read each numbered passage. (Two passages are from "The Luckiest Time of All," and one is about Lucille Clifton.) Underline each pronoun that tells that the passage is told from the third-person point of view. Then, on the lines that follow, briefly describe what you learned from the passage.*

1. Tee's Great-grandmother shook her head and laughed out loud.

   What I learned: _____

2. And they rocked a little longer and smiled together.

   What I learned: _____

3. Lucille Sayles Clifton was born into a large, working-class family in New York State. Although her parents were not formally educated, she learned from their example to appreciate books and poetry.

   What I learned: _____

   _____

Name _____   Date _____

"The Luckiest Time of All" by Lucille Clifton
Vocabulary Builder

Word List

    acquainted   hind   plaited   spied   twine   wonders

A. DIRECTIONS: *Think about the meaning of the underlined Word List word in each sentence. Then, answer the question.*

1. Are mountain climbers likely to use <u>twine</u> to attach themselves to each other while crossing a dangerous crevice? Why or why not?

_____

2. If you are <u>acquainted</u> with someone, are you likely to know where he or she lives? Why or why not?

_____

3. Are women more likely than men to have <u>plaited</u> hair? Why or why not?

_____

4. If you catch an animal by its <u>hind</u> legs, is it likely that you approached it from the front? Why or why not?

_____

5. Is it likely that it would be boring to see one of the Seven <u>Wonders</u> of the World? Why or why not?

_____

6. If you <u>spied</u> an old friend, would you likely be seeing him or her in person? Why or why not?

_____

B. WORD STUDY: The Latin prefixes *ac-/ad-* mean "motion toward," "addition to," or "nearness to." How do the meanings of the prefixes relate to the italicized words in the following sentences?

1. The key allowed me full *access* to the mansion.

_____

2. The toddler had to *adhere* to strict rules after he ran into the street.

_____

"The Luckiest Time of All" by Lucille Clifton
Enrichment: Hyperbole

You have learned that **hyperbole** is a writer's use of exaggeration for effect. Instead of describing a mountain peak as "very high," a writer might say, "The peak is so high that asteroids passing by earth have to swerve to avoid it."

DIRECTIONS: *Read each of the following descriptions. In the line before each one, write* literal *if the description is factual and unexaggerated. Write* hyperbole *if the example is exaggerated for effect.*

_____ 1. Mary Margaret has lots of red hair, and it shines in the sun. People call her Red. When she blushes, her face turns red, too.

_____ 2. It rained so hard that the fish could swim direct from New York to California.

_____ 3. Nicholas is the funniest person I have ever met. After our last class on Friday, he told a joke. By the time we had stopped laughing, it was Monday and time for school again.

_____ 4. The hurricane created tides that were more than 15 feet above normal. Hundreds of thousands of people were evacuated from low-lying areas.

_____ 5. Officials estimated that the wind exceeded 155 miles per hour. The storm was therefore classified as a category 5 hurricane. Damage to property exceeded $5 billion.

_____ 6. The flooding and damage were so extensive that we could not get to work for five days.

_____ 7. Mary Margaret's hair was so bright and red that astronauts on the space shuttle used it to identify Oregon when they flew over the West Coast.

_____ 8. So much rain came down that the rivers held a contest to see which one could widen its banks to cover an entire state.

_____ 9. The wind blew so hard that by the time the hurricane had gone out to sea, the states of Florida and Georgia had changed places.

_____ 10. Nicholas is the funniest person in our class. At lunchtime, he entertains us in the cafeteria. If you do not stop eating while he performs, you might choke on your food because you will be laughing so hard.

from **An American Childhood** by Annie Dillard
"The Luckiest Time of All" by Lucille Clifton
Integrated Language Skills: Grammar

Possessive Nouns

A **possessive noun** is a noun that shows ownership. Ownership is indicated by the use of the apostrophe.

- To form the possessive to a singular noun, add an apostrophe and -*s:*
The black <u>car's</u> tires left tracks.

- To form the possessive of a plural noun that ends in -*s*, add only an apostrophe:
All of the <u>cars'</u> tires left tracks.

- To form the possessive of a plural noun that does not end in -*s*, add an apostrophe and -*s:*
The <u>children's</u> game had unexpected consequences.

A. PRACTICE: *Each of the following sentences is based on* An American Childhood *or* "The Luckiest Time of All." *On the line, rewrite each underlined noun as a possessive. Be sure to place the apostrophe correctly to indicate that the possessive is singular or plural.*

1. The <u>boys</u> games were more exciting to Dillard than the <u>girls</u> activities.

_____   _____

2. The <u>snowball</u> *splat* led the <u>car</u> driver to jump out and chase the children.

_____   _____

3. The <u>boy</u> path took him through the <u>neighbors</u> front yard.

_____   _____

4. Many years later the young <u>women</u> adventure would be the subject of the <u>girl</u> curiosity.

_____   _____

B. Writing Application: *On the line after each description in brackets, write a possessive noun that matches the description. Make sure the possessives you choose make sense in the sentence.*

1. The [*belonging to the singular female adult*] _____ stone hit the [*belonging to the singular animal*] _____ nose.

2. The [*belonging to the plural male children*] _____ games included throwing snowballs at the [*belonging to the plural vehicle*] _____ windows.

3. The [*belonging to the singular adult male*] _____ breath came in gasps and his [*belonging to the legs of his clothing*] _____ cuffs were full of snow.

Name _____ Date _____

from **An American Childhood** by Annie Dillard

"The Luckiest Time of All" by Lucille Clifton

Integrated Language Skills:
Support for Writing a Description That Includes Hyperbole

To prepare to write **descriptions** that include **hyperbole,** complete the following chart, making notes about three qualities or skills a person might have.

Questions About the Quality or Skill	First Quality or Skill	Second Quality or Skill	Third Quality or Skill
What is the quality or skill?			
Who or what might have this quality or skill?			
What is exceptional about this quality or skill?			
How can I exaggerate this quality or skill?			

Now, choose one quality or skill, and use your notes to write a description of it that includes hyperbole.

from **An American Childhood** by Annie Dillard
"The Luckiest Time of All" by Lucille Clifton

Integrated Language Skills: Support for Extend Your Learning

Research and Technology

Use the following chart to record facts for a report on each author's life and career.

Author's Childhood	Author's Career

Name _____ Date _____

"The Luckiest Time of All" by Lucille Clifton
Open-Book Test

Short Answer *Write your responses to the questions in this section on the lines provided.*

1. At the beginning of "The Luckiest Time of All," Elzie Pickens remembers a story. What does she see that reminds her of the story, and why does it remind her? Use details from the story to support your answer.

   _____

   _____

   _____

2. "The Luckiest Time of All" switches from third-person point of view to first-person and then back again. Where does the switch from third to first occur, and how do you know?

   _____

   _____

   _____

3. At the beginning of "The Luckiest Time of All," Elzie remembers her first impressions of the Silas Greene show. She calls it *the world*. Read the description of Silas Greene, and explain what Elzie means by the phrase *the world*.

   _____

   _____

   _____

4. In the middle of "The Luckiest Time of All," young Elzie throws her lucky stone at a dancing dog. How does she feel as soon as she has thrown the stone? Use information from the story to support your answer.

   _____

   _____

5. When Elzie turns to check how close the dog is, she sees Amos Pickens. He is twirling a rope and "grinnin fit to bust." Describe Amos's expression in a way that explains what *grinnin fit to bust* means.

   _____

   _____

6. In the middle of "The Luckiest Time of All," Mr. Pickens comes to Elzie's rescue. He uses some twine as if he were a cowboy. What does he do with the twine, and why is that a good choice for what he does? Explain your answers, using the definition of *twine*.

   _____

   _____

7. Much of "The Luckiest Time of All" is told from the first-person point of view, but some of it is told in third person. Explain why the author switches points of view during the story and whether it is effective. Use details from the story to support your answer.

_____

_____

_____

_____

8. In the middle of "The Luckiest Time of All," Elzie describes how she became *acquainted* with Mr. Pickens. What period of their relationship is she referring to—the beginning, the middle, or the end? How do you know? Use details from the story to help you answer.

_____

_____

_____

_____

9. The author of "The Luckiest Time of All" uses the third-person point of view to allow the reader to explore another character's observations. Use the organizer to write down the other character's name and two of his or her observations as they are stated in the story. On the lines, tell how knowing this character helps you understand more about the story.

_____'s Observations

_____

_____

10. Think about the title "The Luckiest Time of All." Explain the meaning of the title using details from the story.

_____

_____

_____

_____

Essay

Write an extended response to the question of your choice or to the question or questions your teacher assigns you.

11. In "The Luckiest Time of All," readers learn mostly about one character. In a brief essay, describe that character. Tell who the character is, how old he or she might be, and what is most important in the character's life. Use details from the story to help you.

12. In "The Luckiest Time of All," readers learn a little bit about Tee's reactions to her great-grandmother's story. What does she learn about her great-grandfather that might be important to her as she matures into a young woman? In a brief essay, explore some of the lessons Tee might be able to take from her great-grandmother's experience.

13. In "The Luckiest Time of All," Elzie reveals that she once wanted an adventurous life. In an essay, explore whether you believe she ended up having an adventurous life, or whether her life had enough excitement to fulfill her. Use details from the story she tells to support your response.

14. **Thinking About the Big Question: What is the best way to find the truth?**
Think about "The Luckiest Time of All" and the "truth" about how lucky Elzie's life really was. In an essay, explain whether her life was truly lucky and whether she would see it that way. Use story details to support your response.

Oral Response

15. Go back to question 1, 2, 7, or 9 or to the question your teacher assigns you. Take a few minutes to expand your answer and prepare an oral response. Find additional details in "The Luckiest Time of All" that support your points. If necessary, make notes to guide your oral response.

"The Luckiest Time of All" by Lucille Clifton
Selection Test A

Critical Reading *Identify the letter of the choice that best answers the question.*

____ 1. "The Luckiest Time of All" is written from the third-person point of view. Which characteristic is always true of third-person narratives?

   A. The narrator tells the story using the pronouns *I* and *me*.

   B. The narrator is not one of the characters in the story.

   C. The story tells about an older person and a younger person.

   D. The story tells about the narrator's life as a child.

____ 2. At the beginning of "The Luckiest Time of All," why does Elzie say that the dog-wood blooms Tee has brought remind her of the day she met her husband?

   A. Mr. Pickens gave her a gift of dogwood blooms on the day they met.

   B. She and Ovella bought dogwood blooms at the Silas Greene show.

   C. She met Mr. Pickens in the spring, when the dogwood was in bloom.

   D. She and Ovella picked dogwood blooms on their way to the show.

____ 3. Use context clues in this passage from "The Luckiest Time of All" to choose the correct meaning of the underlined expression.

   > "We got there after a good little walk and it was <u>the world</u>, Baby, such music and wonders as we never had seen! They had everything there, or seemed like it."

   A. a store that sells maps and atlases of the world

   B. a place with interesting objects and exciting events

   C. a service that helps people make world travel plans

   D. a place where bands play music from around the world

____ 4. In "The Luckiest Time of All," what does Elzie realize after she throws her lucky stone toward the dancing dog?

   A. She should have thrown a biscuit.

   B. The stone will bring her bad luck.

   C. The stone will hit the dog.

   D. She meant to throw a coin.

____ 5. Use context clues in this passage from "The Luckiest Time of All" to choose the correct meaning of the underlined expression.

   > "Well, he <u>lit out</u> after me, poor thing. He <u>lit out</u> after me and I flew. Round and round the Silas Greene we run."

   A. chased

   B. fled

   C. lay down

   D. barked

____ 6. In "The Luckiest Time of All," Elzie says that Mr. Pickens looked "like an angel coming to help a poor sinner girl." Why does she refer to herself as "a poor sinner girl"?
A. She has stolen dogwood blossoms.
B. She has lost her lucky stone.
C. She has run away from home.
D. She has been late for Sunday school.

____ 7. In "The Luckiest Time of All," how does Mr. Pickens stop the dog?
A. He yells at it.
B. He picks it up.
C. He lassos it with twine.
D. He steps in front of it.

____ 8. In "The Luckiest Time of All," how does Elzie know that Mr. Pickens is kind?
A. He stops the dog from bothering her.
B. He guards her on her way home.
C. He helps her find her lucky stone.
D. He checks to see if the dog is hurt.

____ 9. Use context clues in this passage from "The Luckiest Time of All" to choose the correct meaning of the underlined word.

   "He . . . helped me to find my stone. . . . We searched and searched and at last he spied it!"

A. tripped over
B. found
C. hid
D. lost

____ 10. In "The Luckiest Time of All," why does Elzie think that the day at the show is lucky?
A. She does not get bitten by an angry dog.
B. She wins several prizes at the show.
C. She meets the man she later marries.
D. She loses and finds her lucky stone.

____ 11. In a story told from the third-person point of view, the narrator sometimes lets one character tell most of the story. Which character tells most of the story in "The Luckiest Time of All"?
A. Mr. Pickens
B. Elzie
C. Tee
D. Ovella Wilson

____ 12. In a story told from the third-person point of view, the thoughts of more than one character can be revealed. In addition to Elzie, the thoughts of which other character are revealed in "The Luckiest Time of All"?

A. Mr. Pickens

B. Ovella Wilson

C. Silas Greene

D. Tee

____ 13. To what does the title of "The Luckiest Time of All" refer?

A. Tee's hearing the story from Elzie

B. Ovella's decision to return home from the show

C. Elzie's first meeting with Mr. Pickens

D. the behavior of the dancing dog

Vocabulary and Grammar

____ 14. Someone who is using *twine* is most likely doing what?

A. washing dishes

B. making a cake

C. tying up a package

D. typing a letter

____ 15. Which phrase includes a plural possessive noun?

A. the girls' laughter

B. the dog's dancing

C. the great-granddaughter's questions

D. the stone's luck

Essay

16. "The Luckiest Time of All" is written from the third-person point of view. The reader learns more about Mrs. Elzie F. Pickens than any other character. In an essay, describe what the narrator reveals about Elzie. What do you know about her? What can you tell about her age? What might her life be like? What is important to her?

17. In "The Luckiest Time of All," readers learn little about Tee, the great-granddaughter of Mrs. Elzie F. Pickens. In an essay, discuss what Tee might learn from her great-grandmother's story. You might consider Elzie's plan to join the Silas Greene show, her experience with the lucky stone, or her meeting Mr. Pickens.

18. **Thinking About the Big Question: What is the best way to find the truth?** In an essay, explain whether it is true that Elzie's life was truly lucky in "The Luckiest Time of All." In what kinds of things was she lucky? In what kinds of things was she unlucky? Use details from the story to support your response.

"The Luckiest Time of All" by Lucille Clifton
Selection Test B

Critical Reading *Identify the letter of the choice that best completes the statement or answers the question.*

____ 1. "The Luckiest Time of All" is written from the third-person point of view. Which statement accurately describes every third-person narrative?
   A. There is more than one character in the story.
   B. There is only one main character in the story.
   C. The narrator is not a character in the story.
   D. The story describes the thoughts of only one character.

____ 2. How does the narrator of "The Luckiest Time of All" begin the story?
   A. She introduces Elzie and Tee to the reader.
   B. She describes Elzie on the rocking chair.
   C. She describes Tee's thoughts and feelings.
   D. She has Elzie tell how she met her husband.

____ 3. After introducing Elzie and Tee in "The Luckiest Time of All," whom does the narrator have tell the story of Elzie's meeting with Mr. Pickens?
   A. Tee
   B. Mr. Pickens
   C. Ovella Wilson
   D. Elzie

____ 4. In "The Luckiest Time of All," why do Elzie and Ovella plan to join the Silas Greene show?
   A. They have heard that they can make a lot of money there.
   B. They want to show off the dog they have taught to dance.
   C. They have argued with their parents about going to the show.
   D. They want to travel, see new things, and have a good time.

____ 5. Use context clues in this passage from "The Luckiest Time of All" to choose the best meaning for the underlined expression.

   "Didn't say nothin to nobody but one another. Just up and decided to do it."

   A. We woke up one morning and left.
   B. We suddenly made up our minds to do it.
   C. We thought we would have some fun.
   D. We saved up enough money to do it.

____ 6. In "The Luckiest Time of All," what does Elzie realize as soon as she has tossed her lucky stone toward the dog?
   A. The dog has stopped dancing.
   B. The stone will hit the dog.
   C. The stone will no longer be lucky.
   D. The stone was a gift from Ovella.

____ 7. Use context clues in this passage from "The Luckiest Time of All" to choose the correct meaning of the underlined expression.

"I felt myself slowin down after a while and I thought I would turn around a little bit to see <u>how much gain that cute little dog was makin on me</u>."

A. how angry I had made the dog
B. how badly I had hurt the dog
C. how close the dog was getting to me
D. how quickly someone would rescue me

____ 8. In "The Luckiest Time of All," when does Elzie say she met Mr. Pickens?
A. when he was working as a cowboy
B. when he was working for the Silas Greene show
C. when he was still a boy
D. when he was dressed as an angel

____ 9. In "The Luckiest Time of All," how does Elzie know that Mr. Pickens is kind and gentle?
A. She sees him examine the dog to see if it is hurt.
B. Ovella Wilson tells her that he is.
C. He helps her find her lucky stone.
D. He walks her and Ovella home from the show.

____ 10. Use context clues in this passage from "The Luckiest Time of All" to choose the best meaning of the underlined expression.

"He . . . helped me to find my stone. . . . We searched and searched and at last he <u>spied</u> it!"

A. held it
B. buried it
C. spotted it
D. tied it up

____ 11. After the incident with the dog in "The Luckiest Time of All," Elzie says that she and Ovella "lost heart for shows then." What does she mean by this phrase?
A. They had lost their heart-shaped pins.
B. They had lost interest in joining a traveling show.
C. They had both fallen in love with Mr. Pickens.
D. They had found the traveling show heartless.

____ 12. Toward the end of "The Luckiest Time of All," Tee suggests that Elzie's lucky stone had not been lucky because
A. Elzie had nearly lost it.
B. Elzie had nearly been bitten by the dog.
C. Elzie had met Mr. Pickens.
D. Elzie had not given it to Tee.

___ 13. At the end of "The Luckiest Time of All," Elzie says that her lucky stone "was luckier for me than for anybody, I think. Least mostly I think it." What is another way to word the last sentence?
A. "At least that's what I think most of the time."
B. "That was the most satisfying of my experiences."
C. "Mostly I think I was at least lucky."
D. "I think about it most of the time, at least when I remember."

___ 14. In a story told from the third-person point of view, the thoughts of more than one character can be revealed. In "The Luckiest Time of All," which characters' thoughts are revealed?
A. those of Elzie and Mr. Pickens
B. those of Mr. Pickens and Ovella Wilson
C. those of Elzie and Tee
D. those of Mr. Pickens and Tee

___ 15. Because "The Luckiest Time of All" is told by a third-person narrator, what pronouns does the narrator use?
A. *me* and *my*
C. *I* and *we*
B. *she* and *her*
D. *I, you*, and *they*

Vocabulary and Grammar

___ 16. Which of the following sentences uses the word *acquainted* correctly?
A. Elzie became acquainted with Mr. Pickens.
B. The dog acquainted Elzie and Ovella.
C. Tee acquainted the dogwood blooms.
D. Mr. Pickens acquainted to the lucky stone.

___ 17. Which phrase about "The Luckiest Time of All" includes a plural possessive noun?
A. the dogwoods' blooms
C. the stone's luck
B. the circus's acts
D. the boy's kindness

Essay

18. Readers of "The Luckiest Time of All" learn that Elzie Pickens longed for a life of excitement when she was young. Do you think she has had such a life? Do you think she has been satisfied with the life she has had with Mr. Pickens? In an essay, explain your opinion of Elzie Pickens's life. Support your statements with details from the story.

19. "The Luckiest Time of All" is told by a third-person narrator. In an essay, discuss the role of that narrator in the story. Consider these questions: How much information does the narrator reveal? How much information do the characters reveal in their dialogue? What does the extensive use of dialogue tell you about the narrator's role?

20. **Thinking About the Big Question: What is the best way to find the truth?** Think about "The Luckiest Time of All" and the "truth" about how lucky Elzie's life really was. In an essay, explain whether her life was truly lucky and whether she would see it that way. Use story details to support your response.

Vocabulary Warm-up Word Lists

Study these words from Barrio Boy *and* "A Day's Wait." *Then, complete the activities.*

Word List A

condition [kuhn DISH uhn] *n.* general health or physical fitness
Ryan got himself in good <u>condition</u> for the big race.

foreign [FAWR uhn] *adj.* having to do with or coming from another place
The travel magazine had pictures of <u>foreign</u> countries.

instructions [in STRUHK shunz] *n.* directions for how to do something
The <u>instructions</u> explained how to build a birdhouse.

miserable [MIZ er uh buhl] *adj.* causing great discomfort or unhappiness
The <u>miserable</u> weather spoiled our vacation.

native [NAY tiv] *adj.* belonging to a person because of the place where he or she was born
Spanish is Pilar's <u>native</u> language.

progress [PRAH gres] *n.* an improvement
Katherine's test scores this quarter are much higher, showing that she has made <u>progress</u>.

secure [si KYOOR] *adj.* feeling safe and sure
Because their new home is in a safe neighborhood, the family feels <u>secure</u>.

various [VAYR ee uhs] *adj.* different
We looked at the <u>various</u> desserts and could not decide between apple pie and cheesecake.

Word List B

absolutely [ab suh LOOT lee] *adv.* completely; totally without limit
Alex has no doubt; he is <u>absolutely</u> certain he aced the test.

frequently [FREE kwuhnt lee] *adv.* commonly; happening often
Brianna <u>frequently</u> takes the shortest way home, so she knows the route extremely well.

importance [im PAWR tuhns] *n.* something of high value or interest
We recognize the <u>importance</u> of voting in the election.

influenza [in floo EN zuh] *n.* an illness with sneezing, coughing, fever, and muscle aches
Danielle thought she had <u>influenza</u> because she was coughing and sneezing and running a fever.

menace [MEN is] *n.* a threat or danger
Pollution is a <u>menace</u> to our environment because it can do a great deal of damage.

overcome [oh ver KUHM] *v.* to defeat
The team fought hard to <u>overcome</u> the competition and win the game.

similar [SIM uh luhr] *adj.* alike or the same type
Anthony and William had <u>similar</u> T-shirts; it was hard to tell them apart.

unnecessary [uhn NES uh ser ee] *adj.* not needed
An umbrella is <u>unnecessary</u> on a sunny day.

Name _____ Date _____

Vocabulary Warm-up Exercises

Exercise A *Fill in each blank in the paragraph below with an appropriate word from Word List A. Use each word only once.*

The United States was José's [1] _____ land, but he liked visiting

[2] _____ countries. He often traveled with his father to

[3] _____ parts of the world. His father's strict [4] _____

on how to behave in each country helped him feel [5] _____ in new

situations. Sometimes [6] _____ weather delayed a flight. Sometimes the

[7] _____ of their hotel room was poor. Those were small inconveniences.

Travel gave José a chance to learn new languages. He had already made great

[8] _____ learning French. Knowing many languages made him a good

traveler.

Exercise B *Find a synonym for each word in the following list. Use each synonym in a sentence that makes its meaning clear. Refer to a thesaurus if you need help finding a synonym.*

Example: distasteful   **Synonym:** *unlikable*
   Morgan does not like pepper, so she found the spicy sauce distasteful.

1. importance   **Synonym:** _____
_____

2. frequently   **Synonym:** _____
_____

3. overcome   **Synonym:** _____
_____

4. menace   **Synonym:** _____
_____

5. unnecessary   **Synonym:** _____
_____

6. absolutely   **Synonym:** _____
_____

7. similar   **Synonym:** _____
_____

8. influenza   **Synonym:** _____
_____

Name _____ Date _____

from **Barrio Boy** by Ernesto Galarza
"A Day's Wait" by Ernest Hemingway
Reading Warm-up A

Read the following passage. Pay special attention to the underlined words. Then, read it again, and complete the activities. Use a separate sheet of paper for your written answers.

Schools in the United States enroll a great number of immigrant students every year. The students come from many different nations. They bring with them their <u>native</u> language and culture and their hopes for success. Although they speak the language of their country, they often speak little or no English.

What is it like for an immigrant student entering a public school in the United States for the first time? If you have ever traveled to a <u>foreign</u> country, you have an idea of what it is like. Many things may seem strange. You may be confused and afraid of making mistakes. You may feel shy.

Now imagine what it is like to go to school in a place where you do not know the language. The words on the chalkboard and in the books look like gibberish. You cannot understand the teacher's <u>instructions</u>. Class-mates, who do not know your language, cannot speak to you. In short, not knowing the language makes your ability to adjust extremely difficult. While you may be in good <u>condition</u>, you are likely to feel <u>miserable</u>.

Fortunately, immigrant students usually pick up English quickly. Many attend classes for newcomers at the beginning of their first school year. In those classes, skilled teachers introduce them to the basics of English. Once they have learned the basics, they move to regular classrooms. Still, it takes time before they feel <u>secure</u> in their studies. After several months, many students still need coaching or the help of an interpreter. Learning the <u>various</u> subjects in a new language is difficult because it involves learning more than basic vocabulary.

In spite of all that, immigrant students make tremen-dous <u>progress</u> in their studies. Many graduate with honors. That is an achievement they can be proud of.

1. Underline the phrase that shows the meaning of a <u>native</u> language. Write a sentence using the word *native*.

2. Underline the sentences that tell how you might feel in a <u>foreign</u> country. Do you agree with the description? Why or why not?

3. Underline the phrase that explains why students cannot understand teachers' <u>instructions</u>. How might a teacher make *instructions* understood?

4. Circle the word that describes the <u>condition</u> a student might be in. How do you feel when you are in excellent *condition*?

5. Underline the sentences that tell why a student might feel <u>miserable.</u> What might help a student feel less *miserable*?

6. Underline the sentence that tells why it takes time for a student to feel <u>secure</u>. When might someone feel *secure*?

7. Underline the sentence that tells why learning <u>various</u> sub-jects can be hard. Name the *various* subjects you study.

8. Underline the sentence that shows that students make <u>progress</u>. Tell about a sub-ject in which you are making *progress*.

from **Barrio Boy** by Ernesto Galarza
"A Day's Wait" by Ernest Hemingway
Reading Warm-up B

Read the following passage. Pay special attention to the underlined words. Then, read it again, and complete the activities. Use a separate sheet of paper for your written answers.

A "touch" of influenza, or the flu, is <u>similar</u> to a bad cold. The symptoms are a dry cough, a sore throat, burning eyes, and a stuffy nose. A mild case of the flu is more of a nuisance than a <u>menace</u>. However, a serious attack of influenza can turn deadly.

<u>Influenza</u> is a disease that attacks the respiratory system. Its symptoms include chills, sudden high fever, headache, and aching muscles. Those symptoms <u>frequently</u> lead to pneumonia, and that is what poses the real danger.

This disease has been around since the sixteenth century. Since that time it has caused 31 epidemics. The disease can spread far and fast, infecting millions of people. In 1918, an epidemic caused 20 million deaths throughout the world. About 500,000 people died in the United States.

Fortunately, by the mid-twentieth century, scientists had discovered that a vaccine could control influenza. The discovery was of major <u>importance</u>, but it did not entirely solve the problem. The problem was hard to <u>overcome</u> because research revealed that there are three types of flu viruses. The first two types, A and B, are the ones that cause epidemics. It took scientists several years to create a vaccine that could control those two types.

Most doctors believe it is <u>unnecessary</u> to vaccinate everyone against the disease. However, people in certain age groups and people with respiratory problems should get a flu shot every year. Should you ask your doctor about getting vaccinated? <u>Absolutely</u>.

1. Underline the words that tell what is <u>similar</u> to a bad cold. Write a sentence using the word *similar*.

2. Circle the words that tell what is more a nuisance than a <u>menace</u>. What is the difference between a nuisance and a *menace*?

3. Circle the word that tells what <u>influenza</u> is. What is another name for *influenza*?

4. Underline the words that tell what <u>frequently</u> leads to pneumonia. What *frequently* happens when people get the flu?

5. What discovery was of major <u>importance</u>? Tell why it was of *importance*.

6. Underline the words that tell why the problem was hard to <u>overcome</u>. What problem at school might someone *overcome*?

7. What do most doctors believe is <u>unnecessary</u>?

8. What should everyone <u>absolutely</u> do to protect his or her health?

Unit 1 Resources: Fiction and Nonfiction

from **Barrio Boy** by Ernesto Galarza

"A Day's Wait" by Ernest Hemingway

Writing About the Big Question

What is the best way to find the truth?

Big Question Vocabulary

awareness	believable	conclude	convince	debate
evaluate	evidence	explain	factual	fiction
insight	perceive	reality	reveal	truth

A. *Use one or more words from the list above to complete each sentence.*

1. The scariest stories of all deal with situations that could happen in _____.

2. To _____ how scary a story is, I listen to how hard my heart is pounding.

3. After my little brother watched the horror movie, I had to _____ to him that the "blood" was really red paint.

4. In a good detective story, the _____ is there all along.

B. *Answer the questions.*

1. Describe a situation that you faced that scared you at first.

_____

_____

_____

2. How did you get over your fear? Use two vocabulary words in your answer.

_____

_____

_____

C. *Complete the sentence below. Then, answer the question to write a short paragraph connecting the sentence to the Big Question.*

The most frightening situations are those in which _____

Describe a scary fictional story that you read or a scary movie that you saw. What about it was realistic? What was unrealistic?

_____

_____

_____

_____

from **Barrio Boy** by Ernesto Galarza
"A Day's Wait" by Ernest Hemingway
Literary Analysis: Comparing Fiction and Nonfiction

Fiction is prose writing that tells about imaginary characters and events. Novels, novellas, and short stories are types of fiction. **Nonfiction** is prose writing that presents and explains ideas or tells about real people, places, objects, or events. News articles, essays, and historical accounts are types of nonfiction.

In the excerpt from *Barrio Boy,* the writer tells about an actual event in his life. In contrast, the writer of "A Day's Wait" created a narrator who tells about an imagined event in the lives of an imagined father and son.

DIRECTIONS: *Complete the following chart by answering the questions about the excerpt from* Barrio Boy *and "A Day's Wait."*

Question	*from* **Barrio Boy**	"A Day's Wait"
1. Who tells the story?		
2. Who are the main characters?		
3. Is there important dialogue? If so, summarize it.		
4. What important events make up the action of the story?		
5. What feelings does the main character have as events unfold?		
6. How is the main character's problem resolved?		

from **Barrio Boy** by Ernesto Galarza
"A Day's Wait" by Ernest Hemingway
Vocabulary Builder

Word List

contraption   epidemic   evidently   flushed   formidable   reassuring

A. DIRECTIONS: *Think about the meaning of the italicized word in each question. Then, answer the question.*

1. When there is an *epidemic,* why are infected people kept away from healthy people?
   _____

2. What is an example of a *formidable* school project?
   _____

3. Why might someone call a typewriter a *contraption*?
   _____

4. If Elizabeth is *evidently* healthy, how do you know that she is healthy?
   _____

5. What is a *reassuring* gesture?
   _____

6. When a hunting dog has *flushed* quail from the bushes, what has the dog done?
   _____

B. DIRECTIONS: *For each pair of related words in capital letters, write the letter of the pair of words that best expresses a* similar *relationship.*

____ 1. EPIDEMIC : DOCTORS ::
   A. hospital : nurses
   B. war : soldier
   C. sick : well
   D. medicine : science

____ 2. FORMIDABLE : UNIMPORTANT ::
   A. dangerous : great
   B. square : rectangular
   C. difficult : simple
   D. large : huge

____ 3. EVIDENTLY : SEEMINGLY ::
   A. evidence : trial
   B. slowly : quickly
   C. suddenly : sudden
   D. certainly : surely

Name _____ Date _____

from Barrio Boy by Ernesto Galarza
"A Day's Wait" by Ernest Hemingway
Integrated Language Skills:
Support for Writing to Compare Literary Works

To prepare to write an essay that compares and contrasts the narrators of *Barrio Boy* and "A Day's Wait," use this graphic organizer. Respond to each question by jotting down ideas about how the narrators present their stories.

Question	from *Barrio Boy*	"A Day's Wait"
Who is the narrator? What is the point of view?		
What details about the narrator are revealed?		
How is dialogue used in each work?		
How are the narrator's feelings involved in the work?		
What theme do the narrator's thoughts and actions suggest?		
How do other characters affect the narrator?		
How does the narrator bring the story to a close?		

Now, use your notes to write an essay comparing and contrasting the narrators of *Barrio Boy* and "A Day's Wait."

Name _____ Date _____

from **Barrio Boy** by Ernesto Galarza
"A Day's Wait" by Ernest Hemingway
Open-Book Test

Short Answer *Write your responses to the questions in this section on the lines provided.*

1. In *Barrio Boy*, Ernesto admires Miss Ryan. In each blank oval below, write one of her character traits. Then, on the lines, explain why he admires her so much.

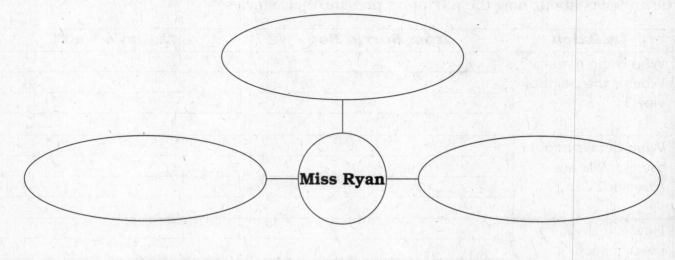

_____

_____

2. Reread the last paragraph of *Barrio Boy*. What does "becoming a proud American" mean to Ernesto? Use details from the essay to support your answer.

_____

_____

_____

3. In "A Day's Wait," the boy is evidently anxious about something. What details in the story show that Hemingway evidently knew about the sport of hunting? Use the definition of *evidently* in your response.

_____

_____

_____

4. In "A Day's Wait," review what the father tells his son after the boy reveals his fear about dying. Consider the tone he takes with the boy. How would you describe the father's reaction to his son's concern? Use details from the story to support your answer.

_____

_____

_____

5. The title of "A Day's Wait" has more than one meaning. Explain what it means for the boy and what it means for his father.

_____

_____

6. At the beginning of *Barrio Boy*, Ernesto does not find the differences he notices in his new school to be reassuring. What reassuring words does the father in "A Day's Wait" give his son? Support your answer by explaining what effect his words have on the boy.

_____

_____

_____

7. Both fiction and nonfiction can use a first-person point of view, in which the narrator is a character participating in the action. Identify the narrators of *Barrio Boy* and "A Day's Wait," and explain how you can tell that both narratives are told from a first-person point of view.

_____

_____

_____

8. What makes *Barrio Boy* a work of nonfiction and "A Day's Wait" a work of fiction? Explain.

_____

_____

_____

9. Contrast how Ernesto's emotions are revealed in *Barrio Boy* with how the boy's emotions are revealed in "A Day's Wait." Use details from the selections to support your ideas.

_____

_____

_____

10. In what way do both Ernesto in *Barrio Boy* and the sick boy in "A Day's Wait" show courage? Explain your answer.

_____

_____

_____

Essay

Write an extended response to the question of your choice or to the question or questions your teacher assigns you.

11. The boys in *Barrio Boy* and "A Day's Wait" are alike in many ways. Think about the problems they have, the emotions they express, the way they overcome obstacles, and the help they get from adults in their lives. In an essay, compare Ernesto with the sick boy. Include details from the selections in your answer.

12. Both Ernesto from *Barrio Boy* and the boy in "A Day's Wait" interact with adults. Ernesto interacts with Miss Ryan, while the sick boy interacts with his father. In an essay, compare and contrast how the boys interact with the adults. Focus on how the boys think of the adults, how the adults react to the boys, and how the boys respond to them. Use details from the selections to support your ideas.

13. Suppose that the excerpt from *Barrio Boy* was fiction and "A Day's Wait" was nonfiction. In an essay, explain how these selections would change and in what ways they would remain the same. Use details from the selections to support your ideas.

14. **Thinking About the Big Question: What is the best way to find the truth?** In an essay, respond to one of the following. Use examples from the selection to support your response.
    * In *Barrio Boy*, Ernesto is wary of his new American school. The truth is that the school is a nurturing place in which he will flourish. In an essay, discuss how he finds, or discovers, this truth. Focus on the experiences in Lincoln School that help him realize his goal of "becoming a proud American."
    * Although the boy in "A Day's Wait" thinks he knows the truth about his situation, he is wrong. In an essay, discuss why the truth escapes the boy at first and how he finally finds it.

Oral Response

15. Go back to question 2, 4, 8, or 10 or to the question your teacher assigns to you. Take a few minutes to expand your answer and prepare an oral response. Find additional details in the excerpt from *Barrio Boy* or "A Day's Wait" that will support your points. If necessary, make notes to guide your response.

from **Barrio Boy** by Ernesto Galarza
"A Day's Wait" by Ernest Hemingway
Selection Test A

Critical Reading *Identify the letter of the choice that best answers the question.*

_____ 1. In the excerpt from *Barrio Boy*, why does Miss Hopley have another boy come to her meeting with Ernesto and his mother?
  A. Ernesto has gotten into a fight with the other boy.
  B. The other boy is Ernesto's older brother.
  C. Ernesto and his mother do not speak English.
  D. The other boy will take Ernesto to his class.

_____ 2. How does Miss Ryan help Ernesto overcome his fear of her?
  A. She does not allow anyone to tease his way of saying "butterfly."
  B. She visits him at his home and talks to his parents in Spanish.
  C. She gives him good grades and announces how well he has done.
  D. She helps him learn English and encourages him in front of the class.

_____ 3. What makes Ernesto similar to several of his classmates?
  A. Other students in the class also do not speak English.
  B. Other students in his class also live in his neighborhood.
  C. Other students in his class are also from Mexico.
  D. Other students in his class are also afraid of Miss Ryan.

_____ 4. In the excerpt from *Barrio Boy*, how does Ernesto learn English?
  A. He learns once he can say "butterfly."
  B. He learns because Miss Hopley insists that all students speak English in class.
  C. He learns because Miss Ryan gives him private lessons in a hall off the classroom.
  D. He learns on the playground, from the other Mexican children in the school.

_____ 5. Who is the narrator of "A Day's Wait"?
  A. the boy
  B. the boy's father
  C. a third person
  D. the writer

____ 6. In "A Day's Wait," what is the boy's temperature when the doctor takes it?

    A. 98.6 degrees

    B. 102 degrees

    C. 104 degrees

    D. 105 degrees

____ 7. To what does the father in "A Day's Wait" compare the different temperature scales?

    A. miles and kilometers

    B. yards and meters

    C. grams and pounds

    D. feet and inches

____ 8. In "A Day's Wait," how can the father's reaction to his son's concern best be described?

    A. impatient

    B. angry

    C. frustrated

    D. understanding

____ 9. What do both Ernesto in *Barrio Boy* and the boy in "A Day's Wait" feel during their stories?

    A. sick and afraid

    B. happy and content

    C. rejected and hurt

    D. fear and anxiety

____ 10. Which of the following statements about *Barrio Boy* and "A Day's Wait" is correct?

    A. *Barrio Boy* is narrated by Ernesto Galarza.

    B. "A Day's Wait" is narrated by the boy who is ill.

    C. Ernesto's mother tells how she feels when she first takes her son to school in America.

    D. The boy in "A Day's Wait" tells how he feels when he thinks he is going to die.

____ 11. Which statement comparing *Barrio Boy* and "A Day's Wait" is correct?

    A. There are more characters in *Barrio Boy.*

    B. There are more characters in "A Day's Wait."

    C. Both stories have many characters.

    D. Both stories have only two characters.

___ 12. How do Ernesto in *Barrio Boy* and the boy in "A Day's Wait" show bravery?

A. Ernesto tells Miss Ryan that he is afraid of her because she is tall; the boy tells his father that he is afraid of dying.

B. Ernesto never says that he is afraid of attending school in America; the boy never says that he is afraid of dying.

C. Ernesto refuses to speak in class until he has mastered the pronunciation of "butterfly"; the boy tells his father that he is afraid of dying.

D. Ernesto makes friends with other children whose families do not speak English at home; the boy declares that he is afraid of dying.

Vocabulary

___ 13. What does it mean if a disease has become an *epidemic*?

A. It is widespread.   C. It cannot be cured.

B. It has been cured.   D. It is not serious.

___ 14. What does it mean if a dog *flushed* birds out of the bushes?

A. The dog splashed water on the birds.

B. The dog chased the birds out of the bushes.

C. The dog hid from the birds in the bushes.

D. The dog caught the birds in the bushes.

___ 15. Which statement describes someone who is *formidable*?

A. The principal smiled warmly as she welcomed the new student.

B. The doctor told the boy's father that the epidemic was not serious.

C. The woman towered above the small boy and spoke sternly.

D. The boy's father sat at the foot of the bed and read a funny story.

Essay

16. In an essay, compare Ernesto in the excerpt from *Barrio Boy* with the boy in "A Day's Wait." Consider these questions: Do the boys have similar problems? Do they express similar emotions? Do they have similar obstacles to overcome? Are there adults in their lives who help them?

17. In an essay, describe the differences between the excerpt from *Barrio Boy* and "A Day's Wait" in terms of fiction and nonfiction. First, define the terms *fiction* and *nonfiction*. Then, tell which selection is a work of fiction and which is a work of non-fiction. Tell who the narrators are and from whose perspective the stories are told.

18. **Thinking About the Big Question: What is the best way to find the truth?** In both *Barrio Boy* and "A Day's Wait," the main character thinks that he knows the truth about his situation, but he later finds out that he does not. In an essay, compare and contrast the ways in which Ernesto and the boy in "A Day's Wait" find out that the truth is different from what they expect it to be.

from **Barrio Boy** by Ernesto Galarza
"A Day's Wait" by Ernest Hemingway
Selection Test B

Critical Reading *Identify the letter of the choice that best completes the statement or answers the question.*

____ 1. Why does Ernesto Galarza compare Lincoln School and his school in Mazatlán?
   A. He wishes to show that he prefers the school he had attended in Mexico.
   B. He wishes to show he is frightened by the "contraption" that shuts the door.
   C. He wishes to show that in Mexico the principal of a school is always a man.
   D. He wishes to show that he feels insecure at a new school in a new country.

____ 2. In *Barrio Boy,* how does Miss Ryan encourage the students that she tutors privately?
   A. She praises their accomplishments before the whole class.
   B. She puts their pictures on the bulletin board in a gold frame.
   C. She invites the best students to sit next to her at lunch.
   D. She places gold stars next to their names on a class list.

____ 3. In "A Day's Wait," the doctor's reaction to the boy's condition can best be described as
   A. unconcerned.   C. greatly concerned.
   B. mildly concerned.   D. panicky.

____ 4. In "A Day's Wait," the fact that the father leaves the boy and goes hunting shows that the father
   A. does not think his son's condition is serious.
   B. is a self-absorbed and neglectful parent.
   C. cannot bear to remain in the boy's presence.
   D. is more attached to his dog than to his son.

____ 5. In "A Day's Wait," the boy's concern about his temperature indicates that he is under the impression that 102 degrees is
   A. far below normal.   C. normal.
   B. far above normal.   D. slightly above normal.

____ 6. Which statement about the narrators of *Barrio Boy* and "A Day's Wait" is correct?
   A. One is a boy in a new school; the other is a boy who thinks he is dying.
   B. One is a man remembering his childhood; the other is a father of a boy.
   C. One is a teacher of a first-grade class; the other is the father of a boy.
   D. One is a first-grader from Mexico; the other is a sick boy in the United States.

____ 7. How are the emotions of Ernesto in *Barrio Boy* and the boy in "A Day's Wait" revealed?
   A. Ernesto's emotions are revealed through his teacher's comments; the boy reveals his emotions by describing his illness.
   B. Ernesto describes his emotions as he speaks directly to the reader; the boy's emotions are not revealed at all.
   C. Ernesto describes his emotions as he speaks directly to the reader; the boy's emotions are revealed through his actions and speech.
   D. Ernesto's emotions are not revealed at all; the boy's emotions are revealed through his father's description.

8. Which statement about the use of dialogue in *Barrio Boy* and in "A Day's Wait" is correct?
   A. There is no dialogue in *Barrio Boy;* the dialogue in "A Day's Wait" is important to the story.
   B. The dialogue in *Barrio Boy* is important to the story; there is no dialogue in "A Day's Wait."
   C. The dialogue in *Barrio Boy* reveals Ernesto's thoughts and feelings; the dialogue in "A Day's Wait" is not important to the story.
   D. The dialogue in *Barrio Boy* is not important to the story; the dialogue in "A Day's Wait" reveals the boy's thoughts and feelings.

9. How are Ernesto's emotions in *Barrio Boy* similar to the boy's emotions in "A Day's Wait"?
   A. Both boys experience fear and anxiety.
   B. Both boys react to unfamiliar surroundings.
   C. Both boys are encouraged by strong women.
   D. Both boys must deal with the fear of dying.

10. What is similar about the resolution of the problems of Ernesto in *Barrio Boy* and the boy in "A Day's Wait"?
    A. Ernesto never learns to speak English, and the boy never learns that he is not fatally ill.
    B. Through communication, Ernesto learns to adjust, and the boy learns he will not die.
    C. Ernesto learns a lesson from Miss Ryan, and the boy learns a lesson from his father.
    D. Ernesto overhears that he is the top first-grader, and the boy overhears that he will live.

11. Although one work is nonfiction and the other is fiction, why do the events in the excerpt from *Barrio Boy* and the events in "A Day's Wait" seem realistic?
    A. Both works are narrated by adult men.
    B. The characters and their emotions are believable.
    C. Adult role models influence the young boys to make real-life choices.
    D. *Barrio Boy* is a true story, and "A Day's Wait" is based on a true story.

12. How is *Barrio Boy* characteristic of nonfiction while "A Day's Wait" is characteristic of fiction?
    A. Ernesto in *Barrio Boy* is a believable character, while the boy in "A Day's Wait" is not believable.
    B. *Barrio Boy* is narrated by the main character, while "A Day's Wait" is told by a third-person narrator.
    C. The dialogue in *Barrio Boy* is realistic, while the dialogue in "A Day's Wait" is unrealistic.
    D. *Barrio Boy* recounts events in the lives of real people; "A Day's Wait" tells about imaginary characters and events.

Vocabulary

____ **13.** If there is an *epidemic* of a disease, the disease
   A. is widespread.   **C.** is incurable.
   B. has been cured.   **D.** is not serious.

____ **14.** In which sentence is the word *evidently* used logically?
   A. The details about hunting ring true; Hemingway evidently knew about that sport.
   B. Ernesto is a new student at Lincoln School; evidently he came from Mexico.
   C. The boy in "A Day's Wait" has a high temperature; evidently he is not sick.
   D. The mechanism that closed the door surprised Ernesto; evidently he had seen one before.

____ **15.** If on the first day of school Miss Ryan's smile is *reassuring* to Ernesto, how does she make him feel?
   A. She makes him happy.   **C.** She causes him to feel uneasy.
   B. She gives him confidence.   **D.** She helps him feel less tired.

Essay

16. In the excerpt from *Barrio Boy*, Ernesto interacts with Miss Ryan; the boy in "A Day's Wait" interacts with his father. In an essay, compare and contrast the boys' interactions with these adults. Consider these questions: How does Ernesto respond to and think of Miss Ryan? How does the boy in "A Day's Wait" respond to and think of his father? How do both boys interact with these adults? What is similar about their interactions? What is different?

17. In an essay, compare and contrast the excerpt from *Barrio Boy* and "A Day's Wait." First, define *fiction* and *nonfiction* and tell which story is a work of fiction and which is a work of nonfiction. Then, describe the narrator of each work. From what point of view does each narrator tell his story? Finally, compare and contrast the main characters and the use of dialogue in each story.

18. Thinking About the Big Question: What is the best way to find the truth? In an essay, respond to one of the following. Use examples from the selection to support your response.

   • In *Barrio Boy*, Ernesto is wary of his new American school. The truth is that the school is a nurturing place in which he will flourish. In an essay, discuss how he finds, or discovers, this truth. Focus on the experiences in Lincoln School that help him realize his goal of "becoming a proud American."

   • Although the boy in "A Day's Wait" thinks he knows the truth about his situation, he is wrong. In an essay, discuss why the truth escapes the boy at first and how he finally finds it.

Writing Workshop—Unit 1, Part 1
Description: Descriptive Essay

Prewriting: Gathering Details

Once you have narrowed down the topic of your description, gather details about that topic by using the following graphic organizer. Write the topic in the center, and then fill in your descriptions.

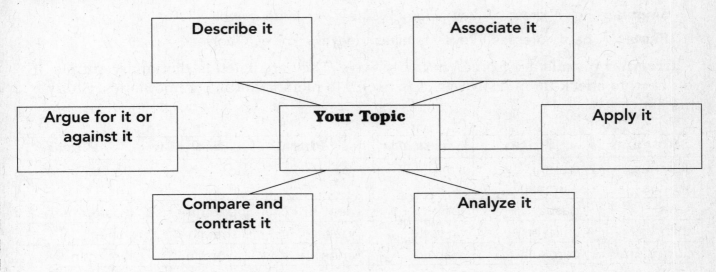

Drafting: Providing Elaboration

After organizing your ideas into an organizational plan, answer the following questions to help you elaborate to create a main impression.

Questions:	Your answers:
What is the main idea of your essay?	
What mood would you like to create in your essay?	
What kind of feelings do you want your audience to feel when reading your essay?	
What sensory details could you include that will strengthen this overall impression?	
How do these sensory details show that your topic is meaningful to you?	

Writing Workshop—Unit 1, Part 1
Descriptive Essay: Integrating Grammar Skills

Revising Incorrect Forms of Plural Nouns

The **singular** form of a noun shows one; the **plural** form shows more than one. Most nouns add *s* or *es* to form the plural. If a noun ends in a consonant + *y*, change the *y* to *i* and add *es*. For some nouns ending in *f* or *fe*, change the *f* to *v* and add *es*.

Singular hat   dress   key   family   leaf   knife   wolf

Plural   hats   dresses   keys   families   leaves   knives   wolves

Irregular plurals are formed in many ways. They are listed in dictionary entries, if you need to check them. However, it is useful to memorize the common ones. Study this list.

Singular	Plural	Singular	Plural	Singular	Plural
alumnus, alumna	alumni, alumnae	deer	deer	ox	oxen
basis	bases	foot	feet	parenthesis	parentheses
child	children	goose	geese	sheep	sheep
curriculum	curricula	man	men	woman	women

Identifying Correct Plural Forms

A. Directions: *Circle the correct form of the noun in parentheses.*

1. Several (alumni, alumnis) visited their old school.
2. They watched a class of older (childs, children) in the science lab.
3. The visitors asked about the new (curriculums, curricula) of the science departments.

Fixing Incorrect Plural Forms

B. Directions: *On the lines provided, rewrite these sentences so that they use correct singular and plural nouns.*

1. The four man went hunting for deers.

_____

2. The dates in parenthesis show when we received the data.

_____

3. The two woman sheared more than a dozen sheeps.

_____

Unit 1: Fiction and Nonfiction
Benchmark Test 1

MULTIPLE CHOICE

Reading Skill: Using Context Clues *Read the selection. Then, answer the questions that follow.*

[1] The tasks of television meteorologists involve much more than standing in front of cameras and forecasting the weather. [2] These professionals must collect and digest vast amounts of data, or information, sent to the studio from several sources, including data from weather satellites high above Earth. [3] They take this highly technical data and translate it into intelligible language that viewers can understand and use in their daily lives.

1. Which word from sentence 1 best helps you understand the meaning of the word *meteorologists*?
   A. forecasting
   B. weather
   C. tasks
   D. cameras

2. Which type of context clue do the words *or information* in sentence 2 provide for the word *data*?
   A. an opposite
   B. a restatement
   C. a contrast
   D. an example

3. Using word position and function, what is the most relevant meaning of the word *digest* in sentence 2?
   A. take into the body and break down
   B. believe
   C. simplify
   D. absorb

4. Using the context clues in sentence 3, what is the most likely meaning for the word *intelligible*?
   A. technical
   B. neutral
   C. understandable
   D. clever

Reading Skill: Locate Types of Information *Read the bus schedule. Then, answer the questions that follow.*

Mojave/California City Intercity Bus Service
(Tuesday & Thursday Only; Saturday, Only Trips 2 & 3 Operate)

		Trip 1	Trip 2	Trip 3
Mojave to California City				
Mojave:	Mojave Motel	4:30 A.M.	8:15 A.M.	5:20 P.M.
	Stater Bros. Market	4:35	8:20	5:25
California City:	Aspen Mall	4:55	8:40	5:45
	City Hall	4:58	8:43	5:48
California City to Mojave				
California City:	Aspen Mall	4:55	8:40	5:45
	City Hall	4:58	8:43	5:48
	Cactus Deli	5:00	8:45	5:50
	Petrol Pavilion	5:02	8:47	5:52
Mojave:	Stater Bros. Market	5:20	9:05	6:10
	Mojave Motel	5:25	9:10	6:15

5. What is the earliest that you could leave Mojave for California City on a Saturday?
   A. 4:30 A.M.
   B. 8:15 A.M.
   C. 8:20 A.M.
   D. 5:20 P.M.

6. If you wanted to go to Mojave, where would you catch the bus in California City at 8:45 A.M.?
   A. Aspen Mall
   B. City Hall
   C. Cactus Deli
   D. Petrol Pavilion

7. To find out what time you should be at the bus stop to travel from City Hall to the Stater Bros. Market on a Saturday morning, which headings would you use?
   A. California City to Mojave / Trip 2
   B. California City to Mojave / Trip 1
   C. Mojave to California City / Trip 2
   D. Mojave to California City / Trip 3

Literary Analysis: Narration *Read the selection. Then, answer the questions that follow.*

When Gibson came into the lives of Katie and Alexa, he was two months old. The girls' task was to train the German shepherd puppy to become a Seeing Eye dog, a type of guide for a blind person. First, they taught Gibson simple commands such as *sit, stay, rest,* and *come.* After he learned the basics, Katie and Alexa took the dog to public places such as shopping malls and baseball games so that he could get used to noises and crowds. Finally, when Gibson was 17 months old, he was returned to the Seeing Eye organization to receive more training. Saying goodbye to Gibson was the hardest part of the girls' task.

8. When do the girls take Gibson to public places?
   A. when he is two months old
   B. after he is fully trained
   C. after he has learned basic commands
   D. when Gibson is 17 months old

9. In which order is the information in this selection presented?
   A. in cause-and-effect order
   B. in spatial order
   C. in order of importance
   D. in chronological order

10. Which of the following answer choices is the best definition of narrative writing?
    A. it tells a story
    B. it explains a concept
    C. it describes characters
    D. it summarizes a story

Literary Analysis: Point of View

11. What point of view would be used in an autobiographical narrative?
    A. third-person omniscient
    B. third-person limited
    C. first-person
    D. objective

Read the selection. Then, answer the questions that follow.

Before Meriwether Lewis set off on his historic journey with William Clark, he had a lot to learn in preparation for the mission. He could scarcely imagine how valuable this knowledge would be on the long trip. Lewis learned from a doctor how to treat medical emergencies. From a botanist, he learned how to categorize plants. Lewis learned to recognize constellations and calculate latitude and longitude. He learned about animals and fossils from an anatomist.

12. Which of the following best applies to the selection?
    A. It is told from a first-person point of view.
    B. It is told from a third-person point of view.
    C. It is told from Lewis's point of view.
    D. It is told from a fictional character's point of view.

13. Given the facts that the narrator chooses to emphasize, what is likely to be the theme of the selection?
    A. Lewis worried unnecessarily about the expedition.
    B. Fields of expertise in the 19th century were very specialized.
    C. Lewis's training was put to the test on the expedition.
    D. Explorers of Lewis's era tended to overprepare.

14. What makes the point of view in the paragraph about Lewis objective?
    A. It is written from one person's perspective.
    B. It describes Lewis's objectives in acquiring new knowledge.
    C. It describes thoughts and feelings.
    D. It presents factual information from a neutral perspective.

Literary Analysis: Elements of Fiction and Nonfiction

15. Which of the following distinguishes fiction from nonfiction?
    A. A narrator describes events in the selection.
    B. One or more characters and events are imagined.
    C. Conversations take place among characters.
    D. Events make up the action in the selection.

16. Which of the following is an example of nonfiction writing?
    A. a novel   C. a novella
    B. a short story   D. an essay

17. Which of the following describes a nonfiction selection?
    A. an explanation of the scientific principles behind gene splicing
    B. a narrative that portrays the life of a famous time-traveler
    C. a story about a horse that can fly
    D. a diary written from the perspective of an interplanetary explorer

Vocabulary: Prefixes

18. Using your knowledge of the prefix re-, what is the meaning of *restore* in the following sentence?

    When will the power company restore our electricity?

    A. bring back   C. cut down on
    B. take away   D. increase

19. Using your knowledge of the prefix in-, what is the meaning of *inadequate* in the following sentence?

    Bob had an inadequate amount of food for his party guests.

    A. more than enough
    B. just enough
    C. not any at all
    D. not enough

20. What is the meaning of the word formed by adding the prefix *trans-* to *plant*?
    A. to make better
    B. to exceed a limit
    C. to relocate
    D. to send an electronic signal

21. Using your knowledge of the prefix *ac-* and the word *climate*, what does the word *acclimate* mean?
    A. move away from your surroundings
    B. adjust to your surroundings
    C. change your point of view
    D. maintain the same point of view

22. Using your knowledge of the prefix *re-*, what is the meaning of the word *refund* in the following sentence?

    The movie theater will refund your money because of the poor sound quality.

    A. give back
    B. take away
    C. add to
    D. save for later

23. The prefix *in-* can mean either "not" or "in." Which one of the following words uses the "not" meaning?
    A. interior
    B. inflexible
    C. internal
    D. inception

Grammar

24. Which sentence contains both a common noun and a proper noun?
    A. Modern telescopes reveal more than earlier ones.
    B. Ancient Greeks were skilled astronomers.
    C. How important was what Copernicus discovered?
    D. What distinguishes Orion from Delphinus?

25. Which word in the following sentence is a common noun?

    Tran wrote an interesting report about the Maori of New Zealand.

    A. Tran
    B. interesting
    C. report
    D. Maori

26. Which of the following sentences contains a singular possessive noun?
    A. The book tells the nation's history.
    B. Some wars begin over minor issues.
    C. My parents' families are from Scotland.
    D. The men's kilts identify their clans.

27. Which of the following is the correct possessive form for the underlined phrase?

   The store manager reviewed the <u>complaints of the customer</u>.

   A. customer complaint's
   B. customers's complaint
   C. customers' complaints
   D. customer's complaints

28. Which of the following is the correct possessive form for the underlined phrase?

   The <u>opinions of the women</u> were varied.

   A. womens' opinions
   B. women's opinions
   C. womans' opinions
   D. womens's opinions

29. In the following sentence, what is the best way to revise *mouse* so that its plural form is correct?

   Four tiny mouse scrambled into the hole.

   A. Change *mouse* to *mouses*.
   B. Change *mouse* to *mice*.
   C. Change *mouse* to *mices*.
   D. Change *mouse* to *mousies*.

30. Which of the following is the correct plural form of *loaf*?
   A. loafs
   B. loafes
   C. loavs
   D. loaves

WRITING

31. What is the most amazing thing you have seen in nature—a strange insect? A gigantic plant? On a separate piece of paper, use hyperbole to write a brief description of what you saw. For example, you might describe an unusual spider by writing, "The rare African spider was less like an arachnid and more like a compact car with eight hairy legs."

32. Think of two narratives you have read. Write a paragraph in which you compare and contrast the narratives. Choose to compare either the setting or a character from each story. Before you begin, jot down your ideas on a separate sheet of paper. Then, think about how to organize your ideas in paragraph form. Include specific details from the narratives as much as possible.

33. On a separate piece of paper, write a brief description of the setting—the time and place—for a fiction or nonfiction narrative that you have read. Your description should contain vivid details that appeal to the five senses.

Name _____

Starting Date _____ Ending Date _____

Unit 1: Fiction and Nonfiction Skills Concept Map—2
What is the best way to find the truth?

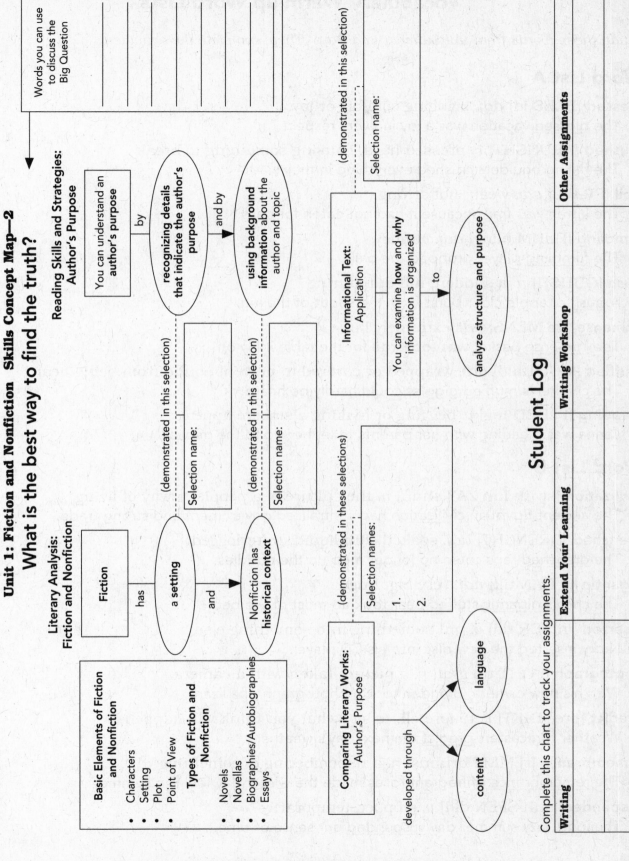

Words you can use to discuss the Big Question

Reading Skills and Strategies: Author's Purpose

You can understand an author's purpose

by → **recognizing details that indicate the author's purpose**

and by → **using background information** about the author and topic

(demonstrated in this selection)

Selection name: _____

(demonstrated in this selection)

Selection name: _____

Informational Text: Application

You can examine **how and why** information is organized

to → analyze structure and purpose

(demonstrated in this selection)

Selection name: _____

Literary Analysis: Fiction and Nonfiction

Fiction

has → a setting

and → Nonfiction has **historical context**

Basic Elements of Fiction and Nonfiction

- Characters
- Setting
- Plot
- Point of View

Types of Fiction and Nonfiction

- Novels
- Novellas
- Biographies/Autobiographies
- Essays

Comparing Literary Works: Author's Purpose

developed through →

- language
- content

(demonstrated in these selections)

Selection names:
1. _____
2. _____

Student Log

Complete this chart to track your assignments.

Writing	Extend Your Learning	Writing Workshop	Other Assignments

Study these words from "All Summer in a Day." Then, complete the activities.

Word List A

blessed [BLES id] *adj.* bringing comfort or joy
The <u>blessed</u> vacation was a joy in every respect.

crushed [KRUHSHT] *v.* pressed hard, causing something to break
The falling boulders <u>crushed</u> everything in their path.

frail [FRAYL] *adj.* weak; not strong
The kitten was <u>frail</u> because it had not eaten for days.

fumbling [FUHM bling] *adj.* clumsy
The <u>fumbling</u> player dropped the ball.

gush [GUHSH] *n.* a sudden, full outpouring
A <u>gush</u> of apple cider burst from the spout of the jug.

immense [im MENS] *adj.* extremely large
The <u>immense</u> basket was too large for the table it lay on.

muffled [MUF uhld] *adj.* wrapped or covered to prevent sound from being heard
The children's <u>muffled</u> giggles could hardly be heard.

pleading [PLEED ing] *v.* begging or making a sincere appeal
Jenna was <u>pleading</u> with her parents to let her go to the movie.

Word List B

civilization [siv ih luh ZAY shun] *n.* the culture of a people; a way of living
The ancient Egyptian <u>civilization</u> had centralized government and strong trade.

drenched [DRENCHT] *adj.* soaked with liquid; waterlogged
The <u>drenched</u> rags could no longer mop up the puddles.

gigantic [jy GAN tik] *adj.* very big; huge
The child's <u>gigantic</u> stuffed bear took up most of the bed.

inserted [in SER tid] *v.* put something into something else
Nicky <u>inserted</u> the new disc into his CD player.

photograph [FOHT uh graf] *n.* a picture taken with a camera
With his new camera, Brandon took a <u>photograph</u> of a lizard.

predict [pree DIKT] *v.* to foretell; to say what you think will happen
Weather forecasters <u>predict</u> the next day's weather.

remembrance [ri MEM bruhns] *n.* a remembering of something
The <u>remembrance</u> of fragrant roses made the winter day feel like summer.

suspended [suh SPEN did] *v.* stopped temporarily
The long, lazy summer day <u>suspended</u> our sense of time.

"All Summer in a Day" by Ray Bradbury
Vocabulary Warm-up Exercises

Exercise A *Fill in each blank in the paragraph below with an appropriate word from Word List A. Use each word only once.*

For Austin, reading adventure stories was a [1] _____ relief from his humdrum life. He enjoyed imagining the challenge each character faced. Most heroes were strong, but a few were small and [2] _____. Not every little hero was a [3] _____ weakling, however; some were skilled adventurers. Naturally, the weak ones often ended up [4] _____ for help. In one book several people were trapped near a volcano. They could barely hear the [5] _____ sound as an eruption began underground. Suddenly, an [6] _____ [7] _____ of lava poured from the crater, an outpouring larger than anyone could imagine, and [8] _____ the trees in its path. What would happen next? Austin could not wait to find out.

Exercise B *Find a synonym for each word in the following list. Then, use each synonym in a sentence that makes its meaning clear. Refer to a thesaurus if you need help finding a synonym.*

Example: muscular **Synonym:** *brawny*
The <u>brawny</u> *athlete lifted weights with ease.*

1. photograph **Synonym:** _____

_____

2. drenched **Synonym:** _____

_____

3. gigantic **Synonym:** _____

_____

4. inserted **Synonym:** _____

_____

5. predict **Synonym:** _____

_____

6. remembrance **Synonym:** _____

_____

7. suspended **Synonym:** _____

_____

8. civilization **Synonym:** _____

_____

"All Summer in a Day" by Ray Bradbury
Reading Warm-up A

Read the following passage. Pay special attention to the underlined words. Then, read it again, and complete the activities. Use a separate sheet of paper for your written answers.

Justin stared at the assignment he had scribbled in his notebook: "Describe your favorite season, telling why it is your favorite." As he gave the matter serious thought, memories of the four seasons came to him.

He remembered hot summer days and swimming at the pool. He remembered the <u>blessed</u> feeling of the cool water against his hot skin and how refreshing that was. He remembered picnics and ballgames. He remembered catching fireflies on warm early-summer nights.

Next, Justin thought of autumn. The sun was weaker then, its light <u>frail</u> compared with the sunshine of summer. The brightly colored leaves produced a special orange-yellow light. Justin remembered raking leaves into piles and the <u>fumbling</u> way in which the younger children walked through them. He remembered scary Halloween stories in which <u>immense</u> giants towered far above everyone and everything else and powerful monsters <u>crushed</u> the weaker creatures.

Justin remembered winter, with its ice and snow and frigid temperatures. He remembered the <u>muffled</u> sounds of traffic after a thick snowfall blanketed the streets.

Finally, Justin thought of spring. He took great enjoyment in remembering the first balmy afternoons when the sun set just a little later every day. Then he was always <u>pleading</u> with his mother, begging to stay outside. In spring he played baseball. He helped plant the vegetable and flower gardens. Best of all, he hiked with his friends along wooded streams and watched as the <u>gush</u> of water from the melting snow swelled the rushing brooks.

How would Justin respond to his homework assignment? It was a toss-up, but he finally decided on spring, the season of renewal.

1. Underline the words that describe the <u>blessed</u> feeling of the water in the swimming pool. Define **blessed**.

2. Underline the words that tell why the autumn light is <u>frail</u>. What does **frail** mean?

3. Circle the words that tell what the children did in a <u>fumbling</u> way. Use **fumbling** in a sentence.

4. Circle the word that tells what was <u>immense</u>. Define **immense**.

5. Circle the words that tell what was <u>crushed</u> by powerful monsters. What else might be **crushed** by something?

6. Underline the words that explain when the sounds of traffic in winter are <u>muffled</u>. Tell what **muffled** means.

7. Circle the word that is a synonym for <u>pleading</u>. Define **pleading**.

8. Underline the words that explain what the <u>gush</u> of water comes from. Use **gush** in a sentence.

"All Summer in a Day" by Ray Bradbury
Reading Warm-up B

Read the following passage. Pay special attention to the underlined words. Then, read it again, and complete the activities. Use a separate sheet of paper for your written answers.

Venus is a fascinating planet. It is almost the same size as Earth. For that reason, scientists have called Venus the sister planet of Earth. For many years, astronomers, people who study planets and stars, thought that life might exist on Venus. They believed there were good reasons to <u>predict</u> that plants and animals might be found there. They even thought that a human <u>civilization</u> might exist on Venus. Contributing to that idea was the fact that a <u>gigantic</u>, dense cloud covers most of Venus's surface. The planet cannot be easily seen, and for a long time scientists could not take a clear <u>photograph</u> of it.

Today, scientists know that the climate of Venus is too hot to support life as we know it. Its cloud cover traps much of the heat the planet absorbs from the sun. The heat is <u>suspended</u> in place above the surface of the planet and is unable to move. Therefore, Venus has the hottest average temperature in our solar system.

Venus is similar to Earth in many ways besides its size, however. It has mountains, valleys, earthquakes, and volcanoes. Scientists have noted formations from lava flows that must have <u>drenched</u> the planet's surface at one time. They wonder whether those formations are the <u>remembrance</u> of a long-past time when Venus's volcanoes erupted.

The information we have today about Venus comes mainly from spacecraft. The vehicles have orbited the planet and <u>inserted</u> probes into its atmosphere. The probes send back a great deal of information. One probe mapped the complete surface of the planet. Another explored the materials that make up Venus's surface. It also recorded the planet's surface temperature.

Venus is indeed a fascinating planet. There is still much on Venus to explore and discover.

1. Underline the words that tell what astronomers had reason to <u>predict</u> about Venus. Define **predict**.

2. Circle the word that tells what kind of <u>civilization</u> there might have been on Venus. What does **civilization** mean?

3. What is an antonym for <u>gigantic</u>? Define **gigantic**.

4. Underline the words that tell why scientists could not take a clear <u>photograph</u> of Venus. Use **photograph** in a sentence of your own.

5. Circle the words that tell what is <u>suspended</u> above Venus. What does it have to do with the high temperature on Venus?

6. Circle the words that tell what once <u>drenched</u> the planet's surface. Define **drenched**.

7. Circle the words that tell what may be a <u>remembrance</u> of a past time on Venus. Use **remembrance** in a sentence.

8. Circle the word that tells what was <u>inserted</u> into Venus's atmosphere. Use **inserted** in a sentence.

Name _____ Date _____

"All Summer in a Day" by Ray Bradbury
Writing About the Big Question
What is the best way to find the truth?

Big Question Vocabulary

awareness	believable	conclude	convince	debate
evaluate	evidence	explain	factual	fiction
insight	perceive	reality	reveal	truth

A. *Use one or more words from the list above to complete each sentence.*

1. A story about someone living on the moon cannot be _____.

2. Scientists who disagree may _____ about the possibility of life on the moon.

3. When something is _____, it is not an opinion.

B. *Answer the questions.*

1. What are the two things you would miss the most if you were away from home for a long period of time?

   _____   _____

2. What do the two things you picked reveal about you as a person? Use at least two vocabulary words in your answer.

   _____

   _____

   _____

C. *Complete the sentence below. Then, write a short paragraph connecting the sentence to the Big Question.*

If I went to live in space, I would want these things from Earth to be present:

_____.

What was true about the fictional story "All Summer in a Day"? What was unrealistic?

_____

_____

_____

_____

"All Summer in a Day" by Ray Bradbury
Reading: Recognize Details That Indicate the Author's Purpose

Fiction writers write for a variety of **purposes.** They may wish to entertain, to teach, to call to action, or to reflect on experiences. They may also wish to inform, to persuade, or to create a mood. **Recognizing details that indicate the author's purpose** can give you a richer understanding of a selection. For example, in this passage from "All Summer in a Day," Bradbury creates a mood:

> Margot stood alone. She was a very frail girl who looked as if she had been lost in the rain for years and the rain had washed out the blue from her eyes and the red from her mouth and the yellow from her hair. She was an old photograph dusted from an album.

DIRECTIONS: *Read these passages from "All Summer in a Day." Then, write the purpose or purposes you think the author had for writing that passage. Choose from these purposes:* to entertain, to inform, to create a mood. *A passage may have more than one purpose.*

1. It had been raining for seven years; thousands upon thousands of days compounded and filled from one end to the other with rain, with the drum and gush of water, with the sweet crystal fall of showers and the concussion of storms so heavy they were tidal waves come over the islands.

   Author's purpose: _____

2. There was talk that her father and mother were taking her back to Earth next year; it seemed vital to her that they do so, though it would mean the loss of thousands of dollars to her family.

   Author's purpose: _____

3. But they were running and turning their faces up to the sky and feeling the sun on their cheeks like a warm iron; they were taking off their jackets and letting the sun burn their arms.

   Author's purpose: _____

4. They walked slowly down the hall in the sound of cold rain. They turned through the doorway to the room in the sound of the storm and thunder, lightning on their faces, blue and terrible. They walked over to the closet door slowly and stood by it.

   Behind the closet door was only silence.

   They unlocked the door, even more slowly, and let Margot out.

   Author's purpose: _____

"All Summer in a Day" by Ray Bradbury
Literary Analysis: Setting

The **setting** of a story is the time and place of the action. In this example from "All Summer in a Day," the underlined details help establish the story's setting.

The sun came out.

It was the color of flaming bronze and it was very large. And the sky around it was a blazing blue tile color. And the jungle burned with sunlight as the children, released from their spell, rushed out, yelling, into the springtime.

- In some stories, setting is just a backdrop. The same story events might take place in a completely different setting.
- In other stories, setting is very important. It develops a specific atmosphere or mood in the story, as in the example above. There, the children joyfully rush outside to feel the sun in the springtime after seven years of constant rain. The setting may even relate directly to the story's central conflict or problem.

DIRECTIONS: *Read the name of the character or characters from "All Summer in a Day" and the passage that follows. Then, on the lines, identify the setting described in the passage and the way the character or characters feel about it. Write your response in a short sentence or two.*

1. Margot: "And once, a month ago, she had refused to shower in the school shower rooms, had clutched her hands to her ears and over her head, screaming the water mustn't touch her head."

   Setting and character's feeling about it: _____

   _____

2. Margot: "They surged about her, caught her up and bore her, protesting, and then pleading, and then crying, back into a tunnel, a room, a closet, where they slammed and locked the door. They stood looking at the door and saw it tremble from her beating and throwing herself against it."

   Setting and character's feeling about it: _____

   _____

3. The children: "The children lay out, laughing, on the jungle mattress, and heard it sigh and squeak under them, resilient and alive. They ran among the trees, they slipped and fell, they pushed each other, . . . but most of all they squinted at the sun until tears ran down their faces, they put their hands up to that yellowness and that amazing blueness and they breathed of the fresh, fresh air."

   Setting and character's feeling about it: _____

   _____

Name _____ Date _____

"All Summer in a Day" by Ray Bradbury
Vocabulary Builder

Word List

intermixed   resilient   savored   slackening   tumultuously   vital

A. DIRECTIONS: *Read each sentence. If the italicized word is used correctly, write* Correct *on the line. If it is not used correctly, rewrite the sentence to correct it.*

1. The speed of the rocket was *slackening* as it prepared to land on Earth.

_____

_____

2. It is said that water is *vital* to life; you can live without it.

_____

_____

3. During the calm before the storm, the wind blew *tumultuously*.

_____

_____

4. Because Margot was *resilient*, she could not get used to the conditions on Venus.

_____

_____

5. During the parade, people were *intermixed* along the packed streets.

_____

_____

6. During the holiday season, we never *savored* the sweet smell of pumpkin pie as it came out of the oven.

_____

_____

B. WORD STUDY: The Latin roots *-vit-* or *-viv-* mean "life." Words containing *-vit-* or *-viv-* include *vitality* ("liveliness"), *survive* ("to live through something"), and *revive* ("to bring back to life"). Write two sentences in which you use all three of these words.

1. _____

_____

2. _____

_____

3. _____

Name _____ Date _____

"All Summer in a Day" by Ray Bradbury
Enrichment: Figurative Language

In "All Summer in a Day," Bradbury uses several kinds of figurative language. This language helps readers see, feel, and hear the events that take place.

For example, a **simile** compares two objects using a word such as *like* or *as:*

All day yesterday they had read in class about the <u>sun</u>. About <u>how like a lemon</u> it was.

Bradbury's simile compares the sun with a lemon. It uses the word *like.*

A **metaphor** compares two objects without using words of comparison:

I think <u>the sun is a flower</u>, / that blooms for just one hour.

Margot's poem compares the sun with a flower without using *like* or *as.*

A. DIRECTIONS: *Read each of the following passages from "All Summer in a Day," and consider the comparison or comparisons it presents. On the line that follows, identify each comparison as a simile or a metaphor. (There may be more than one comparison in a passage.) Then, circle the things that are compared.*

1. [Margot] was an old photograph dusted from an album, whitened away, and if she spoke at all her voice would be a ghost.

   Simile or metaphor: _____

2. But [the children] were running and turning their faces up to the sky and feeling the sun on their cheeks like a warm iron.

   Simile or metaphor: _____

3. [The jungle] was a nest of octopi, clustering up great arms of fleshlike weed.

   Simile or metaphor: _____

4. Then, wildly, like animals escaped from their caves, [the children] ran and ran in shouting circles.

   Simile or metaphor: _____

B. DIRECTIONS: *Choose a noun that is used in "All Summer in a Day," and write your own simile or metaphor to describe it. You might consider the sun, the jungle, the children, the tunnel, or the rain.*

_____

_____

_____

_____

_____

Name _____ Date _____

"All Summer in a Day" by Ray Bradbury
Open-Book Test

Short Answer *Write your responses to the questions in this section on the lines provided.*

1. As "All Summer in a Day" begins, the children await an event the scientists on Venus told them to expect. How does this event relate to the story's setting? Use details from the beginning of the story to respond.

_____

_____

_____

2. Margot is different from the other children in "All Summer in a Day." What is the author's purpose in making her different? Use details from the story to support your answer. Include information about how Margot differs from the other children.

_____

_____

_____

3. In "All Summer in a Day," the children watch as the rain is *slackening*. They become excited and concerned, because they don't want to miss a special experience. How does *slackening* suggest what is about to happen? Use clues from the story to support your answer.

_____

_____

_____

4. As the story of "All Summer in a Day" progresses, the author describes Margot's physical appearance. Why is this description important in helping the reader understand more about her? In your answer, use details from the description to explore how she might be feeling.

_____

_____

_____

5. How is Margot like and unlike the other students in "All Summer in a Day"? Use details from the middle of "All Summer in a Day" to support your response. Include in your answer an explanation that tells why the other children are angry with her.

_____

_____

_____

_____

6. In the middle of "All Summer in a Day," the author calls it a *crime* that Margot came from Earth only five years ago. What is the author's purpose in choosing such a strong word to describe her appearance on Venus? Use examples from the story to justify your response.

_____

_____

_____

7. What conclusion can you draw about how the school showers make Margot feel in "All Summer in a Day"? List two reactions in the organizer. Then, explain why her reaction is so intense.

Margot's Reactions

| |
| |
| |

Conclusion

| |
| |

8. In the middle of "All Summer in a Day," the weeds on the ground are described as *resilient*. How are the children in the story also resilient? Use the definition of *resilient* and details from the story in your answer.

_____

_____

_____

9. In the middle of "All Summer in a Day," the children respond to the change in their setting. How do they react to the appearance and disapperance of the sun? Use details from the story to respond.

_____

_____

_____

10. At the end of "All Summer in a Day," how do the children feel about having shut Margot in the closet? Use details from the end of the story to support your response. Include in your answer information that shows that their feelings about Margot are complicated.

_____

_____

_____

Essay

Write an extended response to the question of your choice or to the question or questions your teacher assigns you.

11. In "All Summer in a Day," the setting of the story plays a strong role in creating a certain mood. In a brief essay, describe the mood of the story. Use details about the setting to support your description.

12. How does the author of "All Summer in a Day" help the reader feel as though he or she is on Venus? In a brief essay, give examples of language used by the author that helps the reader feel connected to the setting, events, and characters in the story.

13. How can Margot's experience in "All Summer in a Day" be compared to an experience that a real child might have? In an essay, use your reading of the story to explore this question. Include in your answer an example of the kind of adjustment a modern child might have to make, along with difficulties he or she would encounter.

14. **Thinking About the Big Question: What is the best way to find the truth?** In "All Summer in a Day," Margot's truth was repeatedly dismissed. In an essay, explore how Margot found the truth and how the other children found the truth. Is one way better than the other? Use examples from the story to support your points.

Oral Response

15. Go back to question 2, 4, 6, or 10 or to the question your teacher assigns you. Take a few minutes to expand your answer and prepare an oral response. Find additional details in "All Summer in a Day" that support your points. If necessary, make notes to guide your oral response.

"All Summer in a Day" by Ray Bradbury
Selection Test A

Critical Reading *Identify the letter of the choice that best answers the question.*

____ 1. What are the children doing as "All Summer in a Day" opens?
   A. They are teasing Margot.
   B. They are reciting poetry.
   C. They are peering out a window.
   D. They are pushing Margot into a closet.

____ 2. What do the details in this passage tell you about the author's purpose?

   It had been raining for seven years; thousands upon thousands of days compounded and filled from one end to the other with rain, with the drum and gush of water.

   A. He wishes to call readers to action.
   B. He wishes to create a mood.
   C. He wishes to amuse.
   D. He wishes to persuade.

____ 3. What does this passage from "All Summer in a Day" suggest about the setting?

   A thousand forests had been crushed under the rain and grown up a thousand times to be crushed again. And this was the way life was forever on the planet Venus.

   A. Venus was a thousand years old.
   B. Venus had rain most of the time.
   C. There had never been forests in Venus.
   D. There were no forests in Venus.

____ 4. What do the details in this passage tell you about Bradbury's purpose?

   And this was the way life was forever on the planet Venus and this was the schoolroom of the children of the rocket men and women who had come to a raining world to set up civilization and live out their lives.

   A. He wishes to inform.   C. He wishes to question.
   B. He wishes to persuade.   D. He wishes to entertain.

____ 5. What does the following passage from "All Summer in a Day" say about Margot?

   She was a very frail girl who looked as if she had been lost in the rain for years and the rain had washed out the blue from her eyes and the red from her mouth and the yellow from her hair.

   A. Margot has been out in the rain for years.
   B. Margot is pale and delicate.
   C. Margot's eyes have no color.
   D. Margot no longer wears lipstick.

_____ 6. Why does Margot refuse to shower or let the water touch her head?

    A. She would rather be dirty than clean.

    B. She does not like to shower in public.

    C. She throws tantrums to get her way.

    D. She is being driven crazy by the rain.

_____ 7. In "All Summer in a Day," what does Margot mean when she says, "But this is the day, the scientists predict, they say, they know, the sun . . ."

    A. The sun appears at predictable times on Venus.

    B. The scientists are playing a joke on the people of Venus.

    C. Margot remembers the last time the sun appeared on Venus.

    D. The scientists know little about the appearance of the sun on Venus.

_____ 8. How do the children show their disrespect for Margot?

    A. They lose her in the tunnel.

    B. They force her to take a shower.

    C. They lock her in a closet.

    D. They push her out the door.

_____ 9. In "All Summer in a Day," why do the children say "Yes!" when their teacher asks, "Are we all here?"

    A. They do not want to wait for Margot.

    B. They have forgotten about Margot.

    C. They are afraid to tell what they did.

    D. They want Margot to miss the sun.

_____ 10. What does the following passage tell you about the setting of "All Summer in a Day"?

    The children lay out, laughing, on the jungle mattress, and heard it sigh and squeak under them, resilient and alive.

    A. The children have put their beds outside.

    B. Venus is covered with thick vegetation.

    C. The vegetation on Venus can talk.

    D. The vegetation on Venus is dangerous.

Vocabulary and Grammar

___ **11.** If wind is *slackening,* which of the following statements is true?

    A. It is not as windy now as it was a little while ago.

    B. It is windier now than it was a little while ago.

    C. The wind is now mixed with rain and sleet.

    D. The wind is creating dangerous driving conditions.

___ **12.** Which sentence from "All Summer in a Day" contains a personal pronoun used as a subject?

    A. Margot stood apart from them.

    B. But then they always awoke to the tatting drum.

    C. The children put their hands to their ears.

    D. A boom of thunder startled them.

___ **13.** Which sentence from "All Summer in a Day" contains a personal pronoun used as an object?

    A. A thousand forests had been crushed under the rain.

    B. She was an old photograph dusted from an album.

    C. A boom of thunder startled them.

    D. They stood in the doorway of the underground.

Essay

14. In an essay, consider how the setting of "All Summer in a Day" contributes to the mood of the story. First, describe the story's setting. Include as many details about the setting as you can think of. Then, tell how the story makes you feel. How does the setting add to or create that feeling?

15. Margot in "All Summer in a Day" suffers greatly from living on a planet where the sun almost never shines. In an essay, tell how Margot's physical appearance and her character have been affected by the absence of sunlight in her life.

16. **Thinking About the Big Question: What is the best way to find the truth?** In "All in a Summer's Day," people doubted the truth that Margot was trying to explain to them. In an essay, explore how Margot found the truth and how the other children found the truth. Is one way better than the other? Use examples from the story to support your points.

"All Summer in a Day" by Ray Bradbury
Selection Test B

Critical Reading *Identify the letter of the choice that best completes the statement or answers the question.*

____ 1. Which statement best describes what the children are doing as "All Summer in a Day" opens?
   A. They are waiting for their teacher.
   B. They are crowding in front of the door.
   C. They are making fun of Margot's poem.
   D. They are looking out the window.

____ 2. What message is conveyed by the following passage from "All Summer in a Day"?
   A thousand forests had been crushed under the rain and grown up a thousand times to be crushed again.

   A. It had been raining for an extremely long time.
   B. The rain on Venus was heavier than the rain on Earth.
   C. The scientists had come to Venus to study the forests.
   D. Timber was the main industry on Venus.

____ 3. What is the most important difference between Margot and her classmates?
   A. She can write poetry, but they cannot.
   B. She remembers the sun, but they do not.
   C. They dream, but she does not.
   D. They are nine years old; she is seven.

____ 4. What does the following passage suggest about the way the setting affects Margot?
   And once, a month ago, she had refused to shower in the school shower rooms, had clutched her hands to her ears and over her head, screaming the water mustn't touch her head.

   A. She hates to take a shower in the public shower rooms.
   B. She experiences the shower in the same way she experiences the constant rain.
   C. She does not trust that the water in the school shower rooms is clean.
   D. She feels isolated from the other children when she is in the shower.

____ 5. In "All Summer in a Day," how does William show his disrespect for Margot?
   A. He refuses to let her play tag with the rest of them.
   B. He refuses to listen when she reads her poem.
   C. He runs away and leaves her alone in the tunnel.
   D. He shoves her and tells her the sun will not shine.

____ 6. After the children lock Margot in the closet, the teacher asks, "Are we all here?" When the children answer "Yes!" why does the teacher check no further?
   A. She does not know how many children are in the class.
   B. She does not want Margot to see the sun.
   C. She is as excited as the children about seeing the sun.
   D. She has miscounted the number of students in her class.

____ **7.** What do the details in this passage from "All Summer in a Day" tell you about the setting?

> It was the color of flaming bronze and it was very large. And the sky around it was a blazing blue tile color. And the jungle burned with sunlight as the children, released from their spell, rushed out, yelling, into the springtime.

A. The sun has set the jungle on fire.
B. It is springtime outside under the sun.
C. The jungle is large and very colorful.
D. A magic spell has brought the sun.

____ **8.** What do the details in this passage tell you about the author's purpose?

> They stopped running and stood in the great jungle that covered Venus, that grew and never stopped growing, tumultuously, even as you watched it. It was a nest of octopi, clustering up great arms of fleshlike weed, wavering, flowering in this brief spring.

A. He wishes to inform.
B. He wishes to persuade.
C. He wishes to create an image.
D. He wishes to teach a lesson.

____ **9.** What does this passage from "All Summer in a Day" suggest about the setting?

> They looked at everything and savored everything. Then, wildly, like animals escaped from their caves, they ran and ran in shouting circles. They ran for an hour and did not stop running.

A. Venus is full of caves.
B. Venus is full of animals.
C. One can feel free on Venus.
D. There is much to see on Venus.

____ **10.** What do the details of this passage tell you about the author's purpose?

> The sun faded behind a stir of mist. A wind blew cool around them. They turned and started to walk back toward the underground house, their hands at their sides, their smiles vanishing away.

A. He wishes to teach a lesson.
B. He wishes to create a mood.
C. He wishes to persuade.
D. He wishes to inform.

____ **11.** Which details does the author of "All Summer in a Day" use to inform readers that the children feel guilty about locking Margot in the closet?

I.   They cannot look into each other's eyes.
II. Their faces are solemn and pale.
III. They run around in the sun.
IV. They look at their hands and feet.
A. I, II, III
B. II, III, IV
C. I, II, IV
D. I, III, IV

Unit 1 Resources: Fiction and Nonfiction

___ 12. In "All Summer in a Day," which setting does the author use to show the children's cruelty?
   A. the shower rooms
   B. the jungle
   C. the schoolroom closet
   D. the underground tunnel

Vocabulary and Grammar

___ 13. Which of the following sentences uses the word *vital* correctly?
   A. It was vital to Margot to return to Earth.
   B. The sky was a vital shade of blue.
   C. The jungle grew to a vital size.
   D. The children were vital to Margot.

___ 14. Which example describes something or someone that is *resilient*?
   A. The forest grew extremely quiet when the rains stopped.
   B. When the sun came out, the windows glistened with light.
   C. The child regained her self-control after being teased.
   D. The children's footprints were soon washed away by the rain.

___ 15. In which of the following sentences is a personal pronoun used as the subject?
   A. She would play no games with them in the echoing tunnels.
   B. "Now, don't go too far," called the teacher after them.
   C. The door slid back and the smell of the . . . world came in to them.
   D. A few cold drops fell on their noses and their cheeks and their mouths.

___ 16. In which of the following sentences is a personal pronoun used as an object?
   A. She knew they thought they remembered a warmness.
   B. And they had written small stories or essays or poems.
   C. They edged away from her, they would not look at her.
   D. And they, they had been on Venus all their lives.

Essay

17. In "All Summer in a Day," the other children do not accept Margot because she is different from them. In an essay, identify the ways in which Margot is different, and explain why those differences cause the children to reject her.

18. As you read "All Summer in a Day," did you feel you were there on Venus, in that classroom, or outside in the sun? Ray Bradbury creates the experience of being there with sensory language—language that appeals to the senses by telling how something looks, how it feels to the touch, how it smells, how it sounds. In an essay, write about sensory images that you remember from the story, and describe how each made you experience the setting.

19. **Thinking About the Big Question: What is the best way to find the truth?** In "All in a Summer's Day," Margot's truth was repeatedly dismissed. In an essay, explore how Margot found the truth and how the other children found the truth. Is one way better than the other? Use examples from the story to support your points.

Vocabulary Warm-up Word Lists

Study these words from "Suzy and Leah." Then, complete the activities that follow.

Word List A

diary [DY uh ree] *n.* a book for writing private thoughts or recording daily activities
   In her <u>diary</u>, Amanda wrote about her dreams for the future.

fever [FEE ver] *n.* a high body temperature often accompanying an illness
   After coming down with the flu, Matthew had a <u>fever</u>.

furious [FYOOR ee uhs] *adj.* filled with wild rage or anger
   Jacob was <u>furious</u> at his sister for playing a trick on him.

pecked [PEKT] *v.* bit at, poked, or picked at something as a bird would do
   Pretending he was a chicken, Anna's little brother <u>pecked</u> at her with his finger.

porcupine [PAWR kyoo pyn] *n.* a rodent covered with long, stiff, sharp spines
   The gel in the man's hair made him look like a <u>porcupine</u>.

prickly [PRIK lee] *adj.* having prickles, or sharp thorny spikes
   The <u>prickly</u> cactus was painful to touch.

shrank [SHRANK] *v.* drawn back in fear
   The shy puppy <u>shrank</u> from the children who were eager to pet it.

trim [TRIM] *n.* the edging on a piece of clothing or on another object
   The sheet of paper was light brown with white <u>trim</u>.

Word List B

appendix [uh PEN diks] *n.* a small saclike organ connected to the large intestine
   Stephanie was in pain because her <u>appendix</u> was inflamed.

assigned [uh SYND] *v.* appointed to carry out a special duty or task
   Natalie was <u>assigned</u> to water the plants in the classroom.

barbed [BAHRBD] *adj.* having sharp points
   The <u>barbed</u> wire kept people from climbing the fence.

false [FAWLS] *adj.* not true or real
   He lied, giving a <u>false</u> answer to the question.

grouch [GROWCH] *n.* an unpleasant, ill-tempered person
   The shopkeeper, known for yelling at customers, was a <u>grouch</u>.

permanent [PER muh nent] *adj.* lasting a long time
   The stain was <u>permanent</u>; it would be on the tablecloth forever.

rickety [RIK it ee] *adj.* unstable or poorly constructed
   The <u>rickety</u> bench collapsed under the weight of three people.

stale [STAYL] *adj.* not fresh
   The <u>stale</u> bread was dry and tasteless.

Name _____ Date _____

"Suzy and Leah" by Jane Yolen
Vocabulary Warm-up Exercises

Exercise A *Fill in each blank in the paragraph below with an appropriate word from Word List A. Use each word only once.*

May 5, 2005

Dear [1] _____,

Today something happened to my puppy, Rufus. He spied an intriguing animal in the
[2] _____, the part of the garden that runs along the edge of our yard.
The animal had [3] _____, sharply pointed spines. Yes! It was a rodent, a
[4] _____. Rufus ran right up and [5] _____ at it,
acting more like a bird than a dog. The critter did not like that. It was
[6] _____. Rufus should have guessed that he was in for trouble. Some
of the rodent's barbs stuck in the puppy's nose. Rufus whined as if he were sick with a
[7] _____, and he [8] _____ from the rodent, showing
just how afraid he was. Rufus has learned an important lesson.

As ever,

Courtney

Exercise B *Answer the questions with complete explanations.*

Example: If a person feels <u>pain</u>, is he or she comfortable?
No; to feel pain is to feel hurt, so a person who feels pain would not be comfortable.

1. If you are <u>assigned</u> to do a job, have you volunteered to do it?
   _____

2. Is there any danger in climbing over <u>barbed</u> wire?
   _____

3. When a person gives a <u>false</u> answer, is he or she lying?
   _____

4. Is a <u>grouch</u> a friendly person?
   _____

5. Is a <u>rickety</u> house likely to be a <u>permanent</u> structure?
   _____

6. Would it be pleasant to take a breath of <u>stale</u> air?
   _____

"Suzy and Leah" by Jane Yolen
Reading Warm-up A

Read the following passage. Pay special attention to the underlined words. Then, read it again, and complete the activities. Use a separate sheet of paper for your written answers.

In September 1939, World War II began. Germany, under the leadership of Adolf Hitler and the Nazi Party, took steps to persecute and then murder the Jews of Europe. At first Jewish families were sent to live in closed communities, or ghettos. With neither homes nor jobs, Jews faced awful living conditions and suffered greatly. Later they were sent to concentration camps. There they were worked to death, starved, and/or systematically murdered.

Survivors have described life in the ghettos. In her diary, one woman wrote that her family endured constant hunger. There was much sickness and fever due to poor nutrition and unclean conditions. A man wrote that the walls around the ghetto made prisoners of all the Jews. At first, Jews were allowed to leave the ghetto at certain times. Then, a new order came: They could never leave the walled communities. Imagine the wall, with its trim of barbed wire like a horrible prickly porcupine. It symbolized the Jews' lost freedom.

A woman wrote that the Jews heard rumors of horrible events. Many Jews would not believe that terrible things could be done to them. They believed that their rights as citizens could never be taken from them. She wrote that they should have known better. She described what happened to her family: In the middle of the night, a soldier with a furious voice and a hateful expression entered her home. He ordered her family to line up outside. She and her brother shrank in fear as the soldier poked and pecked at them with the butt of his rifle. After gathering a few possessions, they were sent to a ghetto.

In 1945, the Germans were defeated. The remaining Jews, those who had not been murdered, were freed. The survivors began new lives. Their memories of the war remained, however. By recording their memories, the survivors have taught us that such events must never happen again.

1. Underline the words that tell what one woman wrote in her diary. Use *diary* in a sentence.

2. Circle the words that tell why people suffered from sickness and fever. Define *fever*.

3. Circle the words that describe the trim on the wall. Define *trim*.

4. Underline the words that tell what looked like a "horrible prickly porcupine." Explain why the thing looked that way.

5. How might the soldier with the furious voice have sounded? What else might sound *furious*?

6. Who shrank in fear? Use *shrank* in a sentence.

7. Underline the words that tell what the soldier used when he pecked at the brother and sister. Use *pecked* in a sentence.

"Suzy and Leah" by Jane Yolen
Reading Warm-up B

Read the following passage. Pay special attention to the underlined words. Then, read it again, and complete the activities. Use a separate sheet of paper for your written answers.

Sean did not like old Mr. Mulligan at all. Mr. Mulligan was Sean's next-door neighbor. As far as Sean was concerned, Mr. Mulligan was the biggest <u>grouch</u> on the planet.

When Sean and his friends played baseball, they dreaded hitting the ball into Mr. Mulligan's backyard. The old man, hearing the noise, would appear at a window and watch as they climbed the <u>rickety</u> fence to retrieve their ball. His face was fixed in a <u>permanent</u> frown. He never showed any other expression. The boys would hurry away the moment they located their ball. "If he doesn't want neighbors," Sean would say, "he should put <u>barbed</u> wire around his house. Then everyone would stay away."

Sean's mother explained that Mr. Mulligan was lonely. He lived by himself and had no family. She said that Mr. Mulligan was not used to children. Sean was not convinced, however.

One day, Sean's mother <u>assigned</u> him the job of taking freshly baked cookies next door. She coaxed him by saying that Mr. Mulligan would appreciate the treat. "I doubt it," said Sean. "He probably loves eating old, <u>stale</u> bread soaked in milk. That would suit him and his <u>false</u> teeth just fine."

Sean knocked on the door. There was no response. Then he heard a cry for help. He pushed open the door and saw that his neighbor was doubled up in pain. "I think it is my <u>appendix</u>," Mr. Mulligan groaned. Sean called for help, and an ambulance came.

Mr. Mulligan's guess was correct. He had appendicitis. Sean and his mother visited him in the hospital. "You saved my life," Mr. Mulligan told Sean. "I want you to have this." It was a silver dollar. That visit was the beginning of Sean and Mr. Mulligan's friendship. Mr. Mulligan never again frowned when Sean's friends hit a baseball into his yard.

1. Underline the words that tell why Sean thinks Mr. Mulligan is a <u>grouch</u>. Define *grouch*.

2. Circle the word that tells what is <u>rickety</u>. What does *rickety* mean?

3. What is a <u>permanent</u> frown? Use *permanent* in a sentence.

4. Why does Sean think that Mr. Mulligan should put up <u>barbed</u> wire? Where else might *barbed* wire be used?

5. What job is <u>assigned</u> to Sean by his mother? Define *assigned*.

6. Circle the word that describes the <u>stale</u> bread. What else could get *stale*?

7. Sean thinks that Mr. Mulligan has <u>false</u> teeth. Define *false*.

8. What is wrong with Mr. Mulligan's <u>appendix</u>? Circle the words that tell you something is wrong with him.

"Suzy and Leah" by Jane Yolen
Writing About the Big Question

What is the best way to find the truth?

Big Question Vocabulary

awareness	believable	conclude	convince	debate
evaluate	evidence	explain	factual	fiction
insight	perceive	reality	reveal	truth

A. *Use one or more words from the list above to complete each sentence.*

1. When writing historical _____, a novelist must research in order to tell the _____ about historical events.

2. The historical facts in the story may _____ readers that the story is believable.

3. Readers must have a(n) _____ of history to know that the book is based on historical events.

4. To _____ whether historical facts are true, the reader can do research.

B. *Answer the questions.*

1. Name three things that you would need to research if you were writing a story that took place one hundred years ago and you wanted to convince your readers that the setting was real.

   _____   _____   _____

2. How is the challenge to write a believable novel that takes place in the future different from the challenge of writing a believable novel that takes place in the past? Explain using at least two vocabulary words.

   _____

   _____

   _____

   _____

C. *Complete the sentence below. Then, write a short paragraph connecting the sentence to the Big Question.*

If I were going to write a story based on a historical event, I would write about

   _____

What kinds of facts in your story would be true? What would be fictional?

   _____

   _____

"Suzy and Leah" by Jane Yolen

Reading: Recognize Details That Indicate the Author's Purpose

Fiction writers may write for a variety of **purposes.** They may wish to entertain, to teach, to call to action, or to reflect on experiences. They may also wish to inform, to persuade, or to create a mood. **Recognizing details that indicate the author's purpose** can give you a richer understanding of a selection. For example, the following passage from "Suzy and Leah" is written to teach readers about the background of some Eastern European Jews:

> I have a little English. But Ruth and Zipporah and the others, though they speak Yiddish and Russian and German, they have no English at all.

DIRECTIONS: *Read these passages from "Suzy and Leah." On the line that follows each passage, write the purpose or purposes you think the author had for writing that passage. Choose from these purposes:* to entertain, to inform, to create a mood. *A passage may have more than one purpose.*

1. Leah: "Today we got cereal in a box. At first I did not know what it was. Before the war we ate such lovely porridge with milk straight from our cows. And eggs fresh from the hen's nest."

   Author's purpose: _____

2. Leah: "But they made us wear tags with our names printed on them. That made me afraid. What next? Yellow stars? I tore mine off and threw it behind a bush before we went in [to the school]."

   Author's purpose: _____

3. Suzy: "Mr. Forest . . . gave me the girl with the dark braids. . . . Gee, she's as prickly as a porcupine. I asked if I could have a different kid. . . . He wants her to learn as fast as possible so she can help the others. As if she would, Miss Porcupine."

   Author's purpose: _____

4. Leah: "One day this Suzy and her people will stop being nice to us. They will remember we are not just refugees but Jews, and they will turn on us. Just as the Germans did. Of this I am sure."

   Author's purpose: _____

5. Suzy: "[Leah's] English has gotten so good. Except for some words, like victory, which she pronounces 'wick-toe-ree.' I try not to laugh. . . . She can't dance at all. She doesn't know the words to any of the top songs."

   Author's purpose: _____

Unit 1 Resources: Fiction and Nonfiction
157

Name _____   Date _____

"Suzy and Leah" by Jane Yolen
Literary Analysis: Setting

The **setting** of a story is the time and place of the action. In this example from "Suzy and Leah," the underlined details help establish the story's setting:

<u>August 5, 1944</u>

Dear Diary,

   Today I walked past *that* place. . . . Gosh, is it <u>ugly</u>! A line of <u>rickety wooden buildings</u> just like in the army. And <u>a fence lots higher than my head</u>. <u>With barbed wire</u> on top.

- In some stories, setting is just a backdrop. The same story events might take place in a completely different setting.
- In other stories, setting is very important. It develops a specific atmosphere or mood in the story, as in the example above. There, the reader is introduced to the refugee camp through the eyes of Suzy, who has lived a privileged life. The setting may even relate directly to the story's central conflict or problem.

DIRECTIONS: *Read the name of the character from "Suzy and Leah" and the passage that follows. Then, on the lines, identify the setting described in the passage and the way the character feels about it. Write your response in a short sentence.*

1. Suzy: "With barbed wire on top. How can anyone—even a refugee—live there?"

   Setting and character's feeling about it: _____

   _____

2. Leah: "But I say no place is safe for us. Did not the Germans say that we were safe in their camps?"

   Setting and character's feeling about it: _____

   _____

3. Leah: "Zipporah braided my hair, but I had no mirror until we got to the school and they showed us the toilets. They call it a bathroom, but there is no bath in it at all, which is strange."

   Setting and character's feeling about it: _____

   _____

4. Suzy: "[Mom] said the Nazis killed people, mothers and children as well as men. In places called concentration camps. . . . It was so awful I could hardly believe it, but Mom said it was true."

   Setting and character's feeling about it: _____

   _____

"Suzy and Leah" by Jane Yolen
Vocabulary Builder

Word List

cupboard   falsely   penned   permanent   porridge   refugee

A. DIRECTIONS: *Read each sentence. If the italicized word is used correctly, write* Correct *on the line. If it is not used correctly, rewrite the sentence to correct it.*

1. The *refugee* fled across the border.

_____

2. The *porridge* made a wonderful dessert.

_____

3. The *permanent* frown on Leah's face disappeared when Suzy offered candy.

_____

4. The teacher was correct when she *falsely* accused Sam of cheating.

_____

5. It is common to keep items like ice cream in the kitchen *cupboard*.

_____

6. It is easy to feel *penned* in when there are a lot of people in a small space.

_____

B. DIRECTIONS: *Read each sentence. If the italicized word is used correctly, write* Correct *on the line. If it is not used correctly, rewrite the sentence to correct it.*

1. The *refugee* fled across the border.

_____

2. The *porridge* made a wonderful dessert.

_____

3. The *permanent* frown on Leah's face disappeared when Suzy offered candy.

_____

_____

C. WORD STUDY: The Latin root *-man-* means "hand." Explain how the meaning of the root *-man-* relates to the following uses of the word *manual.*

1. The men performed ten long hours of <u>manual</u> labor.

_____

2. My new camera allows for both automatic and <u>manual</u> control.

_____

3. The artist showed extraordinary <u>manual</u> dexterity in her work.

_____

Name _____ Date _____

"Suzy and Leah" by Jane Yolen
Enrichment: Communication Skills

"Suzy and Leah" shows how problems can occur when people fail to communicate effectively. In "Suzy and Leah," the two schoolgirls mistrust each other because they do not understand each other's experiences and are unwilling to consider any views except their own. Wherever you are—at home, in school, or in an after-school group—effective communication is important. It can be achieved only when you listen carefully to what others have to say and when you express your own thoughts clearly.

DIRECTIONS: *Choose a classmate to be your partner, and consider the topics listed in the left-hand column of the following chart. Take turns expressing your thoughts about these topics. Do not interrupt each other. Then, in the right-hand column of the chart, write down your partner's main ideas on each topic. Finally, trade charts with your partner. Allow your partner to correct any errors in your summary of his or her ideas. Talk about the similarities and differences in your views.*

Subject	My Partner's Viewpoint	My Partner's Clarification
Our school		
Our library		
Public transportation		
Restaurants in the neighborhood		
Parks in the neighborhood		

"All Summer in a Day" by Ray Bradbury
"Suzy and Leah" by Jane Yolen

Integrated Language Skills: Grammar

A **pronoun** is a word that takes the place of a noun or a group of words acting as a noun. A **nominative pronoun** is a pronoun used as a subject. An **objective pronoun** is a pronoun used as an object.

Suzy met Leah at the camp.	**She** met Leah at the camp.	Nominative pronoun
Suzy met **Leah** at the camp.	Suzy met **her** at the camp.	Objective pronoun

Some important nominative and objective pronouns:

Nominative	**Objective**
I	me
he	him
she	her
we	us
they	them

A. PRACTICE: *Read each sentence based on sentences in "All Summer in a Day" or "Suzy and Leah." Underline each nominative pronoun. Circle each objective pronoun.*

1. They hated her because she had seen the sun.

2. He gave her a shove, but she did not move away from him.

3. The thunder and rain chased them back inside, where they let her out of the closet.

4. When I looked back, she was gone, and I didn't see her again until the next day.

5. They didn't know how to peel oranges, so I taught them.

6. She loves Avi and tries to protect him.

B. Writing Application: *Rewrite each sentence by replacing each underlined noun with a pronoun. Be sure to see the difference between a nominative pronoun and an objective pronoun.*

1. The students wanted to see the sun, so the teacher let the students go outside.

   _____

2. Margot hoped to see the sun, but the students locked Margot in the closet.

   _____

3. William said Margot was a liar, but Margot stuck to Margot's story.

   _____

4. Leah refuses Suzy's candy because Leah doesn't want to look like an animal.

   _____

Name _____ Date _____

"All Summer in a Day" by Ray Bradbury
"Suzy and Leah" by Jane Yolen

Integrated Language Skills: Support for Writing a News Report

"All Summer in a Day": To prepare for your **news report** that tells about the day the sun appeared on Venus, complete this chart.

Question	Information in "All Summer in a Day"
Who sees the sun, and who does not see it?	
What happens when the sun is shining?	
When does the sun shine, and for how long?	
Where do the events take place?	
Why do the characters in the story respond to the sun the way they do?	

"Suzy and Leah": To prepare for your **news report** that tells about the refugee camp where Leah is living, complete this chart.

Question	Information in "Suzy and Leah"
Who is living in the camp that Suzy visits?	
What has brought Suzy to the camp?	
When are the events taking place?	
Where (in what country) is the camp?	
Why has the camp been set up?	

Now, use your notes to write a news report.

Unit 1 Resources: Fiction and Nonfiction

© Pearson Education, Inc. All rights reserved.
162

"All Summer in a Day" by Ray Bradbury
"Suzy and Leah" by Jane Yolen

Integrated Language Skills:
Support for Extend Your Learning

Choose one of the stories from this pairing. Use the following chart as you work with your classmates to write an **annotated bibliography** for a report about either Venus or the Holocaust. Find resources on the Internet or in a library card catalog. Follow the MLA (Modern Language Association) style for listing sources, and write a short description after each source.

Research and Technology: "All Summer in a Day"

Annotated Bibliography for a Report About Venus

Author, Title of Work, and Publication Information	Description of Resources

Research and Technology: "Suzy and Leah"

Annotated Bibliography for a Report on the Holocaust

Author, Title of Work, and Publication Information	Description of Resources

"**Suzy and Leah**" by Jane Yolen
Open-Book Test

Short Answer *Write your responses to the questions in this section on the lines provided.*

1. At the beginning of "Suzy and Leah," the word *refugee* is used to describe Leah. Why are the newcomers described as refugees? Explain the circumstances that brought Leah and the other children to America.

_____

_____

2. How comfortable is the setting in which Leah finds herself in the beginning of "Suzy and Leah"? Support your answer with details from the beginning of the story. In your response, include Suzy's impressions of the setting.

_____

_____

_____

3. Leah's diary entry from September 5 mentions a little boy named Avi. What happened to him in Germany, and how has it affected him? Use details from "Suzy and Leah" to support your answer.

_____

_____

4. In "Suzy and Leah," the author describes the refugee children eating oranges as though they are apples. What is the author's purpose for including this scene? Use details from both Suzy's and Leah's September 2 entries to support your points.

_____

_____

_____

_____

5. Reread Leah's September 5 entry. How does she feel in her new environment? Use details from "Suzy and Leah" to support your answer.

_____

_____

_____

6. Think about how Suzy treats and reacts to the refugees in the first half of "Suzy and Leah." What do her reactions say about her own life? Use details from the story to support your ideas.

_____

_____

_____

_____

7. Reread Leah's entries from September 14 and September 16. How does she feel about school, and why might she feel that way? Use details from the story to support your response.

_____

_____

_____

_____

8. In her September 30 entry, Suzy describes Leah's frown as being *permanent*. Does she expect that Leah is going to become more friendly to her in the future? Use details from the story to explain your answer.

_____

_____

_____

9. In her October 12 entry, Suzy admits to reading Leah's diary. Think about the author's purpose in having this action occur. What does Suzy learn about Leah, and how does this knowledge affect her? Fill in the organizer. Then, write a conclusion about how Suzy changes.

Before Reading Diary   **After Reading Diary**

_____

_____

10. In her October 12 entry, Leah explains why she did not tell anyone she was in pain. Does her explanation make sense? Explain your answer, using details from the story.

_____

_____

_____

_____

Essay

Write an extended response to the question of your choice or to the question or questions your teacher assigns you.

11. How would you compare the settings in which Leah and Suzy live in America? Describe the similarities and differences between them in a brief essay. Use details from "Suzy and Leah" to support your ideas.

12. Throughout "Suzy and Leah," Leah writes to her *Mutti*. Why do you think she writes to her mother as though she is still alive? In a brief essay, use examples from the story to explore Leah's motivation for writing to her mother.

13. Based on your reading of "Suzy and Leah," do you sense that Leah is unique among the refugees, or are there others who are as sensitive to being a refugee as she is? Explore your impressions of Leah in an essay. Use examples from the story that help you better understand who she is.

14. **Thinking About the Big Question: What is the best way to find the truth?** Think about how Suzy finds out the truth about Leah's life. Do you think this is the best way for her to have found out? In a brief essay, explain why or why not. Consider how Suzy reacts to finding the truth. Use details from the selection in your response.

Oral Response

15. Go back to question 3, 4, or 5 or to the question your teacher assigns you. Take a few minutes to expand your answer and prepare an oral response. Find additional details in "Suzy and Leah" that support your points. If necessary, make notes to guide your oral response.

Name _____   Date _____

"Suzy and Leah" by Jane Yolen

Selection Test A

Critical Reading *Identify the letter of the choice that best answers the question.*

____ 1. Where and when does "Suzy and Leah" take place?
   A. in America near the end of World War II
   B. in Europe near the end of World War II
   C. in America just before World War II
   D. in Europe just before World War II

____ 2. This passage describes part of the setting of "Suzy and Leah." What does it tell you the story is about?

   Today I walked past *that* place, the one that was in the newspaper, the one all the kids have been talking about. . . . A line of rickety wooden buildings just like in the army. And a fence lots higher than my head. With barbed wire on top. How can anyone—even a refugee—live there?

   A. people who live near a sleep-away camp and the children at the camp
   B. people who live near a prison and the inmates who are in the prison
   C. people who live near an army camp and people who live in the camp
   D. people who live near a refugee camp and people who live in the camp

____ 3. Which word best describes Leah's reaction to Suzy's first visit to the camp?
   A. joyful
   B. silent
   C. talkative
   D. friendly

____ 4. In "Suzy and Leah," why does Leah refuse Suzy's candy?
   A. She thinks that the candy is poisoned.
   B. She knows that candy is bad for her.
   C. She does not want to act like an animal.
   D. She dislikes everything about America.

____ 5. What does this passage from "Suzy and Leah" tell you about Leah?

   Suzy expects me to be grateful. But how can I be grateful? She treats me like a pet, a pet she does not really like or trust. She wants to feed me like an animal behind bars.

   A. She is well liked.
   B. She is lonely.
   C. She is suspicious.
   D. She is grateful.

_____ 6. Based on this passage from her diary, how would you describe Suzy?

> I wouldn't want to be one of them. Imagine going to school and not being able to speak English or understand anything. . . I can't imagine anything worse.

    A. She has seen much of the world.

    B. She is proud to be an American.

    C. She is sympathetic and kindhearted.

    D. She does not know much about the world.

_____ 7. What does this passage tell you that Leah has learned from her experiences?

> One day soon this Suzy and her people will stop being nice to us. They will remember we are not just refugees but Jews, and they will turn on us. Just as the Germans did.

    A. Germans thought all refugees were Jews.

    B. Strangers should never be trusted.

    C. People are kinder than they seem at first.

    D. Refugees should never be trusted.

_____ 8. What do Leah's diary entries in "Suzy and Leah" reveal about her?

    A. She has a sense of humor.

    B. She is unfriendly by nature.

    C. She feels lost and sad.

    D. She likes America.

_____ 9. What do the details in this passage from "Suzy and Leah" tell you about the author's purpose?

> If I write all this down, I will not hold so much anger. I have much anger. And terror besides. *Terror*. It is a new word for me, but an old feeling.

    A. She is trying to create a mood.

    B. She is trying to entertain readers.

    C. She is trying to teach readers the meaning of *terror*.

    D. She is trying to persuade readers to like Leah better.

_____ 10. In "Suzy and Leah," why does Leah wait to tell anyone about her illness?

    A. She thinks that no one will understand her English.

    B. She is ashamed that she has eaten nonkosher food.

    C. She is shy and does not want to disturb the directors of the refugee camp.

    D. She remembers that sick people in the concentration camps were killed.

____ 11. In "Suzy and Leah," what good comes from Suzy's reading Leah's diary?

    A. Suzy realizes that Leah has liked her all along.

    B. Suzy realizes all that Leah has suffered in the war.

    C. Suzy realizes how lucky she is to have been born in America.

    D. Suzy realizes that to be Leah's friend, she must learn Yiddish.

Vocabulary and Grammar

____ 12. Which of the following sentences describes something that is *permanent*?

    A. Leah's Yiddish accent began to fade as her English improved.

    B. Leah's stay in the hospital lasted less than one week.

    C. Leah's memories of her mother and brother would be with her forever.

    D. Leah's distrust gave way to trust, once Suzy became more understanding.

____ 13. In which of the following sentences is a personal pronoun used as the subject?

    A. There is barbed wire still between us and the world.

    B. The color reminded me of your eyes and the blue skies.

    C. Zipporah braided my hair.

    D. She is ill in her stomach.

____ 14. In which of the following sentences is a personal pronoun used as an object?

    A. I have but a single piece of paper to write on.

    B. But she still never smiles.

    C. What does he know?

    D. If I love her, I will forget you.

Essay

15. "Suzy and Leah" is about two girls who have had very different life experiences. These experiences have affected the way they think about people and about life in general. In an essay, describe ways in which Suzy and Leah are different on account of their experiences. Use examples from the story to develop your ideas.

16. "Suzy and Leah" has four main settings: the refugee camp, the school, Suzy's home, and the hospital. The Nazi concentration camp is a fifth setting, although readers see it only in Leah's memory. Choose one of these settings, and write an essay showing how it relates to the central conflict or problem of "Suzy and Leah."

17. **Thinking About the Big Question: What is the best way to find the truth?**
Think about how Suzy finds out the truth about Leah's life. Do you think this is the best way for her to find out? In a brief essay, explain why or why not. Use details from the selection in your response.

Unit 1 Resources: Fiction and Nonfiction
169

"Suzy and Leah" by Jane Yolen
Selection Test B

Critical Reading *Identify the letter of the choice that best completes the statement or answers the question.*

____ 1. Where and when do the main events of "Suzy and Leah" take place?
A. in an American refugee camp and town before World War II begins
B. in a Nazi concentration camp toward the end of World War II
C. in an American refugee camp and town toward the end of World War II
D. in a Nazi concentration camp after it has been liberated by the Allies

____ 2. These lines reveal details about the setting. What do they tell you about the story?
> I took two candy bars along, just like everyone said I should. When I held them up, all those kids just swarmed over to the fence, grabbing. Like in a zoo.

A. The story is about manners and getting along with others in a group.
B. The story is about people who have had different life experiences.
C. The story is about people and animals.
D. The story is about kindness and generosity.

____ 3. How would you describe Leah's reaction to Suzy's first visit to the refugee camp?
A. excited
B. uncommunicative
C. welcoming
D. uninterested

____ 4. Why does Leah address her diary entries to her *Mutti*, whom she last saw in a Nazi concentration camp?
A. She does not know whether her mother is dead or alive.
B. She knows no other person to write to.
C. She believes that she will see her mother again one day.
D. She takes comfort in imagining that her mother is alive.

____ 5. Which of the following statements best describes Suzy in this passage?
> I wouldn't want to be one of them. Imagine going to school and not being able to speak English or understand anything that's going on. I can't imagine anything worse.

A. Suzy has not had the experiences the refugees have had.
B. Suzy lacks a vivid imagination.
C. Suzy does not want to speak any language except English.
D. Suzy is a kindhearted person.

____ 6. What do the details in this passage from "Suzy and Leah" reveal about the author's purpose?
> And then there is little Avi. . . . He will speak nothing at all. He stopped speaking, they say, when he was hidden away in a cupboard by his grandmother. . . . And he was almost three days in that cupboard without food, without water, without words to comfort him.

A. She is trying to inform her readers.
B. She is trying to persuade her readers.
C. She is trying to entertain her readers.
D. She is trying to amuse her readers.

___ 7. What does Leah mean when she writes, "There is still barbed wire between us and the world"?

A. She has not yet been freed from the German concentration camp.

B. The refugees have not been freed from the American refugee camp.

C. The fear she continues to feel keeps her imprisoned emotionally.

D. She does not realize that the Americans want to help her.

___ 8. How would you describe Leah's response to Suzy's gifts, based on this passage?

She expects me to be grateful. But how can I be grateful? She treats me like a pet, a pet she does not really like or trust. She wants to feed me like an animal behind bars.

A. She feels like an animal trapped in a zoo.

B. She feels like an unloved pet.

C. She feels suspicious and insulted.

D. She feels grateful but unappreciated.

___ 9. What does this passage reveal that Leah has learned from her experiences?

One day soon this Suzy and her people will stop being nice to us. They will remember we are not just refugees but Jews, and they will turn on us. Just as the Germans did.

A. She has learned that the Germans mistreated Jews for centuries.

B. She has learned not to trust people and to keep up her guard.

C. She has learned that people who are cruel at first may become kind.

D. She has learned to hide her thoughts from everyone.

___ 10. What do the details in this passage from "Suzy and Leah," reveal about the author's purpose?

Leah knows a lot about the world and nothing about America. She thinks New York is right next to Chicago, for goodness sakes! She can't dance at all. She doesn't know the words to any of the top songs. And she's so stuck up, she only talks in class to answer questions.

A. She is trying to teach a lesson.

B. She is trying to entertain her readers.

C. She is trying to persuade her readers.

D. She is trying to create a mood.

___ 11. Based on her letters, how would you describe Leah in "Suzy and Leah"?

A. She is emotionally unbalanced.

B. She is happy and well adjusted.

C. She feels lost and grief-stricken.

D. She has a rich imagination.

___ 12. In "Suzy and Leah," why is Suzy impatient with Leah for being "stuck up"?

A. She does not realize how much Leah has suffered.

B. She is basically mean-spirited and self-centered.

C. She thinks that Leah is trying to prove that she is the better student.

D. She does not want to give her clothes to the children in the refugee camp.

_____ 13. In which of the settings in "Suzy and Leah" does Leah begin to realize that she is safe?

    A. the refugee camp   C. Suzy's home

    B. the school   D. the hospital

_____ 14. In "Suzy and Leah," what good comes from Suzy's reading Leah's diary?

    A. She understands that she has betrayed Leah's privacy.

    B. She understands that Yiddish is a hard language to learn.

    C. She realizes how terrible Leah's experiences have been.

    D. She realizes that America was right to enter the war.

Vocabulary and Grammar

_____ 15. What is someone most likely to do with *porridge*?

    A. Plant it in a garden.   C. Eat it for breakfast.

    B. Put it in a salad.   D. Eat it for supper.

_____ 16. Which sentence uses the word *refugee* correctly?

    A. The refugee fled to safety during the war, leaving her belongings behind.

    B. The refugee stopped everyone trying to cross the border to safety.

    C. The refugee stayed safely in his home throughout the war.

    D. The refugee tended the sick and wounded on the battlefield.

_____ 17. In which of the following sentences is a personal pronoun used as the subject?

    A. But I say no place is safe for us.

    B. At least the refugee kids are wearing better clothes now.

    C. Mr. Forest has assigned each of us to a refugee.

    D. Little Avi found me.

_____ 18. In which of the following sentences is a personal pronoun used as an object?

    A. The adults of the Americans say we are safe now.

    B. I took two candy bars along.

    C. But I must call them candies now.

    D. Sometimes when we're having dinner I think of Leah.

Essay

19. In "Suzy and Leah," there is no single narrator telling us about the characters. In an essay, describe how the reader learns about the main characters in this story. What technique does the author use? Use examples from the story to support your points.

20. The setting of a story is the time and place of the action. The setting may be only a background, or it may shape the action. In an essay, discuss how the setting of "Suzy and Leah" relates to the story's central conflict or problem.

21. **Thinking About the Big Question: What is the best way to find the truth?** Think about how Suzy finds out the truth about Leah's life. Do you think this is the best way for her to have found out? In a brief essay, explain why or why not. Consider how Suzy reacts to finding the truth. Use details from the selection in your response.

Vocabulary Warm-up Word Lists

Study these words from "My First Free Summer." Then, complete the activities.

Word List A

accompanied [uh KUM puh need] *v.* went along with
Elizabeth <u>accompanied</u> her family on vacation.

activities [ak TIV uh teez] *n.* actions or pursuits
Jonathan's after-school <u>activities</u> include soccer and chess.

connections [kuh NEK shunz] *n.* influential people with whom one is acquainted
Alexandra got her new job through business <u>connections</u>.

documents [DAHK yoo muhnts] *n.* official papers
Birth certificates were the <u>documents</u> required for identification.

reviews [ri VYOOZ] *v.* examines or inspects
Our teacher <u>reviews</u> each homework assignment carefully.

runway [RUN way] *n.* strip of pavement where planes take off and land
The jet landed smoothly on the <u>runway</u>.

scheduled [SKE joold] *v.* planned for a certain time
The swimming lessons are <u>scheduled</u> for 10 A.M.

terminal [TER muh nuhl] *n.* a transportation station
The bus <u>terminal</u> is never crowded late at night.

Word List B

attending [uh TEND ing] *v.* being present at a place or event
I will be <u>attending</u> the concert tonight.

attitude [AT uh tood] *n.* one's disposition or mind-set
Kyle has a great <u>attitude</u> when it is time to do unpleasant chores.

bliss [BLIS] *n.* extreme happiness or joy
To taste the homemade chocolate was <u>bliss</u> for Chris.

democracy [di MAHK ruh see] *n.* a government ruled by the people
When Dad announced the rules, he said that our family was not a <u>democracy</u>.

endured [en DOORD] *v.* put up with or bore the pain of something
Shelby <u>endured</u> her brother's off-key singing.

escorting [es KAWRT ing] *v.* bringing someone somewhere
The police were <u>escorting</u> prisoners to the jail.

prospects [PRAHS pekts] *n.* expected chances for success
Thomas's <u>prospects</u> for landing the job were good.

summoned [SUHM und] *v.* called together for a meeting
The coach <u>summoned</u> the players to discuss their plans for the next game.

"My First Free Summer" by Julia Alvarez
Vocabulary Warm-up Exercises

Exercise A *Fill in each blank in the paragraph below with an appropriate word from Word List A. Use each word only once.*

When we were little, Paige and I loved to play together. We did not have fancy toys. We just used our imagination. We never [1] _____ our play time—it just happened. Our favorite game was secret agent. We pretended that we had [2] _____ with other spies. Our [3] _____ included spying on our neighbor as he tended his garden. We wrote up important [4] _____, noting everything he did. Then we sent them to a make-believe office. There, we imagined, is someone who [5] _____ them. Next, we would be [6] _____ by an imaginary staff as we hurried to an airline [7] _____. Often our flight would be delayed, and we would wait on the [8] _____. By then we were ready for our next assignment.

Exercise B *Decide whether each statement below is true or false. Circle T or F. Then, explain your answer.*

1. If you are <u>attending</u> the dance, you will not be there.
   T / F _____

2. If Mary has an <u>attitude</u> about cleaning her room, she feels a certain way about it.
   T / F _____

3. <u>Bliss</u> is not the opposite of sorrow.
   T / F _____

4. In a <u>democracy</u>, one ruler makes all the laws.
   T / F _____

5. If you <u>endured</u> a long lecture, you managed to sit through it.
   T / F _____

6. If someone is <u>escorting</u> you, he or she is following you.
   T / F _____

7. If the <u>prospects</u> of a win are good, the team is not likely to have a victory.
   T / F _____

8. If the principal <u>summoned</u> the students, she wanted to meet with them.
   T / F _____

Name _____ Date _____

Read the following passage. Pay special attention to the underlined words. Then, read it again, and complete the activities. Use a separate sheet of paper for your written answers.

Think of a bustling airline <u>terminal</u>, full of busy workers involved in many <u>activities</u>. Flights are <u>scheduled</u>. Computers are programmed to display arrivals and departures. Baggage is tagged and inspected. Security guards check passports and other <u>documents</u> before passengers board the planes. Meanwhile, a ticket agent <u>reviews</u> seat assignments. Outside, mechanics check the aircraft. They ready each <u>runway</u> before a plane lands or takes off. These and many other people are hard at work at every airport.

Many of today's airports are large. They must be big in order to do their job. That job is to move millions of passengers around the country and around the world. It does not matter who the passengers are. Today, air travel is commonplace. Whether you are a movie star or a politician with important contacts and <u>connections</u>, or an ordinary citizen with somewhere to go, flying is a good way to travel. Businesspeople fly to meetings in faraway cities. Children fly across the country to visit grandparents. Families go on vacations to scenic locations.

Airports were not always large and busy. The first airplanes were small, light, and relatively slow. They did not need long runways. Airports then could be built close to the places where people lived.

In the 1930s, multi-engine airplanes were built. They were heavier. They needed long, paved runways for takeoffs and landings. Therefore, larger areas were needed for airports. Those areas were located a distance from major cities, away from tall buildings and other obstructions. Those changes were <u>accompanied</u> by an increase in air travel and eventually led to the construction and expansion of today's airports.

1. Circle the words that tell what kind of <u>terminal</u> is described. Define **terminal**.

2. Underline the sentences that describe the airport workers' <u>activities</u>. What **activities** do you engage in before traveling?

3. Circle the word that tells what is <u>scheduled</u>. Define **scheduled**.

4. Circle the words that tell which <u>documents</u> are checked. Use **documents** in a sentence.

5. Tell what might happen if an agent <u>reviews</u> two tickets with the same seat assignment. Then, tell what **reviews** means.

6. Underline the words that tell what happens on a <u>runway</u>. Define **runway**.

7. Circle a synonym for <u>connections</u>. Describe **connections** that a movie star might have.

8. Underline the words that tell what <u>accompanied</u> the changes in airports. Use **accompanied** in a sentence.

Name _____ Date _____

"**My First Free Summer**" by Julia Alvarez
Reading Warm-up B

Read the following passage. Pay special attention to the underlined words. Then, read it again, and complete the activities. Use a separate sheet of paper for your written answers.

From 1900 to 1914, a record number of immigrants—about nine million—arrived in the United States. Many came from Europe—from Italy, Romania, Greece, Poland, Russia, and the Austro-Hungarian Empire.

In the immigrants' native countries, the <u>prospects</u> for earning a living were not good. In the United States the immigrants' chances for success were much better. In their native lands many immigrants had also <u>endured</u> harsh treatment. Their governments had treated them unfairly. Therefore, the immigrants believed they would have more freedom in a <u>democracy</u>. With courage and a positive <u>attitude</u>, these brave souls boarded steamships headed for the United States.

Most immigrants from Europe entered the United States through Ellis Island in New York Harbor. Imagine the <u>bliss</u> of the travelers as they entered the harbor. What great joy they must have felt as they gazed at the Statue of Liberty. After a long, uncomfortable ocean crossing, they had reached their new home.

Imagine, too, the scene at Ellis Island. Officials would be <u>escorting</u> immigrants, bringing them from station to station in the huge complex of buildings. The immigrants would not be <u>attending</u> formal information sessions, however. There was no such luxury. The immigrants must have felt like strangers in their new land. They did not know what would happen next.

One by one, each immigrant was <u>summoned</u> to meet with a series of officials. The officials checked their documents and gave them a physical examination. If their papers were in order and they were healthy, the immigrants were admitted to the United States. Their new life could begin.

1. Circle the words that tell what kind of <u>prospects</u> were better in the United States than in other lands. Define *prospects*.

2. Circle the words that tell what the immigrants <u>endured</u>. Use *endured* in a sentence.

3. Circle the words that tell what the immigrants believed they would have in a <u>democracy</u>. Tell what a *democracy* is.

4. Circle the word that describes the immigrants' <u>attitude</u>. Do you think this *attitude* helped them reach their goal? Explain.

5. Circle words that mean the same thing as <u>bliss</u>. Describe something that might make someone experience *bliss*.

6. To what places were the officials <u>escorting</u> the immigrants? Define *escorting*.

7. What did immigrants not have the luxury of <u>attending</u>? Name an event that you enjoy *attending*.

8. Whom were the immigrants <u>summoned</u> to meet with? Use *summoned* in a sentence.

Name _____ Date _____

"My First Free Summer" by Julia Alvarez

Writing About the Big Question

What is the best way to find the truth?

Big Question Vocabulary

awareness	believable	conclude	convince	debate
evaluate	evidence	explain	factual	fiction
insight	perceive	reality	reveal	truth

A. *Use one or more words from the list above to complete each sentence.*

1. When an author uses autobiographical information in her writing, she
_____s a personal truth.

2. When reading autobiographical fiction, the reader gains _____
into the author's real life.

3. Some works of fiction can lead to a _____ about
philosophical questions.

B. *Answer the questions.*

1. Describe an event in your life that you perceived differently from someone else.

_____

_____

2. If you were to debate the event with the other person, would you be able to convince
him or her that your version of the truth is correct? Why or why not? Use two
vocabulary words in your answer.

_____

_____

_____

C. *Complete the sentence below. Then, write a short paragraph connecting the sentence
to the Big Question.*

Reflecting on past events _____

How might you incorporate an event from your life into a fictional story? Describe the
event and a story you might create.

_____

_____

_____

_____

"My First Free Summer" by Julia Alvarez

Reading: Use Background Information to Determine the Author's Purpose

One way to determine the **author's purpose,** or reason, for writing a nonfiction work is to **use background information** that you already know about the author and topic. For example, knowing that an author grew up outside the United States might help you determine that she wrote an essay to inform readers about the country where she spent her childhood.

Although she was born in the United States, Julia Alvarez spent much of her childhood in the Dominican Republic. Near the beginning of her essay, she writes,

> That was the problem. English. My mother had decided to send her children to the American school so we could learn the language of the nation that would soon be liberating us.

The author's purpose for providing this background information is to inform readers of her reasons for studying English and attending an American school. Authors provide background information for other purposes as well—for example, to entertain or to create a mood.

DIRECTIONS: *Read each of these passages from "My First Free Summer." Decide whether the author's purpose is* to inform, to create a mood, *or* to entertain. *Write the purpose on the line following the passage. A passage may have more than one purpose.*

1. For thirty years, the Dominican Republic had endured a bloody and repressive dictatorship. From my father, who was involved in an underground plot, my mother knew that *los américanos* had promised to help bring democracy to the island.

   Author's purpose(s): _____

2. Meanwhile, I had to learn about the pilgrims with their funny witch hats, about the 50 states and where they were on the map, about Dick and Jane and their tame little pets, Puff and Spot, about freedom and liberty and justice for all—while being imprisoned in a hot classroom with a picture of a man wearing a silly wig hanging above the blackboard.

   Author's purpose(s): _____

3. The grounds on which the American school stood had been donated by my grandfather. . . . The bulk of the student body was made up of the sons and daughters of American diplomats and business people, but a few Dominicans—most of them friends or members of my family—were allowed to attend.

   Author's purpose(s): _____

Name _____ Date _____

"My First Free Summer" by Julia Alvarez
Literary Analysis: Historical Context

When a literary work is based on real events, the historical context can help you understand the action. **Historical context**—the actual political and social events and trends of the time—can explain why characters act and think the way they do. Read the following passage from "My First Free Summer." Think about what it tells you about the historical context of the selection.

> For thirty years, the Dominican Republic had endured a bloody and repressive dictatorship. From my father, who was involved in an underground plot, my mother knew that *los américanos* had promised to help bring democracy to the island.

DIRECTIONS: *Read each of these passages from "My First Free Summer." On the lines that follow, write a sentence telling how the historical context affects the action.*

1. I didn't know about my father's activities. I didn't know the dictator was bad. All I knew was that my friends who were attending Dominican schools were often on holiday to honor the dictator's birthday, the dictator's saint day, the day the dictator became the dictator, the day the dictator's oldest son was born, and so on.

How context affects action: _____

_____

2. But the yard replete with cousins and friends that I had dreamed about all year was deserted. Family members were leaving for the United States, using whatever connections they could drum up. The plot had unraveled. Every day there were massive arrests. The United States had closed its embassy and was advising Americans to return home.

How context affects action: _____

_____

3. I was about to tell her that I didn't want to go to the United States, where . . . everyone spoke English. But my mother lifted a hand for silence. "We're leaving in a few hours. I want you all to go get ready! I'll be in to pack soon." The desperate look in her eyes did not allow for contradiction. We raced off, wondering how to fit the contents of our Dominican lives into four small suitcases.

How context affects action: _____

_____

4. Next morning, we are standing inside a large, echoing hall as a stern American official reviews our documents. What if he doesn't let us in? What if we have to go back? I am holding my breath. My parents' terror has become mine.

How context affects action: _____

_____

Name _____ Date _____

"My First Free Summer" by Julia Alvarez
Vocabulary Builder

Word List

contradiction   diplomats   extenuating   repressive   summoned   vowed

A. DIRECTIONS: *Something is wrong with the following sentences. Revise each one, using the Word List word in a way that makes the sentence logical.*

1. After her first free summer, Julia *vowed* to pass all her subjects.

   Revision: _____

2. The mission of the *diplomats* was to negotiate the terms of the new car's warranty.

   Revision: _____

3. When Julia's mother *summoned* her daughters, Julia and her sister left for the beach.

   Revision: _____

4. The *repressive* government allowed complete freedom of speech and religion for all of its citizens.

   Revision: _____

5. The judge argued for a harsh sentence because of all the *extenuating* circumstances of the crime.

   Revision: _____

6. When all the witnesses offered a *contradiction* to the defendant's testimony, it was obvious that the defendant was telling the truth.

   Revision: _____

B. WORD STUDY: The Latin root -*dict*- means "to speak, assert." In the following sentences, think about the meaning of -*dict*- in each italicized word. On the line before each sentence, write *T* if the statement is true or *F* if the statement is false. Then, explain your answer.

1. _____ A *prediction* tells what happened in the past. _____

   _____

2. _____ A *dictionary* contains the roots and definitions of words. _____

   _____

3. _____ A *dictator* is the democratically elected head of a country. _____

   _____

"My First Free Summer" by Julia Alvarez
Enrichment: Life and Literature

Julia Alvarez was not kidding when she wrote in "My First Free Summer" that she had to do all her learning at the American school "in that impossibly difficult, rocks-in-your-mouth language of English!" On her Web site, she says that when she and her family moved to the United States, she "couldn't tell where one word ended and another began." It was paying attention to each word that prepared her for a career as a writer.

Alvarez was born in the United States but returned with her family to the Dominican Republic when she was three months old. When her father realized just how brutal the Trujillo dictatorship was, he joined the underground. That action put the family in danger, and they left the country in 1960. Shortly afterward, three Dominican sisters, the Mirabels, were murdered in retaliation for their and their husbands' opposition to the dictatorship. Shortly after that, Trujillo himself was assassinated. Alvarez has written a historical novel about the Mirabel sisters, titled *In the Time of the Butterflies*. Because she survived the dictatorship, she felt that she should use her skills to tell the story of these three brave women who did not survive to tell it themselves.

Alvarez has also shown her commitment to her former country by establishing an organic farm in the Dominican Republic. The farm raises shade-grown coffee. "Shade grown" means that the trees do not have to be cut down for the coffee to be harvested, thus enhancing the land and the economy. Alvarez also writes picture books for the families on the farm who are learning to read.

Alvarez writes in a variety of genres. In addition to the story of a young girl who grows up under a Latin American dictatorship, she has published poetry, folk tales, and autobiographical essays. Her novel *How the García Girls Lost Their Accents* addresses one of her favorite topics—the immigrant experience.

DIRECTIONS: *Answer these questions based on the information in the preceding passage.*

1. What problems did Alvarez have learning English?

   _____

2. What led Alvarez's father to join the underground?

   _____

3. Why did Alvarez write about the Mirabel sisters?

   _____

4. According to the passage, "Alvarez writes in a variety of *genres*." What is a genre? Use context to figure out the meaning of the word. _____

   _____

5. How does Alvarez show her commitment to the country of her childhood?

   _____

   _____

   _____

"My First Free Summer" by Julia Alvarez
Open-Book Test

Short Answer *Write your responses to the questions in this section on the lines provided.*

1. At the beginning of "My First Free Summer," the reader learns how the author spent many of her summers as a young child. Why did she spend her summers in this way? Use details from the selection to explain your answer.

   _____

   _____

2. At the beginning of "My First Free Summer," the author says she vowed to become a better student. Since she vowed to take on this task, what can you assume about the outcome? Use the definition of *vowed* to explain your answer.

   _____

   _____

3. Toward the beginning of "My First Free Summer," the author mentions holidays her friends celebrated in the Dominican schools. How does her description provide a historical context for the selection? Use information from the selection to respond.

   _____

   _____

4. Toward the beginning of "My First Free Summer," the author writes about her school subjects. How does this information help set the historical context? Answer with details from the selection.

   _____

   _____

   _____

   _____

5. In "My First Free Summer," the author explains that it was unlikely that she would ever be thrown out of the American school. Why was that an unlikely possibility? Use details from the selection to support your response.

   _____

   _____

   _____

6. In "My First Free Summer," some of the children at the American school had parents who were diplomats. The diplomats had to know more than one language as part of their jobs. Why was this knowledge important in their jobs? Explain your answer.

   _____

   _____

7. In the middle of "My First Free Summer," the author finally gets a free summer. Unfortunately, her summer does not turn out to be what she had expected. How do the circumstances of that summer reveal the historical context of the selection? Use details from the selection to respond.

_____

_____

_____

_____

_____

8. In "My First Free Summer," Julia Alvarez writes that "not everyone returned" from a small interrogation room at the airport. What is her purpose for explaining what might happen to people who were trying to leave the country? Use details from the selection.

_____

_____

_____

_____

_____

9. Toward the end of "My First Free Summer," the author finally understands that theirs "was not a trip, but an escape." She uses a specific phrase to explain the "light" that went on in her head. What phrase does she use, and for what purpose?

_____

_____

_____

_____

_____

10. What is the author's attitude toward school in "My First Free Summer"? Use the organizer below to indicate how she feels at the beginning, middle, and end of the selection. On the lines, tell how her attitude changes over the course of the selection.

| Beginning: |
| Middle: |
| End: |

_____

_____

Essay

Write an extended response to the question of your choice or to the question or questions your teacher assigns you.

11. At the beginning of "My First Free Summer," the author does not appreciate her school. Why does she lack this appreciation? Explain your response in a brief essay. Use details from the selection to support your description of the author's attitude.

12. What are the political events that surrounded the author's life in "My First Free Summer"? In a brief essay, discuss the historical context of this selection. Use details to support your response.

13. Keeping in mind the author's age during "My First Free Summer," how much do you think she understood about what was happening in her country? In an essay, analyze the perspective of the young girl at the beginning, middle, and end of the selection. Use details from the selection to support your points.

14. **Thinking About the Big Question: What is the best way to find the truth?** In "My First Free Summer," the word *free* has many meanings. In a brief essay, explain the best way to find the true meaning of "free" or "freedom." Consider whether you have to experience the opposite of freedom in order to understand it. Use examples from "My First Free Summer" as support.

Oral Response

15. Go back to question 1, 3, or 7 or to the question your teacher assigns you. Take a few minutes to expand your answer and prepare an oral response. Find additional details in "My First Free Summer" that support your points. If necessary, make notes to guide your oral response.

"My First Free Summer" by Julia Alvarez
Selection Test A

Critical Reading *Identify the letter of the choice that best answers the question.*

____ 1. What idea does the historical context convey in this passage?

> My mother had decided to send her children to the American school so we could learn the language of the nation that would soon be liberating us. For thirty years, the Dominican Republic had endured a bloody and repressive dictatorship.

    A. The Dominican Republic taught English in its schools.

    B. The Dominican Republic was a dictatorship during the author's childhood.

    C. Alvarez was able to learn Spanish at the American school.

    D. Alvarez believed that the United States would soon liberate her country.

____ 2. What does the background information here reveal about Alvarez's purpose?

> Meanwhile, I had to learn about the pilgrims with their funny witch hats, . . . about Dick and Jane and their tame little pets, Puff and Spot, about freedom and liberty and justice for all—while being imprisoned in a hot classroom with a picture of a man wearing a silly wig hanging above the blackboard.

    A. She wishes to make readers laugh.

    B. She wishes to describe the Dominican heat.

    C. She wishes to inform readers of American ideals.

    D. She wishes to let readers know that she feels patriotic.

____ 3. In "My First Free Summer," what subject in school does Alvarez find most difficult?

    A. fractions

    B. U.S. presidents

    C. Mesopotamia

    D. English

____ 4. In "My First Free Summer," what keeps Alvarez from being thrown out of the American school?

    A. She was a very good student.

    B. Her father was a diplomat.

    C. Her mother had promised the principal that Alvarez would work hard.

    D. Her grandfather had donated the land that the school was built on.

____ 5. Why does Alvarez work harder in school when she is in fifth grade?

    A. She is grateful that she has been allowed to go to the American school.

    B. She realizes that she is lucky to be able to go to the American school.

    C. She is happy because all of her friends are now going to the American school.

    D. She realizes that if she works hard, she will not have to go to summer school.

____ 6. What historical context is provided by this passage?

> But the yard replete with cousins and friends that I had dreamed about all year was deserted. Family members were leaving for the United States . . . The plot had unraveled. Every day there were massive arrests. The United States had closed its embassy and was advising Americans to return home.

A. Everyone in the Dominican Republic was moving to the United States.

B. Alvarez's American friends were now living in the U.S. embassy.

C. People involved in a plot against the government were being arrested.

D. Alvarez's mother and father had no connections in the United States.

____ 7. What does the background information here reveal about Alvarez's purpose?

> "It's a trap," I heard my mother whisper to my father.
>
> This had happened before, a cat-and-mouse game the dictator liked to play. Pretend that he was letting someone go, and then at the last minute, their family and friends conveniently gathered together—wham! The secret police would haul the whole clan away.

A. She wishes to describe how the secret police operated.

B. She wishes to create a mood of danger and fear.

C. She wishes to warn of the danger of leaving one's country.

D. She wishes to show that the dictator liked to play games.

____ 8. What does this passage from "My First Free Summer" suggest about the narrator?

> But as the hours ticked away . . . with no plane in sight, a light came on in my head. If the light could be translated into words, instead, they would say: Freedom and liberty and justice for all . . .

A. She realized why her family was leaving.

B. She realized a plane would never arrive.

C. She began to think in English.

D. She decided to study U.S. history.

____ 9. What does the background information here reveal about Alvarez's purpose?

> He checks our faces against the passport pictures. When he is done, he asks, "You girls ready for school?" I swear he is looking at me.
>
> "Yes, sir!" I speak up.
>
> The man laughs. He stamps our papers and hands them to my father. Then wonderfully, a smile spreads across his face. "Welcome to the United States," he says, waving us in.

A. She wishes to inform readers how it feels to be safe.

B. She wishes to inform readers of immigration procedures.

C. She wishes to persuade readers abroad to emigrate to America.

D. She wishes to describe how it feels to be questioned at a U.S. airport.

_____ **10.** The best explanation of the title "My First Free Summer" is that it was the first summer Alvarez was free

   A. to study Spanish.

   B. of her relatives.

   C. of the dictator.

   D. to learn English.

Vocabulary and Grammar

_____ **11.** In which sentence is the word *vowed* used correctly?

   A. We vowed that we would always be friends.

   B. They vowed before the king and queen.

   C. The dogs vowed through the bushes after the rabbit.

   D. A sudden rainstorm vowed to interrupted our picnic.

_____ **12.** How many possessive pronouns are in this passage?

   I wanted to run with the pack of cousins and friends in the common yard that connected all our properties . . . I wanted to be free.

   A. 1

   B. 2

   C. 3

   D. 4

Essay

13. Like many ten-year-olds, Julia Alvarez in "My First Free Summer" would rather be elsewhere than in school. In an essay, compare Alvarez's experiences in school in the Dominican Republic and her attitude toward school with your own experiences and attitudes.

14. In "My First Free Summer," the ten-year-old narrator lives in a complicated political world. Though politics shapes her life, she does not fully understand it. In an essay, consider the information that the narrator reveals about her country. How much of it is she aware of as a ten-year-old? How much of it is she telling from the point of view of an adult looking back on the events of her "first free summer"?

15. **Thinking About the Big Question: What is the best way to find the truth?** In "My First Free Summer," the word *free* has many meanings. In a brief essay, explain what it means to be truly free. Do you have to feel unfree to know what it means to be free? Use examples from "My First Free Summer" to support your answer.

"My First Free Summer" by Julia Alvarez
Selection Test B

Critical Reading *Identify the letter of the choice that best completes the statement or answers the question.*

_____ 1. What is suggested by the following passage from "My First Free Summer"?

I never had summer—I had summer school. First grade, summer school. Second grade, summer school. Thirdgradesummerschoolfourthgradesummerschool.

    A. The narrator rebels against summer school by running her words together.
    B. The narrator never has enough activities to keep her busy during the summer.
    C. The narrator prefers summer school to first, second, third, and fourth grades.
    D. The narrator is never able to escape from having to attend summer school.

_____ 2. What historical context is provided by this passage from "My First Free Summer"?

My friends who were attending Dominican schools were often on holiday to honor the dictator's birthday, the dictator's saint day, the day the dictator became the dictator, the day the dictator's oldest son was born, and so on.

    A. Students in Dominican schools had too many holidays.
    B. The dictator and his oldest son had the same birthday.
    C. The dictator's power was reflected in the country's holidays.
    D. Students in Dominican schools often had their pictures in the paper.

_____ 3. What does the background information in this passage reveal about Julia Alvarez's purpose?

Meanwhile, I had to learn about the pilgrims with their funny witch hats, . . . about Dick and Jane and their tame little pets, Puff and Spot, about freedom and liberty and justice for all—while being imprisoned in a hot classroom with a picture of a man wearing a silly wig hanging above the blackboard.

    A. She wishes to provide an amusing picture of her experiences in school.
    B. She wishes to show readers that her school taught a lot about America.
    C. She wishes to show readers that Dominican summers were extremely hot.
    D. She wishes to tell readers that she has always been interested in America.

_____ 4. What does the narrator of "My First Free Summer" mean when she describes English as "that impossibly difficult, rocks-in-your-mouth language"?
    A. English is difficult to learn and difficult to pronounce.
    B. English words sound heavy when they are spoken.
    C. To learn to speak English correctly, students had to put rocks in their mouths.
    D. Speakers of English never learn to use or pronounce the language correctly.

_____ 5. In "My First Free Summer," why does Alvarez wish to be thrown out of the American school?
    A. She dislikes learning about the history and geography of the United States.
    B. She dislikes learning in English and envies the holidays in the Dominican schools.
    C. She dislikes being known only for her grandfather's contribution to the school.
    D. She dislikes attending school with the sons and daughters of American diplomats.

____ 6. In "My First Free Summer," why does the narrator have to attend summer school?
A. Her mother wants her out of the house and in a safe environment.
B. She has not learned her schoolwork well enough during the school year.
C. She has spent too much time on English and not enough time on fractions.
D. The dictator has declared that all children must attend summer school.

____ 7. What does the background information in this passage reveal about Julia Alvarez's purpose?

Attitude much improved. Her English progressing nicely. Attentive and cooperative in classroom.

A. She wishes to show that even the teachers did not write complete sentences.
B. She wishes to show the comments the teachers made about her academic progress.
C. She wishes to show the comments her mother made about her academic progress.
D. She wishes to show how she described her own progress when she was ten years old.

____ 8. Why is the narrator's family in danger in the Dominican Republic?
A. They do not observe the dictator's holidays.
B. The father is involved in an antigovernment plot.
C. Their airline tickets and papers have been forged.
D. They have not been allowed to enter the U.S. embassy.

____ 9. In "My First Free Summer," when Alvarez's mother tells her and her sister that they are leaving for the United States, she writes that "our mouths dropped." What does she mean?
A. They were shocked.
B. They fell to the floor.
C. They opened their mouths to protest.
D. They both tried to speak at once.

____ 10. What does the background information in this passage reveal about Julia Alvarez's purpose?

This had happened before, a cat-and-mouse game the dictator liked to play. Pretend that he was letting someone go, and then at the last minute, their family and friends conveniently gathered together—wham! The secret police would haul the whole clan away.

A. She wishes to show that people were betrayed by their friends.
B. She wishes to show the fear that people feel under a dictatorship.
C. She wishes to show the danger people are in when they leave a country.
D. She wishes to show how large groups of people left the country together.

____ 11. What does the background information in this passage from "My First Free Summer" suggest?

The terminal lined with soldiers wielding machine guns, checking papers, escorting passengers into a small interrogation room. Not everyone returned.

A. Some interrogations went on for so long that people missed their flights.
B. Airline pilots were afraid to land because of the soldiers in the airport.
C. Leaving the Dominican Republic was neither safe nor easy.
D. Some people got impatient with the delays and went home.

_____ 12. What historical context is provided by this passage from "My First Free Summer"?

Next morning, we are standing inside a large, echoing hall as a stern American official reviews our documents. What if he doesn't let us in? What if we have to go back? I am holding my breath.

A. U.S. immigration officials always review documents with extreme care.

B. Refugees may have to return home if the country they wish to enter will not accept them.

C. Parents may transmit their fears to their children.

D. When children are in unfamiliar situations, they often imagine dangers that do not exist.

Vocabulary and Grammar

_____ 13. In which sentence does the word *diplomats* make the most sense?

A. The diplomats argued all day over the wording of the treaty.

B. A team of seven diplomats tried to scale the highest mountain in Alaska.

C. The diplomats on our team are better passers than those on your team.

D. The diplomats in the emergency room saved my grandmother's life.

_____ 14. Which sentence uses the word *interrogation* correctly?

A. The interrogation was in the fourth quarter when the storm hit.

B. The suspect underwent an all-night interrogation by the detectives.

C. Our city's interrogation reaches from Market Street to the freeway.

D. The rescue planes dropped an interrogation to the trapped hikers.

Essay

15. In "My First Free Summer," Julia Alvarez includes a combination of personal and political information—about the dictator and the holidays he declared, the school she attended, her "first free summer," and the changes that took place in the summer of 1960. What do you think was her main purpose for writing this autobiographical story? Express your opinion in an essay, and use references to the story to support your points.

16. In "My First Free Summer," Julia Alvarez reflects on the events of a politically dangerous time in the Dominican Republic. In an essay, consider the information that the narrator reveals: Which events is the ten-year-old Julia aware of? What information does the adult narrator bring to the story? Then, comment on whether Alvarez is successful in bringing together these two points of view in one story. Back up your opinion with references to the story.

17. **Thinking About the Big Question: What is the best way to find the truth?** In "My First Free Summer," the word *free* has many meanings. In a brief essay, explain the best way to find the true meaning of "free" or "freedom." Consider whether you have to experience the opposite of freedom in order to understand it. Use examples from "My First Free Summer" as support.

Vocabulary Warm-up Word Lists

Study these words from the selection. Then, complete the activities.

Word List A

apparatus [ap uh RAT us] *n.* group of parts that have a specific use
   The stomach and intestines are part of a person's digestive <u>apparatus</u>.

crisis [KRY sis] *n.* important turning point
   When Jared's fever started to go down, we knew the <u>crisis</u> was over.

germs [jermz] *n.* bacteria or other tiny organisms that can cause illness
   Wash your hands often to clean away any <u>germs</u> that could make you sick.

parcel [PAR sul] *n.* small package
   Alan sent his cousin a <u>parcel</u> containing a toy truck.

reciting [ree SYT ing] *v.* saying aloud a poem, or other writing that has been memorized
   Emma is <u>reciting</u> a paragraph that she wrote and learned to repeat last night.

remarkable [ree MAR kuh bul] *adj.* wonderful; standing out by being unusual and good
   She won that race by running with <u>remarkable</u> speed.

stitches [STICH ez] *n.* loops of thread that fasten pieces of material or skin
   Matt used a needle and thread to sew ten <u>stitches</u> to close up the hole in his shirt.

ward [wÔrd] *n.* part of a hospital set aside for a group of patients
   When eight-year-old Mike broke his leg, he slept in the hospital's children's <u>ward</u>.

Word List B

blight [blyt] *n.* word used to describe any one of a number of plant diseases
   A <u>blight</u> turned the leaves of the rose bush yellow with black spots.

circumstances [SER cum STAN siz] *n.* situation in which one finds oneself
   It is thundering and raining hard; under these <u>circumstances</u>, I think we should go indoors.

collapsed [kuh LAPSD] *v.* fell down suddenly
   The tower built out of toothpicks <u>collapsed</u> when Lucy placed a stone on top.

disobedience [DIS oh BEE dee entz] *n.* misbehavior
   After Joe broke his curfew, his parents punished him for his <u>disobedience</u>.

foreign [FÔR en] *adj.* from other countries
   We take classes in <u>foreign</u> languages like Spanish and Chinese.

fortnight [FORT nyte] *n.* period of time lasting two weeks
   With four weeks of vacation, we spent the first <u>fortnight</u> camping and the second two weeks visiting friends.

internal [in TER nul] *adj.* inside the body
   The serious expression on his face did not reveal his <u>internal</u> joy.

torrent [TAW rent] *n.* fast-moving flood
   A <u>torrent</u> of rain pounded the roofs of the town.

from **Angela's Ashes** by Frank McCourt
Vocabulary Warm-up Exercises

Exercise A *Fill in the blanks, using each word from Word List A only once.*

Let me tell you about our Aunt Rose. She is constantly [1] _____ poems about bats because they are her favorite animal. She has an odd way of speaking, which sometimes makes us laugh. For example, instead of telling us she has a stomachache, Aunt Rose might say, "I have consumed a few [2] _____ that have caused a brief, painful illness in my food [3] _____." Still, we all think Aunt Rose is a truly [4] _____ person. If you run out of gas on the highway, or you have left an important [5] _____ on the bus and wonder how to get it back, she is the person to call. Aunt Rose is the calm problem solver in our family. When my brother Cyrus fell off the slide at the playground, Aunt Rose was the one who looked at the cut on his knee and said he needed [6] _____. Then, she stayed with him at the hospital [7] _____ for emergency patients until the [8] _____ was over. Our Aunt Rose may seem a little strange at times, but we do love her.

Exercise B *Answer the questions with complete explanations.*

1. Would a <u>torrent</u> of words be spoken slowly?

   _____

2. Would you put a bandage on an <u>internal</u> injury?

   _____

3. If someone always follows the rules, could you accuse him of <u>disobedience</u>?

   _____

4. What would you try to do to a plant suffering from <u>blight</u>? Explain.

   _____

5. If Ed's boss offers him a <u>fortnight</u> off, does she expect Ed to return in a week?

   _____

6. If your friend suddenly <u>collapsed</u> next to you on the sidewalk, what would you try to do? Explain.

   _____

7. Why do you think people like to visit <u>foreign</u> countries? Explain.

   _____

8. Under what <u>circumstances</u> might a person use crutches?

   _____

from **Angela's Ashes** by Frank McCourt
Reading Warm-up A

Read the following passage. Pay special attention to the underlined words. Then, read it again, and complete the activities. Use a separate sheet of paper for your written answers.

When Carla signed up to volunteer at the children's hospital, she had no idea what kind of work she might do. Still, she was surprised when the lady in charge of volunteers asked her to assist Lulu, the hospital clown.

The lady handed Carla a brown paper parcel. The small package contained a rainbow-colored hat, a matching vest, and pants big enough to fit over her clothes.

Carla put on the costume and went upstairs to meet Lulu on the balloon ward. In this group of patient rooms, walls were painted with pictures of balloons.

Lulu's outfit matched Carla's. The clown also wore a blue wig and a red rubber nose. A silly squeak sounded when they shook hands, and Carla laughed.

Lulu smiled, "I think you're the right person for this job." She showed Carla five kidney-shaped purple pillows, sewn together in a line, that she pretended was her stomach apparatus. That was one of her tricks, she said. Lulu explained that some young patients were still very sick. They had not yet started to get better. These patients and their families were still in the middle of a crisis. "But, happily, most of the kids are getting well fast," Lulu said.

That first day, Carla's favorite patient was Erik, who had stitches where his head had been sewn up after an operation.

"You need jewels for that crown," Lulu told him, pointing at the bandage on his head. While she was twisting balloons, she was also reciting a silly poem. Erik started smiling, then laughing. Carla helped out by blowing up balloons. The remarkable crown was three feet long. It was very silly-looking and shaped like a boat.

The Crown slipped down onto the floor by mistake. Lulu washed it to clean away germs. She handed it to Erik and said, "We must not let bacteria dirty the royal crown!"

Lulu winked at Carla and the two of them bowed as Carla gently placed the crown on Erik's head.

1. Circle the words that have the same meaning as parcel. Use **parcel** in a sentence.

2. Underline the phrase that has the same meaning as ward. Describe some things you might see on a visit to a hospital **ward**.

3. Underline the words that tell what Lulu pretended was her stomach apparatus. Make up a clown trick Lulu might do with her fake **apparatus,** and write a sentence to describe the trick.

4. Underline the words that give a clue to the meaning of crisis. Use **crisis** in a sentence.

5. Circle the words that explain the reason for Erik's stitches. Name some other places where you can find **stitches.**

6. Circle the words that tell what Lulu was reciting. Use **reciting** in a sentence.

7. Tell what made Erik's crown remarkable. Describe something **remarkable** you have seen.

8. Underline the words that give a clue to the meaning of germs. Write a sentence explaining why Lulu might want to keep **germs** away from Erik.

Name _____ Date _____

from **Angela's Ashes** by Frank McCourt
Reading Warm-up B

Read the following passage. Pay special attention to the underlined words. Then, read it again, and complete the activities. Use a separate sheet of paper for your written answers.

For hundreds of years, governments have helped slow the spread of diseases by keeping sick people away from healthy ones. A common name for this practice is "quarantine," from the Italian words *"quaranta giorni"* [kwa RAHNT ah JOHR nee], meaning "forty days."

During the 14th century, millions of people in Europe died from a disease called the plague. There was no cure for it. However, people knew that damage from an incurable disease might be only <u>internal</u> at first. It could take time for a body to show outward signs of a disease. So the city of Venice, Italy, invented some rules. Ships coming to that city were ordered to lower their anchors and wait 40 days before unloading. If someone on a ship <u>collapsed</u> from an incurable disease during the forty days, the whole crew was kept out of the city. The ship's cargo was burned.

The plague spread fast. Sometimes it seemed to rush through cities and towns like a <u>torrent</u> of water. Many other places also had rules ordering sick people to stay away from others. <u>Disobedience</u> of these rules often resulted in a punishment. A person could be fined, arrested, or even put to death.

Nowadays, the <u>circumstances</u> of a quarantine order vary a lot. One person might be exposed to radioactive materials. She might be confined only a few minutes. After she takes a shower, she might be free to go. Another person might have a virus that is hard to cure. He might be ordered to stay in a hospital for a <u>fortnight</u>, or for twice as long as that—an entire month—or longer.

Plants coming to the United States from <u>foreign</u> countries are sometimes quarantined if they are suspected of carrying an infectious <u>blight</u>. Plant parasites and other plant diseases could harm our country's agriculture industry. For this reason, there are many restrictions about bringing plants into the United States. The same is true for live animals.

1. Underline a nearby sentence that gives a clue to the meaning of <u>internal</u>. Use **internal** in a sentence.

2. Underline the words that explain what happened if a crew member <u>collapsed</u> from illness. If you saw someone who **collapsed**, what else beside illness might have caused that to happen?

3. Circle the word that describes what spreads like a <u>torrent</u> of water. Write your own simile using the word **torrent**.

4. Underline the words that describe the punishments for <u>disobedience</u>. Write a word or phrase that means the opposite of **disobedience**.

5. Underline the phrases that explain two different <u>circumstances</u> for modern-day quarantines.

6. Circle the words that explain the meaning of <u>fortnight</u>. How many **fortnights** are in six months?

7. Underline the words that tell what might be quarantined when it arrives from a <u>foreign</u> country. Use the word **foreign** in a sentence.

8. Circle the nearby words that have the same meaning as <u>blight</u>. Use **blight** in a sentence.

from **Angela's Ashes** by Frank McCourt

Writing About the Big Question

What is the best way to find the truth?

Big Question Vocabulary

awareness	believable	conclude	convince	debate
evaluate	evidence	explain	factual	fiction
insight	perceive	reality	reveal	truth

A. *Use one or more words from the list above to complete each sentence.*

1. After some time has passed, it is easier to _____ important life events.

2. Though sometimes an event seems unimportant while it is happening, we may later gain _____ about its importance.

3. Often, in a memoir, the author will _____ the significance of events in his or her past.

B. *Answer the questions. Use one vocabulary word in each answer.*

1. What event in your life so far would you focus on in a short memoir?

_____

_____

2. If you could ask anyone to write a memoir, who would you ask, and why? What would you want them to tell about?

_____

_____

_____

C. *Complete the sentence below. Then, answer the question with a short paragraph connecting the sentence to the Big Question.*

Things that don't seem important while they are happening _____

Give an example of a lesson that an author might learn from personal experience and how he or she may later use this experience in a work of fiction.

_____

_____

_____

from **Angela's Ashes** by Frank McCourt

Reading: Use Background Information to Determine the Author's Purpose

One way to determine the **author's purpose,** or reason, for writing a nonfiction work is to use **background information** that you already know about the author and topic. For example, knowing that an author grew up outside the United States might help you determine that he wrote a story to inform readers about the country where he spent his youth.

Although he was born in the United States, Frank McCourt spent his childhood and teen years in Ireland. The reader learns some of this information in the excerpt from *Angela's Ashes*, which is set in the Irish hospital where the ten-year-old McCourt recovered from typhoid fever. For example, McCourt writes the following about one of the nurses in the hospital:

She's a very stern nurse from the County Kerry and she frightens me.

The author's purpose for writing this sentence is twofold: (a) to inform the reader that the story takes place in Ireland (County Kerry is a southwestern county of Ireland) and (b) to help establish a mood by portraying the harsh and frightening personality of the nurse. In addition to informing or creating a mood, an author might write a passage in order to entertain the reader.

DIRECTIONS: *Read each of these passages from the excerpt from* Angela's Ashes. *Decide whether the author's purpose is to inform, to create a mood, or to entertain. Write the purpose on the line following the passage. A passage may have more than one purpose.*

1. I have diphtheria and something else.

   What's something else?

   They don't know. They think I have a disease from foreign parts because my father used to be in Africa. I nearly died. . . .

   Author's purpose(s): _____

2. There are twenty beds in the ward, all white, all empty. The nurse tells Seamus to put me at the far end of the ward against the wall to make sure I don't talk to anyone who might be passing the door, which is very unlikely since there isn't another soul on this whole floor.

   Author's purpose(s): _____

3. [The nurse] leaves and there's silence for a while. Then Patricia whispers, Give thanks, Francis, give thanks, and say your rosary, Francis, and I laugh so hard a nurse runs in to see if I'm all right. . . .

   Author's purpose(s): _____

Name _____ Date _____

from **Angela's Ashes** by Frank McCourt
Literary Analysis: **Historical Context**

When a literary work is based on real events, the historical context can help you understand the action. Historical context—the actual political and social events and trends of the time—can explain why characters act and think the way they do. Read the following passage from the excerpt from *Angela's Ashes*. Think about what it tells you about the historical context of the selection.

She tells Seamus this was the fever ward during the Great Famine long ago and only God knows how many died here brought in too late for anything but a wash before they were buried and there are stories of cries and moans in the far reaches of the night. She says 'twould break your heart to think of what the English did to us, that if they didn't put the blight on the potato they didn't do much to take it off.

DIRECTIONS: *Read each of these passages from* Angela's Ashes. *On the lines that follow, write a sentence telling how the historical context affects the action.*

1. Mam visits me on Thursdays. I'd like to see my father, too, but I'm out of danger, crisis time is over, and I'm allowed only one visitor. Besides, she says, he's back at work at Rank's Flour Mills and please God this job will last a while with the war on and the English desperate for flour. She brings me a chocolate bar and that proves Dad is working. She could never afford one on the dole.

   Historical context and effect on story: _____

   _____

2. [Seamus] says I'm not supposed to be bringing anything from a dipteria room to a typhoid room with all the germs flying around and hiding between the pages and if you ever catch dipteria on top of the typhoid they'll know and I'll lose my good job and be out on the street singing patriotic songs with a tin cup in my hand, which I could easily do because there isn't a song ever written about Ireland's sufferings I don't know. . . .

   Historical context and effect on story: _____

   _____

3. No pity. No feeling at all for the people that died in this very ward, children suffering and dying here while the English feasted on roast beef and guzzled the best of wine in their big houses, little children with their mouths all green from trying to eat the grass in the fields beyond, God bless us and save us and guard us from future famines.

   Historical context and effect on story: _____

   _____

Name _____ Date _____

Vocabulary Builder

Word List

ban   desperate   guzzle   miracle   patriotic   saluting

A. DIRECTIONS: *Write a sentence that describes each situation and shows the meaning of each vocabulary word.*

1. Why government wants to *ban* a harmful product or chemical:

   _____

   _____

2. Why someone might feel *desperate*:

   _____

   _____

3. Why one might *guzzle* a drink:

   _____

   _____

4. A situation that seems like—or calls for—a *miracle*:

   _____

   _____

5. A *patriotic* ceremony:

   _____

   _____

6. A situation that would call for *saluting*:

   _____

   _____

B. WORD STUDY: The Latin root *-sper-* means "hope." Think about the meaning of *-sper-* in each italicized word. On the line before each sentence, write *T* if the statement is true or *F* if the statement is false. Then, explain your answer.

1. _____ Someone who feels *desperate* on first seeing an exam expects to do well.

   _____

2. _____ A person who is in *despair* has a negative outlook on life.

   _____

3. _____ In a time of *prosperity*, most people are living in poverty.

   _____

Name _____ Date _____

from **Angela's Ashes** by Frank McCourt
Enrichment: Medical Science

In the excerpt from *Angela's Ashes*, each of the major characters—Francis and Patricia—has a serious illness: Francis has typhoid fever, and Patricia has diphtheria. These are both life-threatening conditions that were once much more widespread than they are now. Thanks to advances in modern medicine, both diseases are less common and more treatable now than they were during World War II, the historical setting of this story.

DIRECTIONS: *Use library and Internet resources to provide basic information on these two illnesses. Use the chart below to organize and present your findings.*

	Typhoid Fever	**Diphtheria**
Symptoms		
Cause		
How common in 1940		
How common now		
Diagnosis		
Treatment		

"My First Free Summer" by Julia Alvarez
from **Angela's Ashes** by Frank McCourt
Integrated Language Skills: Grammar

A **possessive pronoun** is a pronoun that shows ownership.

The football that belongs to **me**	**my** football
The video that belongs to **you**	**your** video
The idea that belongs to **her**	**her** idea
The answer that belongs to **him**	**his** answer
The house that belongs to **them**	**their** house
The decision that belongs to **us**	**our** decision

A. PRACTICE: *Underline each possessive pronoun in the sentences below.*

1. Alvarez vowed she would learn her English.
2. My mother decided to send her children to the American school.
3. I had to learn about the pilgrims with their funny witch hats.
4. The soldiers go seat by seat, looking at our faces.
5. While in the hospital, Frank wants his father to visit him.
6. When a nurse is unkind to the children, Seamus takes their side against her.

B. Writing Application: *For each sentence below, change the underlined pronoun into a possessive pronoun.*

1. Alvarez learned <u>she</u> subjects, so she could play with <u>she</u> family that summer.

    _____

2. But, she says, "<u>I</u> family were packing <u>they</u> clothing to move to America."

    _____

3. Frank McCourt liked Patricia Madigan and appreciated <u>she</u> sense of humor.

    _____

4. Mam hopes that Frank's father can keep <u>he</u> job.

    _____

5. The nurses are cruel to Frank and Patricia and take away <u>they</u> fun.

    _____

Name _____ Date _____

Integrated Language Skills: Support for Writing a Letter

For your letter to Julia Alvarez describing what it is like to go to school in the United States or your letter to Frank McCourt describing a favorite story or poem, gather your ideas in one of the charts below.

Letter to Julia Alvarez:

Topics for Letter	My Ideas About These Topics
School hours and holidays and the school year	
Subjects and homework	
After-school activities	
Best and worst things about school	

Letter to Frank McCourt:

Title of favorite story or poem	
Details about events or characters in the story, or about descriptions or sounds in the poem	
A reason you might recommend the story or poem to Frank McCourt	

"**My First Free Summer**" by Julia Alvarez
Integrate Language Skills: Support for Extend Your Learning

Research and Technology

Use the following chart to gather information for a **timeline** of major events in the recent history of the Dominican Republic. See whether you can find an event for each date listed below. Include additional dates if you wish.

Recent Events in the Dominican Republic

1930: Rafael Trujillo becomes president.
1937:
1961:
1963:
1965:
1966:
1974:
1978:
1979:
1984:
1986:
1996:
2000:

Listening and Speaking: "My First Free Summer"

Use the following as you prepare to interview a friend, relative, neighbor, or classmate who has moved to a new country or neighborhood or who has attended a new school.

Questions to ask at the interview:

1. _____

2. _____

Follow-up questions based on your subject's responses to your questions:

1. _____

2. _____

Conclusions to draw in presentation to the class:

1. _____

2. _____

Name _____ Date _____

from **Angela's Ashes** by Frank McCourt
Open-Book Test

Short Answer *Write your responses to the questions in this section on the lines provided.*

1. At the beginning of the excerpt from *Angela's Ashes*, a nurse tells the narrator that his recovery from typhoid is "a miracle." What does the nurse's use of the word *miracle* tell you about typhoid?

   _____

   _____

2. In the excerpt from *Angela's Ashes*, Patricia Madigan is shown to have a sense of humor. Use this diagram to analyze Patricia's sense of humor. In each blank box, write an example of something funny that she says or does. Then, on the line below, briefly explain the author's purpose for including these details.

   ┌──────────────────────────────────┐
   │ **Patricia's Sense of Humor**   │
   └──────────────────────────────────┘

   ┌─────────────────────┐   ┌─────────────────────┐
   │   │   │   │
   │   │   │   │
   └─────────────────────┘   └─────────────────────┘

   _____

3. In the excerpt from *Angela's Ashes*, Mam relates that Frank's father is working at a flour mill. She expresses hope that his job will last as long as the war is going on and the English need flour badly. Why does Frank's mother believe that those factors will allow her husband to keep his job?

   _____

   _____

   _____

4. In the excerpt from *Angela's Ashes*, Mam says that the English are "desperate for flour." In the Fever Hospital, it seems that Frank and Patricia are desperate for something as well. Explain what that is. Base your answer on the definition of *desperate*.

   _____

   _____

5. Think about what Seamus does for the two sick children in the excerpt from *Angela's Ashes*. What kind of person is he? Support your answer by citing a detail from the selection.

   _____

   _____

6. In the excerpt from *Angela's Ashes*, Frank and Patricia grow close in a short period of time. What factors allow them to become close friends very quickly?

_____

_____

7. In the excerpt from *Angela's Ashes*, how does the long-standing conflict between Ireland and England affect Frank and Patricia? Cite a detail from the selection to support your answer.

_____

_____

8. In the excerpt from *Angela's Ashes*, Frank McCourt portrays the nurse from Kerry and Sister Rita. What is McCourt's purpose in describing these two health-care workers? Explain the effect they have on the passage.

_____

_____

_____

9. Toward the end of the excerpt from *Angela's Ashes*, a nurse talks to Frank and Seamus about the Great Famine. On the basis of the nurse's account, describe how the Great Famine affected the relationship between the Irish and the English.

_____

_____

10. At the end of the excerpt from *Angela's Ashes*, Seamus tells Frank about Patricia's death. He says, "Tis a dirty rotten thing to die in a lavatory when you're lovely in yourself." Explain what Seamus means.

_____

_____

_____

Essay

Write an extended response to the question of your choice or to the question or questions your teacher assigns you.

11. Think about the children's experiences in the hospital in this excerpt from *Angela's Ashes*. In particular, consider how the nurses' attitudes and actions affected Frank and Patricia. In an essay, discuss the treatment the two children received in the hospital. Cite two details that show why the hospital was not a comforting place for them.

Name _____ Date _____

12. As you read the excerpt from *Angela's Ashes*, you learn something about young Frank McCourt. Think about the events in the story and Frank's reaction to them. Then, in an essay, describe young Frank. Cite details from the excerpt to support your description of the boy in the hospital. In particular, cite details that suggest that Frank will become a writer later in life.

13. The excerpt from *Angela's Ashes* is written from the point of view of the author, Frank McCourt. Suppose that Patricia had written this story. In an essay, describe how her version might differ from McCourt's.

14. **Thinking About the Big Question: What is the best way to find the truth?** In the excerpt from *Angela's Ashes*, there are two references to the anger felt by many Irish for the English. Frank McCourt conveys the information by quoting Sister Rita and the Kerry nurse, but he does not reveal how he feels. In an essay, discuss how Frank McCourt might best find the truth that lies behind the bad feelings between the Irish and the English. Cite at least one detail from the excerpt to support your ideas.

Oral Response

15. Go back to question 5, 7, or 8 or to the question your teacher assigns you. Take a few minutes to expand your answer and prepare an oral response. Find additional details in the excerpt from *Angela's Ashes* that support your points. If necessary, make notes to guide your oral response.

from **Angela's Ashes** by Frank McCourt
Selection Test A

Critical Reading *Identify the letter of the choice that best answers the question.*

____ 1. In *Angela's Ashes*, why is Patricia in the hospital?
  A. to keep Francis company
  B. to help the nurses care for patients
  C. to be treated for diphtheria
  D. to have her appendix removed

____ 2. In *Angela's Ashes*, Patricia's striking up a conversation with Francis shows that she is
  A. friendly   C. nosy
  B. very ill   D. selfish

____ 3. When Sister Rita hears Francis and Patricia talking, she
  A. expresses disapproval
  B. is delighted
  C. joins in the conversation
  D. brings in another patient to join in the conversation

____ 4. When Sister Rita leaves, Patricia repeats her words to Francis in a tone that can best be described as
  A. respectful   C. puzzled
  B. mocking   D. hateful

____ 5. In *Angela's Ashes*, what is the author's main purpose in having Mam say about her husband's job, "please God this job will last a while"?
  A. to show that Mam is religious
  B. to show that Mam thinks about nothing but money
  C. to show that Mam wants to teach Francis the value of hard work
  D. to show that the family is poor

____ 6. Mam tells Francis that "the English [are] desperate for flour"; what does this remark say about economic conditions that existed at that time?
  A. People tend to work harder during wartime.
  B. There were shortages of basic necessities.
  C. Bread was the favorite dish of the English.
  D. Work at the mill paid high wages.

____ 7. Which passage from *Angela's Ashes* provides an important clue that the story takes place during a war?

A. The nurse says I'm the only typhoid patient. . . .

B. They don't know. They think I have a disease from foreign parts because my father used to be in Africa.

C. I have stitches on my right hand and my two feet where they put in the soldier's blood.

D. You could be giving thanks for your two remarkable recoveries.

____ 8. Mam mentions St. Jude, and the nuns urge Francis to say his rosary. What do these details say about the historical context of *Angela's Ashes*?

A. Ireland had a shortage of hospitals and doctors.

B. Miracles were common in Ireland.

C. Medical science was not very advanced.

D. Ireland was a very religious country.

____ 9. Patricia and Francis have only books to entertain them in the hospital. What does this fact suggest about the historical context of *Angela's Ashes*?

A. The nurses encouraged all kinds of reading by the patients.

B. Many items were in short supply during the war.

C. There was no TV at that time.

D. The educational system in Ireland was very advanced.

____ 10. After the nurse leaves the room, Seamus "whispers" to Francis that he will teach him a few songs. Why does the author include this detail?

A. to show that the Irish love music

B. to show that Seamus knows that the nurses would disapprove

C. to show that Seamus is a sneaky person

D. to show that everyone in the hospital must speak in a low voice

____ 11. Which of the following words best describes Seamus's personality?

A. suspicious   C. kind

B. sneaky   D. strict

____ 12. Which of the following words best describes the personality of the Kerry nurse?

A. sympathetic   C. selfish

B. kind   D. strict

____ 13. Which of the following phrases best describes Francis's feelings for Patricia?

A. polite friendliness   C. casual friendship

B. mild annoyance   D. boyhood crush

14. Why do the nurses move Francis to a separate part of the hospital?
   A. because he has been talking with Patricia
   B. because he is feeling much worse
   C. because he refuses to say the rosary
   D. because he is feeling much better

Vocabulary and Grammar

____ **15.** If you were saluting the American flag, you would be
   A. raising the flag
   B. showing respect
   C. folding it for storage
   D. repairing a tear

____ **16.** A coach says, "It would take a *miracle* for this team to win the championship," What does the coach think the team's chances of winning are?
   A. poor
   B. excellent
   C. average
   D. fair

____ **17.** Which of the following words is a possessive pronoun?
   A. of   B. she   C. here   D. have

____ **18.** Which word from this sentence from *Angela's Ashes* is a possessive pronoun?
   She comes into my room and wags her finger at me.
   A. into   B. my   C. at   D. me

Essay

19. In the selection from *Angela's Ashes* two young people in a hospital support each other by talking and sharing favorite parts of books they are reading. If you were in a hospital recovering from an illness, would you rather have a room to yourself, or would you rather have a roommate that you could talk to? Explain your answer in an essay that uses specific examples to support your opinion.

20. In this excerpt from *Angela's Ashes,* Seamus Heaney helps Francis and Patricia during their stay in the hospital. In what ways does he help them? Explain your answer in an essay supported by examples from the selection.

21. In the excerpt from *Angela's Ashes,* Francis and Patricia form a close friendship. In an essay, explain how they become such close friends even though they are not able to see each other and neither knows what the other looks like.

22. **Thinking About the Big Question: What is the best way to find the truth?** In the excerpt from Angela's Ashes, there are two references to the bad feelings that many Irish had for the English. Frank McCourt gives this information by quoting words of Sister Rita and the Kerry nurse, but he does not show how he feels. In an essay, first write the words spoken by Sister Rita and the Kerry nurse. Then, suggest two or three ways that a person might find the truth that lies behind the bad feelings. What sources would someone use to obtain this information?

from **Angela's Ashes** by Frank McCourt
Selection Test B

Critical Reading *Identify the letter of the choice that best completes the statement or answers the question.*

_____ 1. In *Angela's Ashes*, Francis is suffering from what disease?
A. pneumonia
B. dysentery
C. diphtheria
D. typhoid

_____ 2. In Angela's Ashes, why does Patricia sound disappointed when Francis tells her his age?
A. His voice is squeaky.
B. He sounds terribly ill.
C. He is too young.
D. He sounds shy.

_____ 3. Francis's reference to receiving the blood of soldiers is the reader's first hint that the story is set in what historical context?
A. peace
B. wartime
C. ancient times
D. the present

_____ 4. Which word best describes Francis's and Patricia's reaction to Sister Rita after she scolds them for talking to each other?
A. fearful
B. respectful.
C. hateful
D. mocking

_____ 5. In *Angela's Ashes*, Mam's description of her husband's job reveals what about the historical context of Francis's family life?
A. They are a poor working-class family.
B. They are a wealthy family.
C. The men are all involved in military service.
D. The family is on welfare.

_____ 6. What does the following passage from *Angela's Ashes* tell the reader about the historical context of Ireland during the time of this story?

He's [Francis's father] sure St. Jude pulled me through the crisis because he's the patron saint of desperate cases and I was indeed a desperate case.

A. Ireland was a very religious country.
B. Most children in Ireland grew up in desperate circumstances.
C. Ireland was a very poor country.
D. Ireland was at war.

_____ 7. In *Angela's Ashes*, what is the author's purpose in having the nuns scold Seamus for singing?
A. to show that Seamus is irresponsible and careless
B. to show that the nuns are cold and serious
C. to show that the nuns care for their patients above all else
D. to show that Ireland was a deeply religious country

____ 8. What is the author's purpose in describing Patricia's offer of a history book to Francis in *Angela's Ashes*?

A. to show that she knows she is seriously ill

B. to show that she has no respect for authority

C. to show that she is desperate for attention

D. to show that she is smart and generous

____ 9. Francis is so enthusiastic about the poem "The Highwayman" because it reflects strong feelings that he has about

A. his illness

B. the nurses

C. Patricia

D. his parents

____ 10. How do the nurses punish Francis for listening to Patricia recite of "The Highwayman"?

A. They move him to a different room.

B. They forbid his parents from visiting.

C. They confiscate his book on English history.

D. They make him go without dinner.

____ 11. In *Angela's Ashes,* the nurse puts Francis in the big ward upstairs to make sure that he

A. feels comfortable

B. has plenty of books to read

C. is isolated from other patients

D. feels safe

____ 12. In *Angela's Ashes,* when the nurse tells Francis that "Patricia Madigan will never know a gray hair," she means that

A. Patricia takes great pride in her personal appearance.

B. Patricia will always have a youthful quality.

C. Patricia has a calm, worry-free personality.

D. Patricia is going to die soon.

Vocabulary and Grammar

____ 13. If a state instituted a *ban* on cell phone use while driving, that means that the use of cell phones in that situation would

A. be encouraged

B. continue as before

C. be illegal

D. increase

____ 14. Which of the following is a *patriotic* act?

A. bringing an apple to your teacher

B. donating your time or money to a charity

C. remembering your sister's birthday

D. singing the national anthem before a ballgame

—— 15. If you were to *guzzle* a soft drink, that would most likely mean that you
    A. were very thirsty   C. believed in sharing with others
    B. were sipping it politely   D. did not care for that flavor

—— 16. Which sentence from *Angela's Ashes* contains a possessive pronoun?
    A. Patricia says she has two books by her bed.
    B. One is a poetry book and that's the one she loves.
    C. The other is a short history of England and do I want it?
    D. She gives it to Seamus, the man who mops the floors every day, and he brings it to me.

—— 17. Which word in this sentence from *Angela's Ashes* is a possessive pronoun?
    The history writer says this is what Catherine says to the Cardinal, who is trying to have her head cut off.
    A. this   C. who
    B. what   D. her

Essay

18. In this excerpt from *Angela's Ashes*, Francis and Patricia use books and literature to keep them from the gloom of the hospital and their illnesses. Nowadays patients have other forms of entertainment in the hospital, including television and, in some cases, Internet access. Which form of entertainment—books and literature, or television and the Internet—do you think would be a better form of entertainment during a long hospital stay? Explain your answer in an essay supported by specific examples.

19. In the excerpt from *Angela's Ashes*, the nurses and Seamus take very different approaches to helping Francis and Patricia. In an essay, describe these differences, and discuss whose approach—Seamus's or the nurses'—in your opinion, is better for the health and well-being of these patients. Support your answer with specific examples from the story.

20. In *Angela's Ashes*, Patricia and Francis form a close friendship by sharing and talking about books and poetry. In an essay, discuss the ways in which literature and books help these two young patients form a friendship that helps them through the loneliness and unhappiness of a serious illness and a long stay in the hospital. Support your answer with specific examples from the text.

21. **Thinking About the Big Question: What is the best way to find the truth?** In the excerpt from *Angela's Ashes*, there are two references to the deep bad feelings many Irish have for the English. Frank McCourt gives the information by quoting Sister Rita and the Kerry nurse, but he does not show how he feels. In an essay, discuss how Frank McCourt might best find the truth that lies behind the bad feelings between the Irish and the English. Include at least one detail from the selection to support your ideas.

Vocabulary Warm-up Word Lists

Study these words from the selections. Then, complete the activities.

Word List A

confident [KAHN fi dent] *adj.* sure of oneself or some outcome
Tara was <u>confident</u> that she did well on her spelling test.

frantic [FRAN tik] *adj.* frenzied or wild with worry, pain, or anger
Lou's <u>frantic</u> calls for the lost puppy sounded through the park.

formed [FAWRMD] *v.* made or organized
The freezing rain <u>formed</u> icicles on the trees.

incidents [IN sud uhntz] *n.* events that happen; occurrences
Certain historic <u>incidents</u> have had a great effect on future events.

nervous [NER vuhs] *adj.* worried or uneasy about something
Cliff was <u>nervous</u> about his first day of seventh grade.

occasions [uh KAY zhuhnz] *n.* times or events
The dance recitals are festive <u>occasions</u>.

persuaded [per SWAYD id] *v.* convinced someone to do or believe something
Linda <u>persuaded</u> her friends to go to the movies instead of to the mall.

suspected [suh SPEKT id] *v.* guessed or supposed
Tim <u>suspected</u> that Daniel was not telling the truth.

Word List B

accustomed [uh KUS tuhmd] *adj.* used to or familiar with something
Sue was <u>accustomed</u> to celebrating holidays with her family.

afterwards [AF ter werdz] *adv.* later
The couple stopped for dinner; <u>afterwards</u>, they walked in the park.

apprehension [ap ree HEN shun] *n.* feeling of dread or worry
Dave's <u>apprehension</u> about the math test grew because he had not studied.

cease [SEES] *v.* to stop
I wish my alarm clock would <u>cease</u> its ringing.

detected [dee TEKT id] *v.* discovered or caught
The cat <u>detected</u> a mouse under the kitchen sink.

evidence [EV i dens] *n.* sign of proof
The dent in Joe's car was <u>evidence</u> of his recent automobile accident.

onward [AHN werd] *adv.* toward a position or time ahead
The soldiers marched <u>onward</u> into the forest.

solemn [SAHL uhm] *adj.* very serious
My brother's last dinner at home before moving away was a <u>solemn</u> occasion.

"Stolen Day" by Sherwood Anderson
"The Night the Bed Fell" by James Thurber
Vocabulary Warm-up Exercises

Exercise A *Fill in each blank in the paragraph below with an appropriate word from Word List A. Use each word only once.*

Max [1] _____ a checkers club at his school last week. Because the club was new, he was [2] _____ that no one would come to the first meeting. Max's friend, Nancy, [3] _____ him to make flyers. After posting the flyers, Max was [4] _____ that enough students would want to join his club. He was right! Nearly fifty students showed up. The games moved at a [5] _____ pace. Still, there were many [6] _____ when students had to wait nearly twenty minutes before playing. Max vowed to bring more boards to the next meeting to avoid such [7] _____. Max never [8] _____ that so many students enjoyed checkers as much as he did. His checkers club became the largest club at school.

Exercise B *Revise each sentence so that the underlined vocabulary word is used in a logical way. Be sure to keep the vocabulary word in your revision.*

Example: The cars drove <u>onward</u> when the traffic light turned red.
The cars drove <u>onward</u> when the traffic light turned green.

1. Tom was very <u>solemn</u> and always laughed and told jokes. _____
   _____

2. Jane fell asleep, and <u>afterwards</u>, she read a book. _____
   _____

3. Lynn <u>detected</u> smoke, so she hung up with 911 and called Gina. _____
   _____

4. Carl was <u>accustomed</u> to waking up early since he had never done it before. _____
   _____

5. The full box in Drake's room is <u>evidence</u> that he ate the cookies. _____
   _____

6. Mary's <u>apprehension</u> was so great that she entered the cave willingly. _____
   _____

7. Dark clouds indicated that the rain was about to <u>cease</u>. _____
   _____

"Stolen Day" by Sherwood Anderson
"The Night the Bed Fell" by James Thurber
Reading Warm-up A

Read the following passage. Pay special attention to the underlined words. Then, read it again, and complete the activities. Use a separate sheet of paper for your written answers.

When Kurt woke up Tuesday morning, he scratched his head. Suddenly, his left arm began to itch, followed by his right leg, his stomach, and his two big toes. Before he knew it, his entire body itched. Kurt guessed that he had the chicken pox. He also <u>suspected</u> that he had got them from Bill Hansen.

Bill had come down with the chicken pox on Monday and had left school before lunchtime. However, at the morning assembly, before Bill began to itch, Kurt had sat next to him. Kurt and Bill always sat next to each other during such <u>occasions</u>; Kurt's last name was Haley, and the teacher insisted that they sit in alphabetical order.

Kurt, as he lay in bed itching, tried to recall each of yesterday's events that had put him in contact with Bill. He listed <u>incidents</u> in his head: when the class <u>formed</u> a line to go outside, when they walked through the halls to the library, and when they traded homework papers to grade. He had spent nearly the entire morning near his classmate! Kurt was now <u>confident</u> that he had the chicken pox, and he didn't appreciate the knowledge. He panicked and let out a <u>frantic</u> cry.

"Mom! Come here! I've got the chicken pox!" he yelled. "What's going to happen to me?"

His mother came in and took a look at his arm. "Let me see," she said, spotting several small, reddish marks that had begun to appear. "You sure did. Don't worry, though. There's no need to be <u>nervous</u>. We'll get some lotion to stop the itch and you'll be fine."

"Really?"

"Of course. But you'll have to stay home from school for a while," replied his mother.

With those words, Kurt's mother <u>persuaded</u> him that having the chicken pox might not be so bad after all.

1. Circle the word that is a synonym for <u>suspected</u>. Write a sentence using the word **suspected**.

2. Underline the words that describe the <u>occasions</u> when Kurt always sits next to Bill. Define **occasions**.

3. Underline the three <u>incidents</u> that put Kurt in contact with Bill. Write a sentence using the word **incidents**.

4. Circle the word that tells what the class <u>formed</u>. Use the same meaning of **formed** in a sentence of your own.

5. Underline the sentence that tells why Kurt became <u>confident</u> that he had caught the chicken pox. Write a synonym for **confident**.

6. Circle the word that gives a clue to the meaning of <u>frantic</u>. Use **frantic** in a sentence.

7. Circle the word that gives a clue to the meaning of <u>nervous</u>. What makes you **nervous**?

8. Underline what Kurt's mother said that <u>persuaded</u> him that having the chicken pox might not be so bad after all. Write a synonym for **persuaded**.

"Stolen Day" by Sherwood Anderson
"The Night the Bed Fell" by James Thurber
Reading Warm-up B

Read the following passage. Pay special attention to the underlined words. Then, read it again, and complete the activities. Use a separate sheet of paper for your written answers.

Sally couldn't sleep. She had been lying in bed for nearly an hour, but the deep, rumbling sound coming from down the hall was keeping her wide awake. It was clear by now that the noise was not going to <u>cease</u> on its own, so Sally decided she would have to be the one to stop it.

One problem kept her from leaping out of bed. She was terrified. She was certain that a sound so frightening could only be <u>evidence</u> of the monster that had lived for years in the hall closet next to her bedroom. Certainly, this noise was proof that the monster was real.

Sally slipped out of bed and tiptoed out into the hallway. She caught a glimpse of her <u>solemn</u> expression in the hall mirror and was momentarily surprised by how serious she looked. The grumbling raged on. She craned her neck forward and listened carefully. Shockingly, she <u>detected</u> that the sound was coming from within her parents' room!

Sally was afraid, but knew she could not turn back. She had to help her parents, and so she crept <u>onward</u>. The growls grew fiercer and Sally became more frightened. Her <u>apprehension</u> mounted as she put her hand on the doorknob to her parents' room. She gathered her courage and swung open the door. Her parents were fast asleep on the bed, and alongside them, snoring loudly enough to wake the entire town, was Peanut the dog.

There was no monster. Even if there had been, Sally was certain that the dog's snoring would have been enough to scare it away. Relieved, she quietly eased the door shut and started back toward her bedroom. As she tucked herself back into her bed, she wondered how her parents were able to sleep through such a racket. Then, Sally realized that after having spent fifteen years living with the dog, they must have become <u>accustomed</u> to his snoring. Sally was sure she could never get used to such an obnoxious noise. Her thoughts began to drift, and a short time <u>afterwards</u>, she fell fast asleep.

1. Circle the word that is a synonym for <u>cease</u>. Write a sentence using the word **cease**.

2. Underline the phrase that tells what Sally felt the sound was <u>evidence</u> of. Write a synonym for the word **evidence**.

3. Circle the word that tells what was <u>solemn</u> about Sally. Write a synonym for the word **solemn**.

4. Underline the phrase that describes what Sally <u>detected</u>. Write a sentence using the word **detected**.

5. Circle the two words that together describe the opposite of <u>onward</u>. Use the word **onward** in a sentence.

6. Underline the sentence that gives clues to the meaning of <u>apprehension</u>. Describe something that might cause **apprehension**.

7. Underline the sentence that gives clues to the meaning of <u>accustomed</u>. What are things you are **accustomed** to?

8. Sally's thoughts drifted. Circle the words that tell what happened <u>afterwards</u>. Define **afterwards**.

"Stolen Day" by Sherwood Anderson
"The Night the Bed Fell" by James Thurber

Writing About the Big Question

What is the best way to find the truth?

Big Question Vocabulary

awareness	believable	conclude	convince	debate
evaluate	evidence	explain	factual	fiction
insight	perceive	reality	reveal	truth

A. *Use one or more words from the list above to complete each sentence.*

1. When there are several different versions of _____, it does not mean that someone is not telling the _____.

2. People describe events differently when they _____ them differently.

3. Four different stories of the same event by four different witnesses can all be _____.

B. *Answer the questions.*

1. What are two things that you and a family member may disagree on?

   _____   _____

2. In a debate about what really happened to start an argument between you and your sibling, how do you convince your family members that your version of the truth is the correct version? Use two vocabulary words in your answer.

   _____

   _____

   _____

C. *Complete the sentence below. Then, use the writing prompt to write a short paragraph connecting the sentence to the Big Question.*

Family members may experience the same event differently because _____

_____

Write two versions of the same event. One will be your perception of the truth. The other will be a different perspective—a fictional account that someone else might think was the truth.

_____

_____

_____

_____

Name _____ Date _____

"Stolen Day" by Sherwood Anderson
"The Night the Bed Fell" by James Thurber
Literary Analysis: Comparing Characters

A **character** is a person or an animal that takes part in the action of a literary work. In literature, you will find characters with a range of personalities and attitudes. For example, a character might be dependable and intelligent but also stubborn. One character might hold traditional values, while another might rebel against them. The individual qualities that make each character unique are called **character traits.**

Writers use the process of **characterization** to create and develop characters. There are two types of characterization:

- **Direct characterization:** The writer directly states or describes the character's traits.
- **Indirect characterization:** The writer reveals a character's personality through his or her words and actions, and through the thoughts, words, and actions of other characters.

DIRECTIONS: *To analyze the use of characterization in "Stolen Day" and "The Night the Bed Fell," complete the following chart. Answer each question with a brief example from the story. Write* not applicable *if you cannot answer a question about one of the characters.*

Character	Words that describe the character directly	What the character says and does	How other characters talk about or act toward the character
The narrator of "Stolen Day"			
The mother in "Stolen Day"			
Briggs Beall in "The Night the Bed Fell"			
The mother in "The Night the Bed Fell"			

"Stolen Day" by Sherwood Anderson
"The Night the Bed Fell" by James Thurber
Vocabulary Builder

Word List

affects   culprit   deluge   ominous   perilous   pungent   solemn

A. DIRECTIONS: *Read each sentence, paying attention to the italicized word from the Word List. If the word is used correctly, write* Correct *on the line. If it is not used correctly, write a new sentence using the word.*

1. The girl's smile was *ominous* as she happily and gently hugged her new puppy.

   _____

2. The *deluge* of rain caused the river to overflow.

   _____

3. The boy was *solemn* after he heard the good news.

   _____

4. A week of rainy weather often *affects* a person's mood negatively.

   _____

5. The mountain climbers had the most *perilous* stretch at the tip of the peak.

   _____

6. The sweet taste of peppermint ice cream was *pungent*.

   _____

7. The old lady was considered the most likely *culprit* when her purse was stolen.

   _____

B. DIRECTIONS: *Write the letter of the word that is most similar in meaning to the word from the Word List.*

____ 1. solemn
   A. joyful   B. silent   C. serious   D. cheerful

____ 2. perilous
   A. happy   B. tired   C. safe   D. dangerous

____ 3. pungent
   A. sharp   B. silly   C. serious   D. light

____ 4. culprit
   A. judge   B. criminal   C. jury   D. lawyer

____ 5. ominous
   A. easy   B. huge   C. threatening   D. pleasant

____ 6. deluge
   A. flood   B. water   C. storm   D. lightening

____ 7. affects
   A. enjoys   B. praises   C. allows   D. changes

Name _____ Date _____

Support for Writing to Compare Literary Works

Before you **write an essay comparing and contrasting** the narrator in "Stolen Day" and "The Night the Bed Fell," jot down your ideas in this graphic organizer. In the overlapping section of each set of boxes, write details that are true of both characters. In the sections on the left, write details that describe the narrator of "Stolen Day," and in the sections on the right, write details that describe the narrator of "The Night the Bed Fell,"

"What are some of each character's traits?

Narrator of "Stolen Day":	Both:	Narrator of "The Night the Bed Fell":

What problems does each character face? How much responsibility does each character have in creating his problem?

Narrator of "Stolen Day":	Both:	Narrator of "The Night the Bed Fell":

What does the character learn from his situation? Which character learns more?

Narrator of "Stolen Day":	Both:	Narrator of "The Night the Bed Fell":

Now, use your notes to write an essay that compares and contrasts the two characters.

"**Stolen Day**" by Sherwood Anderson
"**The Night the Bed Fell**" by James Thurber
Open-Book Test

Short Answer *Write your responses to the questions in this section on the lines provided.*

1. Why does the boy in "Stolen Day" begin to think he has inflammatory rheumatism rather than some other disease? Use details from the story to support your answer.

   _____

   _____

   _____

2. Why does the boy in "Stolen Day" relate the story of the drowned Wyatt boy? Use details from the story to support your answer.

   _____

   _____

   _____

3. Find two examples of description or dialogue from the first two pages of "Stolen Day" that show something about the narrator. Tell what each example reveals. Then, write a brief description of the narrator's character.

Example	What It Reveals

   _____

   _____

4. In "Stolen Day," the narrator describes his brother Earl as solemn. Is the family's reaction to the narrator at the end of the story solemn? Explain.

   _____

   _____

   _____

5. Think about the different members of the narrator's family in "The Night the Bed Fell." Consider what they all have in common. How would you describe them? Explain your answer.

   _____

   _____

   _____

6. In "The Night the Bed Fell," the narrator's family hears ominous creakings. How would you feel if you heard ominous sounds? Explain.

_____

_____

_____

7. Think about the families presented in "Stolen Day" and "The Night the Bed Fell." Both include mothers, fathers, and siblings. How are these same characters presented differently? Use details from the selections in your answer.

_____

_____

_____

8. Contrast the mother in Anderson's "Stolen Day" with Thurber's mother in "The Night the Bed Fell." What is the major difference in how the two women are portrayed? Use details from the selections to support your answer.

_____

_____

_____

9. In what way is the boy in "Stolen Day" a more sympathetic character than Thurber in "The Night the Bed Fell"? Explain your answer.

_____

_____

_____

10. Both the boy in "Stolen Day" and Thurber in "The Night the Bed Fell" have problems dealing with their families. Which boy is more successful, and why? Use details from the selections to support your answer.

_____

_____

_____

Essay

Write an extended response to the question of your choice or to the question or questions your teacher assigns you.

11. Think about how the characters act in "Stolen Day" and "The Night the Bed Fell." In an essay, explain how one character from each of these two selections is ridiculous. Then, tell what this characteristic adds to the selections. Use details from the selections to support your ideas.

12. Consider the main characters from "Stolen Day" and "The Night the Bed Fell." In an essay, discuss which character learns the most and which one learns the least. Use details from the selections to support your ideas.

13. Suppose that the main characters from "Stolen Day" and "The Night the Bed Fell" met. In an essay, describe what they would probably talk about, on which topics they might agree, and on which they might disagree. Use details from the selections to support your ideas.

14. **Thinking About the Big Question: What is the best way to find the truth?**
Choose either "Stolen Day" or "The Night the Bed Fell." In an essay, explain how the selection shows the best way to find the truth. Use examples from the selection to support your response.

Oral Response

15. Go back to question 1, 4, 5, or 8 or to the question your teacher assigns to you. Take a few minutes to expand your answer and prepare an oral response. Find additional details in "Stolen Day" or "The Night the Bed Fell" that support your points. If necessary, make notes to guide your response.

"Stolen Day" by Sherwood Anderson
"The Night the Bed Fell" by James Thurber
Selection Test A

Critical Reading *Identify the letter of the choice that best answers the question.*

_____ 1. In "Stolen Day," when do the narrator's legs begin to hurt?
A. after a long day on the playing field
B. after an accident at recess
C. after he sees Walter fishing
D. after tripping on the way to school

_____ 2. In "Stolen Day," why does the narrator's pain begin to go away as he walks away from the school?
A. The exercise warms his muscles and eases the stiffness of his joints.
B. The farther from the school he gets, the less he thinks about his pain.
C. At first he walks uphill, so when the road levels off, walking becomes easier.
D. He is trying to be brave, and he is using willpower to make the pain go away.

_____ 3. What does the narrator of "Stolen Day" mean when he describes himself as "pretty sore at Mother"?
A. He knows that she is in pain.
B. He loves her and misses her.
C. He feels hurt because she scolded him.
D. He is angry with her for ignoring him.

_____ 4. How does the narrator of "Stolen Day" feel after he catches the big carp?
A. proud   B. disappointed   C. ashamed   D. panicky

_____ 5. The narrator of "Stolen Day" says that his family often laughs at him. How does he react when they do?
A. He wishes he were an orphan.
B. He dislikes everyone he knows.
C. He appreciates the attention.
D. He dislikes being teased.

_____ 6. When the narrator of "Stolen Day" tells his family he has inflammatory rheumatism, their reactions make him
A. cry and run upstairs.
B. feel better in his legs.
C. want to go fishing again.
D. want to visit Walter.

_____ 7. What does the last line from "Stolen Day" say about the narrator?
I was sick all right, but the aching I now had wasn't in my legs or in my back.
A. He has more health problems than he thought.
B. His mother needs to take him to a doctor.
C. He is feeling embarrassed by his family.
D. His headache is getting worse in his room.

____ 8. According to "The Night the Bed Fell," the narrator's aunt believes that burglars have been getting into her house every night for forty years. Which word best describes this belief?

    A. reasonable   **B.** untruthful   **C.** understandable   **D.** unreasonable

____ 9. What starts the confusion in "The Night the Bed Fell"?

    A. Burglars enter the narrator's aunt's house.

    B. Briggs Beall stops breathing while he sleeps.

    C. The cot the narrator is sleeping on collapses.

    D. Gracie Shoaf throws her shoes down the hall.

____ 10. What can you conclude about Briggs Beall in "The Night the Bed Fell"?

    A. He is sleeping soundly through the yelling.

    B. He has stopped breathing.

    C. He is dreaming of demons.

    D. He is awakened easily by the mother.

____ 11. In "The Night the Bed Fell," why does the narrator's mother tug on the attic door?

    A. She is checking to see if Grandfather is asleep in the attic.

    B. She believes her husband's bed has collapsed on top of him.

    C. She needs her husband's help because Briggs has stopped breathing.

    D. She needs her husband's help because her son's cot has collapsed.

____ 12. How would you describe the members of the narrator's family in "The Night the Bed Fell"?

    A. slow and lazy   **C.** witty and clever

    B. unusual and humorous   **D.** wild and dangerous

____ 13. In "The Night the Bed Fell," what is the father's reaction to the scene he discovers when he opens the attic door?

    A. He is ready to chase a burglar.   **C.** He wants to know what's happened.

    B. He's worried someone's been hurt.   **D.** He's glad that everyone is all right.

____ 14. Which characters in "Stolen Day" and "The Night the Bed Fell" seek to gain family sympathy with an ailment?

    A. the narrator of "Stolen Day" and the father in "The Night the Bed Fell"

    B. the father in "Stolen Day" and Briggs Beall in "The Night the Bed Fell"

    C. the mother in "Stolen Day" and the narrator of "The Night the Bed Fell"

    D. the narrator of "Stolen Day" and Briggs Beall in "The Night the Bed Fell"

___ 15. What is similar about the problems faced by the narrators in "Stolen Day" and "The Night the Bed Fell"?

A. Both characters face problems within their families.

B. Both characters are pressured into making a bad decision.

C. Both characters face problems within themselves.

D. Both characters make emotional decisions after being teased.

___ 16. Both narrators in "Stolen Day" and "The Night the Bed Fell" are school-age boys. What do we learn about the narrator in "Stolen Day" that we do not learn about the narrator of "The Night the Bed Fell"?

A. his relationship with his father   C. the kind of house he lives in

B. his interior thoughts and feelings   D. his relationships to cousins

Vocabulary

___ 17. Which sentence below most accurately uses the word *affects*?

A. The family affects the dinner table each night.

B. The trip to the pond affects the fishing poles.

C. Catching a fish affects the boy's mood.

D. Illness affects the medicine cabinet.

___ 18. In "Stolen Day," the narrator's brother Earl is described as *solemn*. How would he most likely act?

A. He would lecture his family.   C. He would be serious and quiet.

B. He would giggle and make jokes.   D. He would be happy and talkative.

___ 19. Which word best describes the odor of the camphor in "The Night the Bed Fell"?

A. ominous   B. pungent   C. perilous   D. solemn

Essay

20. The writers of both "Stolen Day" and "The Night the Bed Fell" portray a boy within his family. Apart from the narrator of each story, which family members does each writer develop? In an essay, describe one minor character from each story. Consider the following questions: What do the characters' words or actions reveal? What do the narrators from each story think of the character?

21. The writers of both "Stolen Day" and "The Night the Bed Fell" develop the characters of school-age boys. In an essay, describe the narrator of "Stolen Day" and the narrator of "The Night the Bed Fell." Begin by telling what each boy is like. Then, consider these questions: What do the boys say? What do they do? How do other characters react to them?

22. **Thinking About the Big Question: What is the best way to find the truth?** People sometimes see their own "truth" in a situation, even if it turns out to be untrue later on. In an essay, explain how either "Stolen Day" or "The Night the Bed Fell" shows the best way to find the truth. Use examples from the selection to support your response.

"**Stolen Day**" by Sherwood Anderson
"**The Night the Bed Fell**" by James Thurber
Selection Test B

Critical Reading *Identify the letter of the choice that best completes the statement or answers the question.*

_____ 1. When the narrator of "Stolen Day" observes Walter fishing at the pond, his reaction can best be described as

A. angry.   C. bitter.

B. sympathetic.   D. envious.

_____ 2. What does the following passage reveal about the narrator of "Stolen Day"?

It was then that my own legs began to hurt.

A. He lacks physical strength.   C. He has a vivid imagination.

B. He may be seriously ill.   D. He cannot keep from lying.

_____ 3. In "Stolen Day," the relationship between the narrator and his mother can best be described as

A. somewhat distant.   C. somewhat tender.

B. extremely tense.   D. extremely close.

_____ 4. In "Stolen Day," the narrator thinks he has inflammatory rheumatism because

A. he wants to go home from school and go fishing.

B. he feels that his mother is not paying enough attention to him.

C. he believes that he has caught the disease from Walter.

D. he knows a lot about the disease and recognizes its symptoms.

_____ 5. What does this passage from "Stolen Day" reveal about the narrator's character?

"So," I thought, "they'll miss me and there'll be a search made. Very likely there'll be someone who has seen me sitting by the pond fishing, and there'll be a big alarm and all the town will turn out and they'll drag the pond."

A. He loves to pull pranks and play practical jokes.

B. He feels neglected and unappreciated by his family.

C. He needs to be at the center of attention all the time.

D. He hopes to find a good excuse for missing school.

_____ 6. The narrator of "Stolen Day" may best be characterized as someone who

A. is afraid of dying.   C. wants to win family sympathy.

B. wants to be like his friends.   D. cannot keep from lying.

_____ 7. In "Stolen Day," how does catching the big carp change the way the narrator's family sees him?

A. He is ignored by his mother.   C. He is a hero in the family.

B. He is laughed at by his brothers.   D. He is not considered a sick boy.

____ 8. In "The Night the Bed Fell," why might the narrator's father have decided that sleeping in the attic is the best way "to be away where he can think"?

A. He has an office in the attic.

C. He is trying to annoy his wife.

B. The attic door has a lock on it.

D. The attic is the only quiet place.

____ 9. What characteristic of the narrator in "The Night the Bed Fell" ends up being a key element in the story?

A. He is a deep sleeper who is slow to arouse.

B. He is a funny boy who is always making a joke.

C. He is a bit strange, like his family members.

D. He is sympathetic and nice toward his family.

____ 10. In "The Night the Bed Fell," what characteristic of the narrator's mother drives the other characters' misunderstanding?

A. She is afraid that the house is on fire.

C. She is overly protective of her sons.

D. She is afraid that the father will die.

B. She has strange dreams.

____ 11. What contributes to the humor in this passage from "The Night the Bed Fell"?

"He's dying!" she shouted.

"I'm all right!" Briggs yelled to reassure her, "I'm all right!"

A. The narrator's mother is talking about her husband, not Briggs.

B. Everyone already knows that no one is in any danger.

C. Everyone is yelling at once, and the dog is barking at Briggs.

D. Briggs is not all right; he is in danger of suffocating.

____ 12. Which character could be described as the most reasonable in "The Night the Bed Fell"?

A. the mother

C. the narrator

B. Aunt Gracie Shoaf

D. Briggs Beall

____ 13. How does the dog, Rex, contribute to the humor and the confusion in the story?

A. He climbs the attic stairs.

C. He jumps on the mother.

B. He barks at Briggs.

D. He tries to rescue the narrator.

____ 14. Both narrators in "Stolen Day" and "The Night the Bed Fell"

A. struggle with their families.

C. feel confident in their abilities.

B. think they are dying.

D. cannot keep from lying.

____ 15. What is a common element to both "Stolen Day" and "The Night the Bed Fell"?

A. false information

C. strict family rules

B. loving mother figures

D. sick children

Vocabulary

____ 16. When the father of the narrator in "Stolen Day" says that inflammatory rheumatism *affects* the heart, he means that it
A. improves its condition.   C. causes it to weaken.
B. causes a change in it.   D. makes it beat faster.

____ 17. Which sentence below most accurately uses the word *solemn*?
A. The mourners were solemn at the funeral.
B. The boys were solemn on the playground.
C. The parents were solemn at the picnic.
D. The hunters were solemn in the forest.

____ 18. What does James Thurber mean by describing his cot as *perilous* when its sides are up?
A. It is unsafe.   C. It is balanced.
B. It is uncomfortable.   D. It is comfortable.

____ 19. A *pungent* odor is one that is
A. pleasing.   B. strong.   C. dangerous.   D. poisonous.

Essay

20. The writers of both "Stolen Day" and "The Night the Bed Fell" portray a boy within his family. Apart from the narrator of each story, which family members does each writer develop? In an essay, compare one minor character from each story. Consider the following questions: How do the writers of "Stolen Day" and "The Night the Bed Fell" develop their characters through *indirect characterization?* How are these characters similar to or different from one another? Cite examples from each text to support your answer.

21. The writers of both "Stolen Day" and "The Night the Bed Fell" develop characters of school-age boys. In an essay, compare the characterizations of each narrator. Consider these questions: What does each writer reveal about the character through indirect characterization? Cite examples from the stories to support your points. What conclusions about the characterization of the main characters of these stories can you draw?

22. **Thinking About the Big Question: What is the best way to find the truth?** Choose either "Stolen Day" or "The Night the Bed Fell." In an essay, explain how the selection shows the best way to find the truth. Use examples from the selection to support your response.

Name _____ Date _____

Narration: Autobiographical Narrative

Prewriting: Gathering Details

Now that you have a focused topic, gather details for your narrative by creating a timeline like the example shown.

Event 1: I met Mark

Event 2: We decided to join the swim team

Event 3: Mark and I compete in the freestyle

Detail 1:
Mark has red hair, carries his knapsack everywhere

Detail 2:
Cold day—everybody lines up nervously by the pool waiting for the coach

Detail 3:
I feel funny about trying to beat Mark. He is probably my best friend.

Event 1:

Event 2:

Event 3:

Detail 1:

Detail 2:

Detail 3:

Drafting: Show, Don't Tell

Bring your story to life by including precise descriptions of places, people, and events and by using dialogue.

1. What specific details can you add to your writing about the person, place, or event?

   _____

   _____

2. How can you make your descriptions of people, places, or events more precise?

   _____

   _____

3. What interesting conversations can you add to your narrative?

   _____

   _____

4. How do these conversations show the characters' feelings and thoughts as they react to events?

   _____

   _____

Writing Workshop—Unit 1, Part 2

Autobiographical Narrative: Integrating Grammar Skills

Checking Agreement Between Pronouns and Antecedents

Pronouns are words that take the place of nouns or other pronouns. The **antecedent** is the word or words to which a pronoun refers. The pronoun you choose must agree with its antecedent in person, number, and gender.

Person	Number	Gender	Pronouns
first (person speaking or writing)	singular plural	male or female male, female, or mixed	I, me, my, mine, myself we, us, our, ours, ourselves
second (person spoken or written to)	singular plural	male or female male, female, or mixed	you, your, yours, yourself you, your, yours, yourselves
third (person spoken or written about)	singular singular singular singular plural	male female male or female neuter male, female, neuter, or mixed	he, him, his, himself she, her, hers, herself he or she, him or her, his or hers, himself or herself it, its, itself they, them, their, theirs, themselves

Identifying Correct Pronoun-Antecedent Agreement

A. DIRECTIONS: *Circle the pronoun in parentheses that correctly completes each sentence. Underline the antecedent with which the pronoun agrees.*

1. Everyone needed to study (his or her, their) notes for the test.
2. Most of the students wrote (his or her, their) notes in spiral notebooks.
3. A few of my friends copied (his or her, their) notes onto a computer.
4. Neither Jack nor Leon could find (his, their) notes.

Fixing Incorrect Pronoun-Antecedent Agreement

B. DIRECTIONS: *Rewrite these sentences so that they use the correct pronouns.*

1. Most of the students enjoyed his or her art classes.

   _____

2. Carlos was learning the skills that you needed to become a sculptor.

   _____

3. Everyone in the pottery class had their chance to use the potter's wheel.

   _____

4. Either Sonya or Penny had two of their fashion designs made into dresses.

   _____

Unit 1 Vocabulary Workshop—1
Using a Dictionary and Thesaurus

A **dictionary** provides information about the origins, meanings, and uses of words. Here is a sample dictionary entry.

Each entry word appears in alphabetical order.

These symbols show how to pronounce the word and divide it into syllables.

This abbreviation shows the word's part of speech. *Destroy* is a verb.

The **etymology** shows the word's origin. This word came into modern English from a Middle English word, which came from an Old French word, which originally came from a Latin word.

destroy ([dis troi´]) *v.* [[ME *destroien* < OFr *destruire* < L *destruere* < *de-*, down + *struere*, to build]] **1** to tear down or demolish **2** to spoil totally; ruin **3** to bring to complete defeat; crush

These are the word's various definitions.

[callout 1—keyed to **destroy**: Each entry word appears in alphabetical order.]
[callout 2—keyed to pronunciation: These symbols show how to pronounce the word and divide it into syllables.]
[callout 3—keyed to *v.*: This abbreviation shows the word's part of speech. *Destroy* is a verb.
[callout 4—keyed to origins: The **etymology** shows the word's origin. This word came into modern English from a Middle English word, which came from an Old French word, which originally came from a Latin word.]
[callout 5—keyed to definitions: These are the word's various definitions.]

A. DIRECTIONS: *Use a dictionary to find the answers to these questions.*

1. How many syllables are in the word **geraniol**? _____

   _____

2. What is the part of speech of **mignonette**? _____

   _____

3. What is the etymology of **evaporate**? _____

   _____

4. How many definitions are listed for **gondola**? _____

   _____

5. What is the definition of **echidna**? _____

   _____

Name _____ Date _____

Unit 1 Vocabulary Workshop—2
Using a Dictionary and Thesaurus

In a **thesaurus,** you will find synonyms, or words that have similar meanings, for most words. If a word can be used as different parts of speech, the thesaurus will provide synonyms for each part of speech. Here is a sample thesaurus entry.

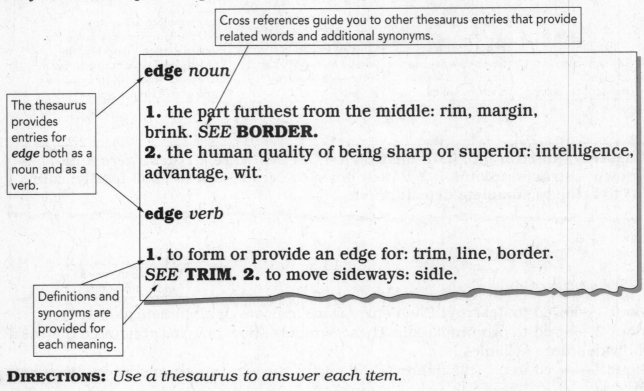

Cross references guide you to other thesaurus entries that provide related words and additional synonyms.

The thesaurus provides entries for *edge* both as a noun and as a verb.

edge *noun*

1. the part furthest from the middle: rim, margin, brink. *SEE* **BORDER.**
2. the human quality of being sharp or superior: intelligence, advantage, wit.

edge *verb*

1. to form or provide an edge for: trim, line, border. *SEE* **TRIM. 2.** to move sideways: sidle.

Definitions and synonyms are provided for each meaning.

B. DIRECTIONS: *Use a thesaurus to answer each item.*

1. What is the part or parts of speech of **smile**? _____

_____

2. What is the definition of the word **express** when it is used as a noun? _____

_____

3. List three synonyms for the verb **laugh.** _____

_____

4. Use a thesaurus to find a synonym for *went* that makes the following sentence more vivid and interesting. Rewrite the sentence using your synonym.

   Sentence: Eager to spread the happy news, Hank *went* home.

   Rewrite: _____

_____

5. Rewrite the following sentence twice, using two different synonyms for the verb *said*. Be sure that your synonyms give the sentences different meanings or tones.

   Sentence: "I don't have time to talk to you now," Sarah *said*.

   Rewrite 1: _____
   Rewrite 2: _____

_____

Unit 1 Resources: Fiction and Nonfiction

Name _____ Date _____

Organizing and Delivering a Narrative Presentation

After choosing your fictional story, fill out the following chart to help you organize and deliver your presentation to the audience you chose.

Title of Fictional Story: _____

What is the central problem of the story?
Who are the main characters?
What are the characters like?
Where and when does the story take place?
How does the story end?
What comment is the story making about people or life in general?

Unit 1: Fiction and Nonfiction
Benchmark Test 2

MULTIPLE CHOICE

Reading Skill: Author's Purpose *Read the selection. Then, answer the questions that follow.*

There's good news and bad news about grizzly bears in the American West. The good news? Their numbers have been increasing in recent years. In 1975, grizzlies made the threatened-species list under the federal Endangered Species Act. The bad news? Some politicians want to abandon federal protection for the bears. Powerful energy corporations want to invade bear habitats to look for oil and gas. Developers want to build houses and shopping malls in bear territory. The bears are also losing their natural food source. Disease is killing the Whitebark Pines that grizzlies eat. If you care about these great bears, please help us save them.

1. Which of the following best expresses the author's purpose in the selection?
   A. to entertain the reader
   B. to convey a mood
   C. to persuade the reader
   D. to reflect on an experience

2. Which of the following sentences provides a clue that helps you determine the author's purpose in the selection?
   A. Their numbers have been increasing in recent years.
   B. In 1975, grizzlies made the threatened-species list.
   C. Disease is killing the Whitebark Pines that grizzlies eat.
   D. If you care about these great bears, you'll want to save them.

3. Which answer choice best expresses the meaning of the term *author's purpose*?
   A. an author's main reason for writing
   B. an author's opinion of a topic
   C. strategies used by an author
   D. a reader's opinion about a topic

Read the selection, which was written by a farmer who suffered a recent drought that threatened his crops. Then, answer the questions that follow.

Sometimes you'll take desperate steps when you have to. Months had gone by without a trace of rain. We needed relief, and lots of it. Our crops were dying. Relief finally came from above: a small airplane sprayed chemicals into the clouds to cause rain. The plane "seeded" the clouds with salt and silver oxide, which caused water droplets that usually evaporate to form clusters and fall as rain. And that's what caused the seeds on the ground to grow.

4. Which background information helps you determine the author's purpose in the selection?
   A. Clouds are seeded using chemicals.
   B. The author is a farmer who underwent a drought.
   C. Some people will take desperate steps.
   D. Cloud seeding is accomplished using a small plane.

5. Which answer choice best expresses the author's purpose in writing this selection?
   A. to express an opinion
   B. to persuade readers
   C. to inform or explain
   D. to entertain readers

Reading Skill: Analyze Structure and Purpose: Workplace Documents

6. What is the difference in purpose between an application and a contract?
   A. An application gives the details of an agreement, whereas a contract protects rights and lists obligations.
   B. An application protects rights and lists obligations, whereas a contract gives the details of an agreement.
   C. An application gives the details of an agreement, whereas a contract helps a person provide information.
   D. An application helps a person provide information, whereas a contract gives the details of an agreement.

7. Which structural feature is likely to be used to organize information in an application?
   A. a diagram with labels
   B. a heading with a blank line
   C. a table of contents
   D. a numbered list of responsibilities

8. Which structural feature is likely to be used to organize information in a contract?
   A. a diagram with labels
   B. a heading with a blank line
   C. a chart displaying data
   D. a numbered list of responsibilities

Literary Analysis: Setting *Read the selection. Then, answer the questions that follow.*

The last wisps of light dissolved. The campers huddled in their flimsy tent, inert and discouraged by the increasingly colder temperature. No one, it seems, had thought to check a weather forecast. Ted brooded silently, a blanket wrapped tightly around his body. Arturo sighed heavily and wracked his brain to think of a plan. James fussed at the others, who ignored him. Outside, the wind moved heavily through the pine trees. When James stuck an arm outside the tent, the air felt cold and moist.

9. What is one element of the setting of this selection?
   A. a campsite in the woods
   B. the characters' thoughts
   C. the author's purpose
   D. the plot of the story

10. Which of the following best describes the mood of the selection?
    A. hopeful
    B. lonely
    C. threatening
    D. energetic

11. Which of the following is part of the setting?
    A. time
    B. tone
    C. dialogue
    D. plot

Literary Analysis: Historical Context *Read the selection. Then, answer the questions that follow.*

During a 17-season baseball career, from 1923 to 1939, legendary first baseman Lou Gehrig led the New York Yankees to eight American League championships and seven World Series championships. Those were the years before baseball became big business and players' stats and records were more newsworthy than their salaries. Gehrig was tagged the "Iron Horse" because he was tireless and tough. He played well, no matter how hot or cold or wet the weather. He played in spite of fevers and bruises and broken bones. He would have been the most famous baseball player of his time, except for one thing: the Babe. Gehrig played in the shadow of Babe Ruth, the most popular player in the sport. Ruth was so loved that even when he struck out, the fans cheered for him. Gehrig once said that, following Ruth at bat, he could have stood on his head at home plate and no one would have noticed.

12. Which of the following best defines the term *historical context*?
    A. the time and place of a story
    B. people who influence events in history
    C. a fictional story based on real events
    D. real events and trends of the story's time

13. According to the author, which of these was important to the public in the early years of baseball?
    A. a player's salary
    B. a player's record
    C. the business of baseball
    D. the management of teams

14. In which way did historical context affect Lou Gehrig?
    A. He led the Yankees to many victories.
    B. He played baseball for seventeen seasons.
    C. He was nicknamed the "Iron Horse."
    D. He found himself overshadowed by fan favorite Babe Ruth.

Literary Analysis: Comparing Characters

15. Which of the following is an example of direct characterization?
    A. two characters explain why they are angry with a friend
    B. the story's narrator describes a character's personality and appearance
    C. one character reacts to another's unkind remark
    D. one character reveals a secret about another

16. Which of the following devices is used in the sentence below?

    The captives heard the guard laugh cruelly as he shut the heavy metal door and left them in darkness.

    A. direct characterization
    B. personification
    C. indirect characterization
    D. simile

17. Which of these character traits best describes Paul?

Paul hurried from sun up to sun down: He fed the livestock, helped his father in the fields, and cared for his little sister when his mother fell ill.

A. hard-working   C. selfish

B. tired   D. intelligent

Vocabulary: Roots

18. What is the meaning of the root -*dict*-, which is shared by *contradict* and *dictate*?

A. to read   C. to speak

B. to write   D. to guess

19. How does the meaning of the word *revitalize* reflect the meaning of the root -*vit*-?

A. When you revitalize something, you put new life into it.

B. When you revitalize something, it takes a different form.

C. When you revitalize something, you set it free.

D. When you revitalize something, you place it somewhere else.

20. Using your knowledge of the root -*manere*-, what does the word *manse* mean in the following sentence?

The manse of the minister was large and imposing.

A. body   C. personality

B. residence   D. church

21. Using your knowledge of the root -*dict*-, what does the word *predict* mean in the following sentence?

My grandmother says that she can predict the weather.

A. approximate   C. wish for something

B. tell beforehand   D. change by will

22. Using your knowledge of the root -*manere*-, what is a key quality of a permanent marker?

A. its ink is very bright   C. its ink does not come off

B. its ink is very dark   D. its ink washes off easily

23. Using your knowledge of the root -*vit*-, what does the word *vital* mean in the following sentence?

The heart is a vital organ.

A. necessary to life   C. located centrally

B. not very important   D. higher than others

Grammar

24. Which sentence contains a personal pronoun that functions as the subject?
    - **A.** Ariel greeted him with a broad smile.
    - **B.** I had not expected to enjoy the play.
    - **C.** Keneshia used her best memory trick.
    - **D.** The officer caught them trying to flee.

25. Which sentence contains a personal pronoun that functions as a direct object?
    - **A.** Mr. Alvarez helped me choose a topic.
    - **B.** We cheered for the rescued sailors.
    - **C.** My best time to exercise is noon.
    - **D.** Are you sure we are not lost?

26. Which personal pronoun in the following sentence functions as a direct object?

    He and I taught them how to tie their shoelaces.
    - **A.** He
    - **B.** I
    - **C.** them
    - **D.** their

27. Which of the following sentences contains a possessive pronoun?
    - **A.** The voice on the recording is mine.
    - **B.** We ate peaches fresh from the tree.
    - **C.** Did I tell you about the movie?
    - **D.** Everyone except Ben has eaten.

28. Which word in the following sentence is a possessive pronoun?

    Kai's brother told me that his dream is to get us a job on a film crew.
    - **A.** Kai's
    - **B.** me
    - **C.** his
    - **D.** us

29. What is the antecedent of the pronoun *its* in the following sentence?

    The book had Julian's name written inside its cover.
    - **A.** book
    - **B.** Julian's
    - **C.** name
    - **D.** cover

30. Which pronoun best completes the following sentence?

    Many actors travel around the country to promote _____ latest movies.
    - **A.** her
    - **B.** theirs
    - **C.** their
    - **D.** his

WRITING

31. Write the "lead," or introductory paragraph, for a news report about a recent event at school, in your neighborhood, or in your town. Answer the questions *who, what, when, where, why,* and *how* in the paragraph. Do not use more than four sentences in your paragraph.

32. Imagine that you have an idea for a magazine article and you would like to have it published. Write a brief letter to the editor of an imaginary magazine in which you convince him or her that your story is worth publishing. Before you write, jot down the topic of your article, a summary of what you intend to say about the topic, and at least two reasons why readers would be interested in the topic. Remember to include a date, a greeting, a closing, and a signature in your letter.

Name _____ Date _____

33. Think of a humorous event that happened to you recently or in the past. Imagine that you are preparing to write an autobiographical narrative in which you describe the event. Make a timeline of the event. On the timeline, list at least three important details in chronological order. Use complete sentences to write the details.

Name _____ Date _____

Vocabulary in Context

Identify the answer choice that best completes the statement.

1. Because of the rain, all activities today will take place in the _____ .
   A. gym
   B. community
   C. laboratory
   D. university

2. His face quickly changed to a puzzled _____ .
   A. exertion
   B. expression
   C. exercise
   D. evidence

3. Happily, all of my three wishes were _____ .
   A. granted
   B. dodged
   C. inspected
   D. attended

4. When Randi asked to drive, her mother _____ .
   A. contrasted
   B. concerned
   C. consented
   D. constructed

5. Draw a circle and measure its _____ .
   A. oval
   B. triangle
   C. diameter
   D. kilometer

6. He knew he was dreaming when he saw a _____ in the water.
   A. tuna
   B. squid
   C. muskrat
   D. mermaid

7. Instead of fruit, she chose a _____ .
   A. limes
   B. melon
   C. sausage
   D. strawberries

8. A penalty was called by the _____ .
   A. referee
   B. majority
   C. criminals
   D. communists

9. The mother looked at her son with love and _____ .
   A. affection
   B. objection
   C. profession
   D. combination

10. This water is so clean because it has been _____ .
    A. reduced
    B. revived
    C. filtered
    D. tempered

11. When you add the numbers, you must do so _____ .
    A. absolutely
    B. accurately
    C. occasionally
    D. apologetically

12. There were so many people at the concert that they were too _____ to count.
    A. mild
    B. positive
    C. powerful
    D. numerous

13. She became a great cook because she was _____ by her mother.
    A. inherited
    B. inspired
    C. indicated
    D. identified

14. She held a daisy and, one at a time, picked off the _____ .
    A. petals
    B. carnations
    C. dandelions
    D. undergrowth

15. The baby's curls formed what appeared to be a _____ around his head.
    A. guardian
    B. shrine
    C. virtue
    D. halo

16. She loved to dance and was thrilled to be a _____ .
    A. boxer
    B. pianist
    C. challenger
    D. ballerina

17. Dad's pictures and his descriptions of them are glued in this _____ .
    A. bible
    B. textbook
    C. photograph
    D. scrapbook

18. I meant to do the right thing, and I assure you that I had good _____ .
    A. traditions
    B. destiny
    C. intentions
    D. traits

19. When she left the room, she left the door _____ .
    A. anew
    B. carelessly
    C. ajar
    D. pried

20. Don't eat too much or too little—eat _____ .
    A. dolefully
    B. moderately
    C. listlessly
    D. simultaneously

Diagnostic Tests and Vocabulary in Context
Use and Interpretation

The Diagnostic Tests and Vocabulary in Context were developed to assist teachers in making the most appropriate assignment of *Prentice Hall Literature* program selections to students. The purpose of these assessments is to indicate the degree of difficulty that students are likely to have in reading/comprehending the selections presented in the *following* unit of instruction. Tests are provided at six separate times in each grade level—a *Diagnostic Test* (to be used prior to beginning the year's instruction) and a *Vocabulary in Context,* the final segment of the Benchmark Test, appearing at the end of each of the first five units of instruction. Note that the tests are intended for use not as summative assessments for the prior unit, but as guidance for assigning literature selections in the upcoming unit of instruction.

The structure of all Diagnostic Tests and Vocabulary in Context in this series is the same. All test items are four-option, multiple-choice items. The format is established to assess a student's ability to construct sufficient meaning from the context sentence to choose the only provided word that fits both the semantics (meaning) and syntax (structure) of the context sentence. All words in the context sentences are chosen to be "below-level" words that students reading at this grade level should know. All answer choices fit *either* the meaning or structure of the context sentence, but only the correct choice fits *both* semantics and syntax. All answer choices—both correct answers and incorrect options—are key words chosen from specifically taught words that will occur in the subsequent unit of program instruction. This careful restriction of the assessed words permits a sound diagnosis of students' current reading achievement and prediction of the most appropriate level of readings to assign in the upcoming unit of instruction.

The assessment of vocabulary in context skill has consistently been shown in reading research studies to correlate very highly with "reading comprehension." This is not surprising as the format essentially assesses comprehension, albeit in sentence-length "chunks." Decades of research demonstrate that vocabulary assessment provides a strong, reliable prediction of comprehension achievement— the purpose of these tests. Further, because this format demands very little testing time, these diagnoses can be made efficiently, permitting teachers to move forward with critical instructional tasks rather than devoting excessive time to assessment.

It is important to stress that while the Diagnostic and Vocabulary in Context were carefully developed and will yield sound assignment decisions, they were designed to *reinforce*, not supplant, teacher judgment as to the most appropriate instructional placement for individual students. Teacher judgment should always prevail in making placement—or indeed other important instructional—decisions concerning students.

Diagnostic Tests and Vocabulary in Context
Branching Suggestions

These tests are designed to provide maximum flexibility for teachers. Your *Unit Resources* books contain the 40-question **Diagnostic Test** and 20-question **Vocabulary in Context** tests. At *PHLitOnline,* you can access the Diagnostic Test and complete 40-question Vocabulary in Context tests. Procedures for administering the tests are described below. Choose the procedure based on the time you wish to devote to the activity and your comfort with the assignment decisions relative to the individual students. Remember that your judgment of a student's reading level should always take precedence over the results of a single written test.

Feel free to use different procedures at different times of the year. For example, for early units, you may wish to be more confident in the assignments you make—thus, using the "two-stage" process below. Later, you may choose the quicker diagnosis, confirming the results with your observations of the students' performance built up throughout the year.

The **Diagnostic Test** is composed of a single 40-item assessment. Based on the results of this assessment, make the following assignment of students to the reading selections in Unit 1:

Diagnostic Test Score	Selection to Use
If the student's score is 0–25	more accessible
If the student's score is 26–40	more challenging

Outlined below are the three basic options for administering **Vocabulary in Context** and basing selection assignments on the results of these assessments.

1. For a one-stage, quicker diagnosis using the *20-item* test in the *Unit Resources:*

Vocabulary in Context Test Score	Selection to Use
If the student's score is 0–13	more accessible
If the student's score is 14–20	more challenging

2. If you wish to confirm your assignment decisions with a *two-stage* diagnosis:

Stage 1: Administer the 20-item test in the *Unit Resources*	
Vocabulary in Context Test Score	**Selection to Use**
If the student's score is 0–9	more accessible
If the student's score is 10–15	(Go to Stage 2.)
If the student's score is 16–20	more challenging

Stage 2: Administer items 21–40 from *PHLitOnline*	
Vocabulary in Context Test Score	**Selection to Use**
If the student's score is 0–12	more accessible
If the student's score is 13–20	more challenging

3. If you base your assignment decisions on the full 40-item **Vocabulary in Context** from *PHLitOnline:*

Vocabulary in Context Test Score	Selection to Use
If the student's score is 0–25	more accessible
If the student's score is 26–40	more challenging

Name _____ Date _____

Grade 7—Benchmark Test 1
Interpretation Guide

For remediation of specific skills, you may assign students the relevant Reading Kit Practice and Assess pages indicated in the far-right column of this chart. You will find rubrics for evaluating writing samples in the last section of your Professional Development Guidebook.

Skill Objective	Test Items	Number Correct	Reading Kit
Reading Skill			
Context Clues	1, 2, 3, 4		pp. 2, 3
Locate Types of Information	5, 6, 7		pp. 4, 5
Literary Analysis			
Narration	8, 9, 10		pp. 6, 7
Point of View	11, 12, 13, 14		pp. 8, 9
Fiction and Nonfiction	15, 16, 17		pp. 10, 11
Vocabulary			
Prefixes *re-, in-, trans-, ac-*	18, 19, 20, 21, 22, 23		pp. 12, 13
Grammar			
Common and Proper Nouns	24, 25		pp. 14, 15
Possessive Nouns	26, 27, 28		pp. 16, 17
Plural Nouns	29, 30		pp. 18, 19
Writing			
Description with Hyperbole	31	Use rubric	pp. 22, 23
Comparison-and-Contrast Essay	32	Use rubric	pp. 20, 21
Description	33	Use rubric	pp. 24, 25

Name _____ Date _____

Grade 7—Benchmark Test 2
Interpretation Guide

For remediation of specific skills, you may assign students the relevant Reading Kit Practice and Assess pages indicated in the far-right column of this chart. You will find rubrics for evaluating writing samples in the last section of your Professional Development Guidebook.

Skill Objective	Test Items	Number Correct	Reading Kit
Reading Skill			
Author's Purpose	1, 2, 3, 4, 5		pp. 26, 27
Analyze Structure and Purpose: Workplace Documents	6, 7, 8		pp. 28, 29
Literary Analysis			
Setting	9, 10, 11		pp. 30, 31
Historical Context	12, 13, 14		pp. 32, 33
Comparing Characters	15, 16, 17		pp. 34, 35
Vocabulary			
Roots -vit-, -manere-, -dict-	18, 19, 20, 21, 22, 23		pp. 36, 37
Grammar			
Personal Pronouns	24, 25, 26		pp. 38, 39
Possessive Pronouns	27, 28		pp. 40, 41
Pronoun-Antecedent Agreement	29, 30		pp. 42, 43
Writing			
News Report	31		pp. 46, 47
Letter	32	Use rubric	pp. 48, 49
Autobiographical Narrative	33	Use rubric	pp. 50, 51

ANSWERS

Big Question Vocabulary—1, p. 1

1. evaluate; He needs to judge how good each act is.
2. conclude; She wants to bring the meeting to a close.
3. reveal; He wants to make the thief's identity known.
4. convince; She wants to persuade them to share her opinion.
5. perceive; We were trying to see the mountain.

Big Question Vocabulary—2, p. 2

A.
1. No; Fiction is about imaginary people and events. A work of nonfiction would be a better source.
2. Yes; Photographs and eyewitness reports would provide facts about the sporting event.
3. No; A debate is a discussion between people with different, and opposing, views.

B. Answers will vary. Possible responses are shown.
1. Fiction is about imaginary people and events, while reality is real life. A short story is an example of fiction; a news story reflects reality.
2. black smoke, extreme heat, crackling sounds, sparks

Big Question Vocabulary—3, p. 3

Answers will vary. Possible responses are shown.

1. Cats have four legs. Cats are small mammals. Cats have good eyesight.

   It is strange, but believable, that cats can see clearly in the dark of night.

2. It is a middle school. It is located in Austin, Texas. It is named after Rosa Parks.

   Factual information about my school includes this statement: It is a middle school.

3. They need to know about sharp tools. They need to know about bicycle safety. They need to know to protect themselves from strangers.

   It's important to explain to young children about bicycle safety.

4. Friends are helpful. They provide good company. They share your interests.

   An important insight I have about friendship is that friends make good company.

5. Some have leaves. Some have needles. All have roots.

   There are many truths about trees, including that some have leaves and others have needles.

Diagnostic Test 1, p. 5

MULTIPLE CHOICE

1. ANS: C
2. ANS: D
3. ANS: B
4. ANS: A
5. ANS: C
6. ANS: D
7. ANS: B
8. ANS: B
9. ANS: C
10. ANS: D
11. ANS: A
12. ANS: C
13. ANS: A
14. ANS: A
15. ANS: C
16. ANS: D
17. ANS: A
18. ANS: B
19. ANS: A
20. ANS: C
21. ANS: D
22. ANS: B
23. ANS: D
24. ANS: A
25. ANS: A
26. ANS: C
27. ANS: C
28. ANS: D
29. ANS: B
30. ANS: D
31. ANS: A
32. ANS: B
33. ANS: B
34. ANS: C
35. ANS: A
36. ANS: C
37. ANS: D
38. ANS: C
39. ANS: D
40. ANS: A

"Three-Century Woman" by Richard Peck
"The Fall of the *Hindenburg*" by Michael Morrison

Vocabulary Warm-up Exercises, p. 14

A.
1. anchor
2. reputation
3. broadcasting
4. angle
5. technology
6. interview
7. achievement
8. photographer

B. Sample Answers

1. F; If your voice is wavering, it is shaky and uncertain.
2. T; It would be unpleasant to be around a person who is in a foul mood.
3. F; Only human beings are members of humanity.
4. F; A majestic person shows dignity, beauty, and grandeur, so you would not be likely to pity him or her.
5. T; *Fantastic* means "terrific" or "amazing," so if you had a fantastic time, you would probably want to return.
6. F; *Pondered* means "considered carefully," so if you pondered a decision, you took a long time to think about it; you did not make a snap judgment.
7. F; *Approximately* means "about," so if you know the exact number you know the precise number, not the approximate number.
8. T; If you have many complaints about you health, you are dissatisfied with your health or have discomforts, so you should see a doctor.

Reading Warm-up A, p. 15

Words that students are to circle appear in parentheses.

Sample Answers

1. (newscasters or news analysts); A news anchor coordinates a news broadcast.
2. you must be able to write and speak clearly and effectively; Devin has a reputation as an excellent chess player.
3. it takes a great deal of training and preparation; An achievement I am proud of is learning first aid.
4. (satellite); Technology is the methods or machines of applied science.
5. (witnesses and experts); I would ask what was the most difficult story he or she ever covered and why it was so difficult.
6. taking pictures at the scene of breaking stories; If I were a professional photographer, I would most enjoy taking pictures of wild animals.
7. slant; For a story about a lost dog, I would use the angle of the child whose dog was lost.
8. take courses in radio and television news and production; *Broadcasting* means "having to do with radio or television."

Reading Warm-up B, p. 16

Words that students are to circle appear in parentheses.

Sample Answers

1. what it will be like to grow old; "thought about"
2. (Old age); *human*
3. wonderful; The skiing this winter has been fantastic.
4. (weakened lung function); Two complaints about old age that I have heard are aching muscles and a poor memory.

5. (unpleasant); One thing that can put me in a foul mood is a week of gloomy weather.
6. uncertainly; Because the old man was wavering when he walked, the doctor recommended that he use a cane.
7. always exercised regulary; *Majestic* means "having or showing great dignity, beauty, and grandeur."
8. 80 percent of the strength he or she had at age twenty-five; *Approximately* means "about" or "around."

Richard Peck

Listening and Viewing, p. 17

Sample answers and guidelines for evaluation:

Segment 1. Richard Peck was first inspired by his students and now gets ideas by listening to and observing young people interacting. Students may suggest that they would write about their own experiences, friendships, and families and other things that are important to them.

Segment 2. Fiction can be "truer" to readers because the characters can make a greater impression and be more convincing. Students may suggest that viewpoint, voice, dialogue, and action can make fiction more realistic and convincing, so that it seems almost true.

Segment 3. Richard Peck believes that the first chapter holds clues to the ending, so once he has written the ending, he must add clues to the first chapter. Students may suggest that they would do research, use a typewriter, take notes, or remove twenty words from each page because those methods contribute to the completion or improvement of a draft.

Segment 4. Richard Peck believes that readers have an advantage because literature is omnipresent and readers have access to much more information than nonreaders do. Students may point to books that have had a particularly strong impact on them, teaching them about themselves or someone else.

Unit 1: Learning About Fiction and Nonfiction, p. 18

A. 1. fiction
2. nonfiction
3. nonfiction
4. fiction
5. nonfiction

B. fiction; It involves a family traveling to a distant galaxy.

"The Three-Century Woman" by Richard Peck

Model Selection: Fiction, p. 19

1. Megan (the narrator), her mother, her great-grandmother, news reporters
2. inside
3. It is told from the first-person point of view.

4. The clues that reveal that the story is told from the first-person point of view are the narrator's use of the pronouns *me, my, I,* and so on.

5. The story takes place on January 1, 2001.

6. The story takes place in an "elder care facility" in a suburb somewhere in the United States.

7. The setting is realistic. The car, the mall, the Christmas tree in the lobby of the elder care facility, and Mrs. Breckenridge's bare room are all realistic details.

8. realistic

9. Realistic plot elements include Megan's attitude about visiting her great-grandmother, her interest in the mall, and her mother's cell-phone conversation with her aunt.

10. The conflict is between Mrs. Breckenridge and the news reporters: she is annoyed with them because she believes they see her as a news story rather than a person.

"The Fall of the *Hindenburg*"
by Michael Morrison

Model Selection: Nonfiction, p. 20

A. 1. It discusses the crash of the *Hindenburg*.

2. The crash took place on May 6, 1937, at the Lakehurst Naval Air Station, in New Jersey.

3. Sample answer: The airship weighed 242 tons; it burst into flames as it tried to land; thirty-six people died in the fire.

4. It was a tragedy, and the cause of the fire is still uncertain.

5. Sample answer: The Nazis were in power in Germany.

B. Sample answer: Morrison's purpose was to inform readers about an event that happened almost seventy years ago.

"The Three-Century Woman" by Richard Peck
"The Fall of the *Hindenburg*"
by Michael Morrison

Open-Book Test, p. 21

Short Answer

1. It is fiction. The events are made up—we do not have the technology to send manned missions to Jupiter.
   Difficulty: *Easy*   **Objective:** *Literary Analysis*

2. It is nonfiction. An eyewitness is someone who saw what happened. A journal entry is that person's record of events.
   Difficulty: *Average*   **Objective:** *Literary Analysis*

3. I need to know if the people and events are real or made up. If the book tells about real people and events, it is nonfiction. If it tells about made-up characters or events, even if parts of it are real, it is fiction.
   Difficulty: *Average*   **Objective:** *Literary Analysis*

4. An intersection is a place where two or more roads cross. Megan's mother seems to speed up and not pay much attention as she drives through it without looking for other cars.
   Difficulty: *Average*   **Objective:** *Vocabulary*

5. Mom says, "They've got her done up like a Barbie Doll." She is annoyed because she thinks someone at the nursing home has dressed Great-grandma in a way that looks ridiculous.
   Difficulty: *Challenging*   **Objective:** *Interpretation*

6. Great-grandma is not telling the truth, but she wants the reporters to think that she is. So she takes a minute to ponder, or think deeply, to make it appear as if she's trying to remember what happened.
   Difficulty: *Challenging*   **Objective:** *Vocabulary*

7. Sample answer: Although Great-grandma refers to real disasters such as the San Francisco earthquake and the explosion of the Hindenburg, she is a character, not a real person. Characters are an element of fiction.
   Difficulty: *Average*   **Objective:** *Literary Analysis*

8. Sample answer: Great-grandma is a venerable person. She is more than 100 years old, so she is worthy of respect by reason of age.
   Difficulty: *Average*   **Objective:** *Vocabulary*

9. He meant "How awful it is to see this tragedy happening to people." He is watching the blimp burn and explode, and he sees some people jumping and others not making it out.
   Difficulty: *Challenging*   **Objective:** *Interpretation*

10. Sample answer: Facts: May 1937; traveling from Europe; landed at Lakehurst, New Jersey; Fiction: she was on it; she walked away; her dress burned. She added the details to make the story sound believable.
    Difficulty: *Average*   **Objective:** *Interpretation*

Essay

11. Students should note that the article is filled with facts about a real-life event and should list facts from the article. Some may point out that headings make information easy to find and quotes are included from people who witnessed the event.
    Difficulty: *Easy*   **Objective:** *Essay*

12. Students should choose a character to discuss. For example, the narrator has mixed feelings about the nursing home. She says she "hated going" and notes that the locked door keeps "the inmates from escaping," but she also acknowledges that it doesn't smell bad. The action of the story also brings the setting of a TV studio to the nursing home. Their difference is emphasized by the fact that the narrator observes that while Great-grandma is usually dozing, today she is dressed up for the cameras.
    Difficulty: *Average*   **Objective:** *Essay*

13. Students should write a brief news report. Some students may write that Great-grandma is still deserving of respect and find it funny that she fooled a roomful of

reporters. Others may write that she should not be as respected because she lied.

Difficulty: *Challenging* **Objective:** *Essay*

14. Students should observe that Great-grandma knows perfectly well that what she is telling the reporters is not wholly true. She uses true facts she has read in books but then makes up other parts of the stories so that if someone checks her version of the truth, she won't be found out. Great-grandma knows that the truth of the matter is she is interesting only because she is old, a truth that she does not particularly like. By taking matters into her own hands, she creates a truth that she does like.

Difficulty: *Average* **Objective:** *Essay*

Oral Response

15. Oral responses should be clear, well organized, and well supported by appropriate examples from the selections.

Difficulty: *Average* **Objective:** *Oral Interpretation*

Selection Test A, p. 24

Learning About Fiction and Nonfiction

1. ANS: B	DIF: Easy	OBJ: Literary Analysis
2. ANS: C	DIF: Easy	OBJ: Literary Analysis
3. ANS: B	DIF: Easy	OBJ: Literary Analysis
4. ANS: D	DIF: Easy	OBJ: Literary Analysis
5. ANS: A	DIF: Easy	OBJ: Literary Analysis

Critical Reading

6. ANS: A	DIF: Easy	OBJ: Literary Analysis
7. ANS: D	DIF: Easy	OBJ: Literary Analysis
8. ANS: B	DIF: Easy	OBJ: Comprehension
9. ANS: A	DIF: Easy	OBJ: Comprehension
10. ANS: B	DIF: Easy	OBJ: Interpretation
11. ANS: C	DIF: Easy	OBJ: Comprehension
12. ANS: D	DIF: Easy	OBJ: Comprehension
13. ANS: B	DIF: Easy	OBJ: Comprehension
14. ANS: D	DIF: Easy	OBJ: Interpretation
15. ANS: B	DIF: Easy	OBJ: Comprehension

Essay

16. Students should note that Mrs. Breckenridge probably means that although she is old and frail, she was once as young and strong as Megan. She may mean that someday Megan, too, will be old. She may be hoping that Megan will understand what it is like to live for a hundred years.

Difficulty: *Easy*

Objective: *Essay*

17. Students might note any of the factual material contained in the beginning of the article: the size and weight of the airship, its composition and layout, the number of passengers and crewmen on board, where it

had taken off from, and so on. They should include the information that would have been available to an eye-witness: where the ship was landing, how it was being landed, what happened, how quickly it happened, how passengers and crew members reacted, and so on.

Difficulty: *Easy*

Objective: *Essay*

18. Students should observe that Great-grandma knows well that what she is telling the reporters is not totally true. She uses facts she has read in books but then makes up other parts of the stories. That way, if someone checks her version of the truth, she won't be found out. Great-grandma knows that people think she is interesting only because she is old. This is a fact that she does not particularly like. By making up her own version of things, she creates a truth that she does like.

Difficulty: *Average*

Objective: *Essay*

Selection Test B, p. 27

Learning About Fiction and Nonfiction

1. ANS: C	DIF: Average	OBJ: Literary Analysis
2. ANS: D	DIF: Average	OBJ: Literary Analysis
3. ANS: B	DIF: Average	OBJ: Literary Analysis
4. ANS: A	DIF: Challenging	OBJ: Literary Analysis
5. ANS: C	DIF: Average	OBJ: Literary Analysis
6. ANS: D	DIF: Challenging	OBJ: Literary Analysis

Critical Reading

7. ANS: A	DIF: Average	OBJ: Literary Analysis
8. ANS: B	DIF: Average	OBJ: Literary Analysis
9. ANS: A	DIF: Average	OBJ: Comprehension
10. ANS: C	DIF: Average	OBJ: Comprehension
11. ANS: B	DIF: Average	OBJ: Interpretation
12. ANS: A	DIF: Challenging	OBJ: Interpretation
13. ANS: C	DIF: Average	OBJ: Interpretation
14. ANS: C	DIF: Challenging	OBJ: Interpretation
15. ANS: A	DIF: Average	OBJ: Comprehension
16. ANS: B	DIF: Average	OBJ: Literary Analysis
17. ANS: C	DIF: Challenging	OBJ: Literary Analysis
18. ANS: A	DIF: Challenging	OBJ: Comprehension
19. ANS: C	DIF: Challenging	OBJ: Interpretation
20. ANS: B	DIF: Average	OBJ: Literary Analysis

Essay

21. Students should note that Megan shows that she has enjoyed herself and has perhaps learned something about people during the visit. She kisses her great-grandmother and tells her that she will visit more often. Students should recognize that Megan has gained respect and admiration for her great-grandmother.

Difficulty: *Average*

Objective: *Essay*

22. Students should note that the airship, like an ocean-liner or a jet, could travel long distances (across the Atlantic Ocean) and carry passengers and a crew. It was like an oceanliner in that it contained sleeping quarters, a library, a dining room, and a lounge. They should note that unlike a ship or a jet, it was fueled by hydrogen, and for its size it carried relatively few passengers and a relatively large crew.

Difficulty: *Average*

Objective: *Essay*

23. Students should observe that Great-grandma knows perfectly well that what she is telling the reporters is not wholly true. She uses facts she has read in books but then makes up other parts of the stories so that if some-one checks her version of the truth, she won't be found out. Great-grandma knows that the truth of the matter is she is interesting only because she is old, a truth that she does not particularly like. By taking matters into her own hands, she creates a truth that she does like.

Difficulty: *Average*

Objective: *Essay*

"Papa's Parrot" by Cynthia Rylant

Vocabulary Warm-up Exercises, p. 31

A. 1. stroll
2. twilight
3. bins
4. roasted
5. maple
6. furnace
7. sample
8. merely

B. Sample Answers
1. No, an ambulance is a vehicle that carries people to a hospital, so if you were in an ambulance, you would not be going home.
2. No, a batch is a number of things, more than just two.
3. Yes, operas are plays set to music, so if you listen to operas, you will hear a lot of music.
4. No, a strawberry milkshake is flavored with strawberries.
5. Yes, someone would most likely feel embarrassed, or uncomfortable, if his or her private writing was made public.
6. No, a romantic novel would describe adventure, love, or excitement, not ordinary people doing ordinary things.
7. No, a table near a smelly garbage can would be a bad place for a picnic because the odor from the garbage would be unpleasant.
8. No, if someone were arriving somewhere, he or she would be coming to a place, not leaving it.

Reading Warm-up A, p. 32

Words that students are to circle appear in parentheses.

Sample Answers
1. (dim); In March, there was more daylight.
2. After cutting a gash in a maple tree, workers collected the sap in a bucket. They heated the sap over hot stones or an open fire. At last the fire would get hot enough to boil the sap; I eat maple-flavored smoked turkey.
3. a furnace heats fuel to warm a house; A furnace is a machine that burns fuel to make heat.
4. (meat and vegetables); I eat roasted peanuts.
5. (candies); Another word for *bins* is *containers*.
6. (sweets); *Sample* means "to try one of a group of items to see if you like it."
7. (maple sugaring); *Merely* means "only" or "simply."
8. (among the maple trees); I like to stroll along the street and look at shop windows.

Reading Warm-up B, p. 33

Words that students are to circle appear in parentheses.

Sample Answers
1. (in her hometown); The passengers were arriving at the gate to board the plane.
2. (She did not know the woman well); *Embarrassed* means "uncomfortable" or "ashamed."
3. (her perfume); *Smelly* means "having a bad odor."
4. She had ridden in an ambulance and saved soldiers' lives. She had had many adventures; *Romantic* means "having a mood or spirit of love, adventure, or excitement."
5. An ambulance takes sick or wounded people to a hospital, and a nurse is trained to care for the sick and wounded. If a nurse rode in an ambulance, she or he could care for people on the way to the hospital.
6. Soap operas are dramatic daytime television shows with continuing stories. Musical operas are plays in which the words are sung.
7. (homemade cookies); A batch is a number of things made in a group.
8. (ice cream)

Writing About the Big Question, p. 34

A. 1. insight
2. reveal
3. perceive
4. conclude

B. Sample Answers
1. Yes. My cousin, Steven would never talk to me, and I thought that was **evidence** that he hated me.
2. Yes. One day, I was upset because I had a fight with my best friend. Steven was really nice to me. Later, he **explained** that he never talked to me because he is shy and I am so outgoing. I found his explanation **believable**.

my grandma's illness/my parents took me aside to talk to me about it.

I could use this in a fictional story about a character whose grandmother was dying. I could change the names and even the feelings involved and use the facts about the illness. Or I could use the feelings in the story and change the facts about the illness.

"Papa's Parrot" by Cynthia Rylant

Reading: Use Context Clues to Unlock the Meaning, p. 35

Sample Answers

1. Clue: "and were still"; Meaning: continued to be
2. Clue: "joked"; Meaning: annoying by poking fun
3. Clues: "fat," "stomach"; Meaning: fat (like the fat of a whale, called blubber)

Literary Analysis: Narrative Writing, p. 36

A. 5
B. 7
C. 9
D. 3
E. 10
F. 6
G. 1
H. 4
I. 2
J. 8

Vocabulary Builder, p. 37

A. 1. Yes, they were pleased that Mr. Tillian was back and the shop was open again.
2. No, they were not pleased because Harry was not paying attention to them.
3. Yes. He held on tight to his stand in the cage.
4. Harry stepped in to handle the deliveries of candy and the daily business.
5. Yes, he didn't think very highly of it.
6. candies and nuts, such as jawbreakers and peppermints

B. 1. It means you like it because *replay* means to play again.
2. He is placing the players in different places because *reposition* means to position again.
3. No, it means you are thinking about it again with some doubt because *rethink* means to think again.

Enrichment: Science, p. 38

Sample Answers

1. The number of parrots has decreased because parrots have been captured to be sold as pets and because their habitat has been destroyed to make way for farming and housing.
2. They are setting aside reserves where wildlife is protected. They are building imitation trees in which parrots can build their nests. They are raising parrot chicks in captivity and releasing them in the wild.
3. Both people who live in the tropics and tourists enjoy seeing parrots.

Open-Book Test, p. 39

Short Answer

1. The word *merely* means "only." Its meaning is suggested by the words *Though* and *owned a candy and nut shop*. The author is hinting that owning a candy and nut shop is not a big accomplishment.
   Difficulty: *Challenging*   **Objective:** *Reading*
2. Harry and his father had been close, and Harry had stopped in to see his father at the store. Then, when Harry entered junior high school, he didn't come by as often because he became interested in other things like video games, records, and going to burger places.
   Difficulty: *Easy*   **Objective:** *Interpretation*
3. Because Harry is not visiting the store anymore, Mr. Tillian decides to buy a pet so he can have company. He chooses a parrot, an animal that can talk, to have someone to talk to.
   Difficulty: *Average*   **Objective:** *Interpretation*
4. Ignored means "paid no attention to." Mr. Tillian may have pretended not to listen to Harry. He also continued to keep the parrot as a pet, which shows he paid no attention to Harry's concerns.
   Difficulty: *Easy*   **Objective:** *Vocabulary*
5. After Harry's father goes to the hospital, Harry starts to feel a sense of responsibility toward his father and the store that he didn't feel before. He decides to help out in the store while his father is in the hospital.
   Difficulty: *Challenging*   **Objective:** *Literary Analysis*
6. "To resume" means to "begin again; continue." If he were unable to resume his work, the candy would have been left unsorted.
   Difficulty: *Average*   **Objective:** *Vocabulary*
7. Harry realizes that the parrot is repeating things he has heard from Mr. Tillian about missing Harry's presence in the store. It's difficult for Harry to accept that he has hurt his father, even if he didn't do it on purpose.
   Difficulty: *Challenging*   **Objective:** *Interpretation*
8. The word *checked* and the phrase *so the bird wouldn't get cold* suggest the meaning of the word. A *furnace* is a heating device.
   Difficulty: *Average*   **Objective:** *Reading*
9. Sample answer: Beginning: Harry comes to the store with his friends; Middle: Harry is busy with new activities and friends; Mr. Tillian buys a parrot; End: Mr. Tillian goes to the hospital; Harry helps out in the store. The events happen over a period of years begin-

ning in Harry's early childhood and going until Harry is in junior high.

Difficulty: *Average* **Objective:** *Literary Analysis*

10. Students may say that "Papa's Parrot" tells a story or that it is in written in chronological order.

Difficulty: *Easy* **Objective:** *Literary Analysis*

Essay

11. At first, Harry is a young child who enjoys being "friends" with his father. Then, as he grows up, Harry is busy with new activities and friends. Finally, however, Harry realizes he cares deeply about his father.

Difficulty: *Easy* **Objective:** *Essay*

12. Sample answer: The most important thing Rocky says is "Where's Harry?" This question clearly shows Harry that his father has been wondering why Harry doesn't come to the store anymore, and it makes Harry rethink his behavior.

Difficulty: *Average* **Objective:** *Essay*

13. Sample answer: It seems that Mr. Tillian understands that Harry is growing up. He doesn't scold Harry for neglecting to come visit him, and he buys a parrot to keep him company. Certainly, he is hurt, but he would never tell Harry this. They have a loving relationship at home, and Mr. Tillian knows that his son is a good boy.

Difficulty: *Challenging* **Objective:** *Essay*

14. Students should explain that Harry finds the truth about his father's feelings when Rocky repeats things he has heard. Students may say this is the best way for Harry to find the truth because it allows him to hear it without confrontation or embarrassment. Others may say it is not the best way because it does not come directly from his father. A conversation between the two of them would have let his father know the truth, too.

Difficulty: *Average* **Objective:** *Essay*

Oral Response

15. Oral responses should be clear, well organized, and well supported by appropriate examples from the selection.

Difficulty: *Average* **Objective:** *Oral Interpretation*

Selection Test A, p. 42

Critical Reading

1. ANS: C	DIF: Easy	OBJ: Comprehension
2. ANS: B	DIF: Easy	OBJ: Comprehension
3. ANS: D	DIF: Easy	OBJ: Literary Analysis
4. ANS: D	DIF: Easy	OBJ: Interpretation
5. ANS: C	DIF: Easy	OBJ: Reading
6. ANS: B	DIF: Easy	OBJ: Comprehension
7. ANS: A	DIF: Easy	OBJ: Reading
8. ANS: A	DIF: Easy	OBJ: Interpretation
9. ANS: C	DIF: Easy	OBJ: Reading
10. ANS: B	DIF: Easy	OBJ: Literary Analysis
11. ANS: C	DIF: Easy	OBJ: Interpretation

Vocabulary and Grammar

12. ANS: C	DIF: Easy	OBJ: Vocabulary
13. ANS: A	DIF: Easy	OBJ: Vocabulary
14. ANS: C	DIF: Easy	OBJ: Grammar

Essay

15. Students should note that Mr. Tillian enjoys Rocky's company, whereas Harry is embarrassed by the bird's presence. Mr. Tillian spends a lot of time with Rocky, talks to him, feeds him, cleans his cage, and watches television with him. They have an affectionate relationship. Harry simply ignores the bird—until Mr. Tillian becomes ill. Then, he learns from the parrot's chatter how lonely his father has been, and he realizes how the bird has taken his place as his father's companion. At first, Harry takes out his emotions on the bird, yelling at him and throwing candy at him. Then, in what appears to be an act of love for his father, he tends to the bird, treating him with respect.

Difficulty: *Easy*

Objective: *Essay*

16. Students should note that at the beginning of the story, Harry likes his father and the two are "friends." Harry enjoys stopping by the store after school with his friends and visiting with his father. After Harry enters junior high school, however, he and his friends develop new interests and have more money to spend, so they no longer stop by the store. Harry seems to be outgrowing his father and is not aware of how that change is affecting Mr. Tillian. After Mr. Tillian buys the parrot and begins talking to the bird, Harry becomes embarrassed by his father and avoids him. Students may also note that despite these changes, Harry and his father continue to be "friends" at home. After Mr. Tillian becomes ill, however, Harry learns from the parrot just how much his father has missed him. He feels guilty and perhaps develops a new sympathy for and understanding of his father.

Difficulty: *Easy*

Objective: *Essay*

17. Students should explain that Harry finds the truth about his father's feelings when Rocky the parrot repeats things he has heard. Students may say this is the best way for Harry to find the truth because it allows him to hear it without having to deal directly with his father. Others may say it would be better for him to hear it directly from his father.

Difficulty: *Average*

Objective: *Essay*

Selection Test B, p. 45

Critical Reading

1. ANS: C	DIF: Average	OBJ: Literary Analysis
2. ANS: A	DIF: Average	OBJ: Comprehension
3. ANS: B	DIF: Challenging	OBJ: Interpretation
4. ANS: A	DIF: Average	OBJ: Interpretation

5. ANS: B	DIF: Average	OBJ: Reading
6. ANS: D	DIF: Average	OBJ: Comprehension
7. ANS: A	DIF: Average	OBJ: Reading
8. ANS: B	DIF: Average	OBJ: Reading
9. ANS: D	DIF: Average	OBJ: Literary Analysis
10. ANS: B	DIF: Average	OBJ: Comprehension
11. ANS: A	DIF: Average	OBJ: Literary Analysis
12. ANS: C	DIF: Challenging	OBJ: Interpretation
13. ANS: C	DIF: Challenging	OBJ: Comprehension
14. ANS: A	DIF: Challenging	OBJ: Interpretation

Vocabulary and Grammar

15. ANS: C	DIF: Average	OBJ: Vocabulary
16. ANS: A	DIF: Average	OBJ: Vocabulary
17. ANS: A	DIF: Average	OBJ: Grammar
18. ANS: B	DIF: Average	OBJ: Grammar

Essay

19. Some students may say that Mr. Tillian was wise to allow Harry the freedom to grow independent and to cope with his loneliness by developing a relationship with Rocky. Others may contend that Mr. Tillian might have lessened the growing distance between him and his son by speaking more honestly to him. About Harry's responsibility in the relationship, many students may think that Harry should have recognized his father's loneliness and paid more attention to him. Other students may say that Harry was acting the way any other twelve-year-old would have acted and that he should not have had to take care of his parent.

Difficulty: *Average*

Objective: *Essay*

20. Students should explain that Harry finds the truth about his father's feelings when Rocky repeats things he has heard. Students may say this is the best way for Harry to find the truth because it allows him to hear it without confrontation or embarrassment. Others may say it is not the best way because it does not come directly from his father. A conversation between the two of them would have let his father know the truth, too.

Difficulty: *Average*

Objective: *Essay*

"mk" by Jean Fritz

Vocabulary Warm-up Exercises, p. 49

A. 1. emergency
2. fake
3. deceive
4. difficulty
5. immediate
6. Generally
7. education
8. verge

B. Sample Answers

1. The minister opened her Bible and read the story of Noah.
2. Hannah will commit herself to the project, so she will be very involved in it.
3. Historians are likely to talk about topics that have to do with the past.
4. Being ignorant of the schedule, Andrew was always late.
5. Because Megan was informed of the date, she marked it on her calendar.
6. The normal time to eat dessert is after the main dish is served.
7. The president's oath was a serious promise to serve the country.
8. Gym class has three sessions a week, so students meet for gym on Mondays, Wednesdays, and Fridays.

Reading Warm-up A, p. 50

Words that students are to circle appear in parentheses.

Sample Answers

1. (listen to me); A synonym for *generally* is *usually*.
2. I was nervous before I left; *Difficulty* means "the condition of being hard to do."
3. I thought about coming down with a fake attack of the flu the night before camp started. She was nervous about going to work as a camp counselor.
4. A fake attack of the flu might include phony sneezing and coughing and claims of weakness and aches. *Fake* means "false."
5. I have learned a great deal about working with people. Her education gave her the knowledge to be a scientist.
6. She sounded the siren and rescued the boy. *Emergency* means "unexpected and requiring immediate attention."
7. (At once); A cut or gash that bleeds a lot requires immediate attention.
8. I felt both joy and relief because I had saved a little boy; Graduation would put me on the verge of tears.

Reading Warm-up B, p. 51

Words that students are to circle appear in parentheses.

Sample Answers

1. people who study the events of the past; The historians are writing a book on colonial America.
2. (did not know); The judges were not informed of their duties.
3. group of judges met; I might attend sessions of scout meetings or music classes.
4. The judges were ignorant of their powers. *Ignorant* means "having little knowledge."
5. The *Bible* is the sacred book of Christianity. The minister reads from the Bible at church.

6. *promise;* The president also takes an oath.
7. No, it did not, because the judges did not have a clear idea of their job.
8. <u>to decide only the most important issues;</u> *Normal* means "being or feeling the usual way."

Writing About the Big Question, p. 52

A. 1. fiction
   2. reality/truth
   3. believable

B. Sample Answers
   1. In <u>Harry Potter</u>, I was convinced that the author must have had evil adults in her life who treated her like Harry Potter's aunt and uncle treated him.
   2. The way the aunt and uncle treated Harry so poorly and their own son so well was very realistic to me. I could see people really doing that. They gave him a closet to sleep in and food to eat that was not as good as the food their son ate.

C. Sample Answer
   about the time I got lost on the beach when I was three. I would get lost, the same way I did—by wandering off while my parents were talking to each other. Instead of being found quickly by my worried parents, I would create a whole adventure that happened when I was lost. The adventure would take place under the sea. When my parents finally found me, I would use their true reactions in the story.

Reading: Use Context Clues to Unlock the Meaning, p. 53

Sample Answers
1. Clues: "couldn't let on how I really felt," "fake tears"; Meaning: mislead
2. Clues: "boys were supposed to sign up," "if her card wasn't filled up"; Meaning: someone who looks on while others dance
3. Clues: "across," "America," "the Rocky Mountains, the Mississippi river, flat ranch land, small towns, forests"; Meaning: any one of the large land areas of the earth
4. Clues: "Didn't their teachers teach them anything?"; Meaning: uneducated

Literary Analysis: Narrative, p. 54

A. 5
B. 7
C. 2
D. 9
E. 3
F. 6
G. 8
H. 1
I. 10
J. 4

Vocabulary Builder, p. 55

A. 1. ignorant
   2. quest
   3. adequate
   4. transformation
   5. relation
   6. deceive

B. 1. C; 2. B 3. D

C. 1. There are many choices in a candy aisle, and an indecisive person is someone who does not decide things quickly.
   2. Drivers without experience would benefit from extra safety instruction.

Enrichment: Making History Live, p. 56

Sample Answers
1. She wrote in a journal in order to escape her loneliness.
2. As the child of American parents in China, she was curious about the United States. After she arrived in this country, she felt she had to make up for lost time, so she read about U.S. history. She also likes stories, and history is full of stories.
3. She finds unusual facts about her subjects.
4. She never makes up dialogue for real people. She uses only their own words, which she finds in letters, diaries, and journals.

"Papa's Parrot" by Cynthia Rylant
"MK" by Jean Fritz

Integrated Language Skills: Grammar, p. 57

A. Proper nouns / common nouns:
   1. Rocky, Mr. Tillian / company
   2. Rocky / shipments, candy, nuts
   3. Harry / father, store, day, school, boxes
   4. Jean, British School, Wuhan / grade
   5. American, Shanghai / women, children, boat
   6. Mr. Barrett, Shanghai / home, wife, porch

Sample Answers
B. 1. Jean Fritz lived in China when she was young.
   2. Harry was disappointed when Mr. Tillian bought Rocky.
   3. Jean Fritz moved to the United States.
   4. Rocky showed by his speech that Mr. Tillian missed Harry.

"MK" by Jean Fritz

Open-Book Test, p. 60

Short Answer
1. As an MK, the author understood that she was always an outsider in China. MKs always knew they would be leaving China at some point in time, and that knowledge colored all of their thoughts and feelings.

Difficulty: *Average*   **Objective:** *Literary Analysis*

2. The author sounds somewhat sad. She recognized even as a child that the MKs were different and knew they would not stay in China forever.

   Difficulty: *Challenging* **Objective:** *Interpretation*

3. All American women and children were sent to Shanghai to get away from the approaching army. Because the army had "done so much damage" to another village, the Americans assumed the same thing would happen in Wuhan.

   Difficulty: *Easy* **Objective:** *Interpretation*

4. Sample answer: The words *protected* and *steel* suggest the meaning of the word *barrier*, because they give a sense of something that protects.

   Difficulty: *Easy* **Objective:** *Reading*

5. Sample answer: Mrs. Barrett might have preferred a hug or a kiss on the cheek to show more feeling. The word *adequate* means "enough," and by raising her eyebrows, Mrs. Barrett showed that she thought a handshake was not enough. This reaction is emphasized when she added, "Have you become so grown up, Jean, that I'm no longer your 'Auntie Barrett'?"

   Difficulty: *Average* **Objective:** *Vocabulary*

6. Sample answer: As a person who traveled a lot and felt out of place in another country, the author may have felt a strong connection to the Pilgrims, who were strangers in a new land. She probably drew comfort from their story and hoped she would find success in America too.

   Difficulty: *Challenging* **Objective:** *Interpretation*

7. The author had little control over her life. She lived in China because her parents were missionaries there. When the British school closed, she was sent to the American School. Though she expected to stay in China through seventh grade, her family left for America early.

   Difficulty: *Average* **Objective:** *Literary Analysis*

8. Sample answers: Event - cheerleaders practicing; Reaction - not impressed; Event - hair cut; Reaction - felt ugly; Event - talk parties; Reaction - enjoyed being popular.

   Difficulty: *Average* **Objective:** *Interpretation*

9. Sample answer: She thought they were *ignorant* because their questions revealed that they did not know anything about China that was based on facts: they asked about living in mud huts and eating dog.

   Difficulty: *Easy* **Objective:** *Vocabulary*

10. Sample answer: "When he thought his work was over at the end of the Revolution, he agreed to work on the Constitution." Washington did what was needed for the country, despite what he might have preferred personally. Washington needed to be persuaded to run for president again because "he could hardly wait to go back home and be a farmer again." He had to be talked into it by others who "had confidence" in his abilities.

    Difficulty: *Challenging* **Objective:** *Reading*

Essay

11. Students may say the author's feelings about being a Missionary Kid seem complicated. On the one hand, she learned a lot that helped her in later life, because she learned to adapt to new situations. She also could appreciate feeling more settled when she finally came to America. On the other hand, it seems that she often felt out of control of her life and that she did not belong anywhere.

    Difficulty: *Easy* **Objective:** *Essay*

12. Students may say the author's dislike of Fletcher was partly based on his being two years younger than she. She had little patience for him and his enthusiastic kind of love, and because they were thrown together by circumstance, she hadn't chosen his friendship. She was justified in her reaction, because their being thrown together was one more example of her lack of control over her life.

    Difficulty: *Average* **Objective:** *Essay*

13. Sample answer: Through identifying with the Pilgrims' experience and understanding the story of George Washington's life and accomplishments, the author is able to explore some of her feelings about what it means to be a "real" American. As she notes at the end of "MK," she had to carry her Chinese experience with her, just as the Pilgrims carried their history with them, even as she became an American.

    Difficulty: *Challenging* **Objective:** *Essay*

14. Students may say the author found her first truths about America in books that she read as a child living in China. She developed her own ideas of what life in America would be like and what it meant to be an American. When she finally got to America, however, reality and her "truths" did not match. At first, the new truth did nothing but disappoint her, but as she got older she realized that she could combine the truths of her storybook heroes and the world she saw around her.

    Difficulty: *Average* **Objective:** *Essay*

Oral Response

21. Oral responses should be clear, well organized, and well supported by appropriate examples from the selection.

    Difficulty: *Average* **Objective:** *Oral Interpretation*

Selection Test A, p. 63

Critical Reading

1.	**ANS:** C	**DIF:** Easy	**OBJ:** Interpretation
2.	**ANS:** D	**DIF:** Easy	**OBJ:** Interpretation
3.	**ANS:** B	**DIF:** Easy	**OBJ:** Reading
4.	**ANS:** A	**DIF:** Easy	**OBJ:** Interpretation
5.	**ANS:** C	**DIF:** Easy	**OBJ:** Literary Analysis
6.	**ANS:** C	**DIF:** Easy	**OBJ:** Comprehension
7.	**ANS:** C	**DIF:** Easy	**OBJ:** Comprehension
8.	**ANS:** B	**DIF:** Easy	**OBJ:** Literary Analysis
9.	**ANS:** D	**DIF:** Easy	**OBJ:** Reading
10.	**ANS:** B	**DIF:** Easy	**OBJ:** Reading
11.	**ANS:** A	**DIF:** Easy	**OBJ:** Comprehension

Vocabulary and Grammar

12. ANS: B	DIF: Easy	OBJ: Vocabulary
13. ANS: C	DIF: Easy	OBJ: Vocabulary
14. ANS: B	DIF: Easy	OBJ: Grammar

Essay

15. Students should notice that at the beginning of the selection, Jean does not feel a strong tie to China. As a child, she knows that she will leave China for America after she finishes seventh grade, and she says that China's problems have nothing to do with her. She is mostly concerned with becoming an American as quickly as possible. Yet, when she enters school in America, she is disappointed to find that she does not seem to fit in. Later, she realizes that China is part of who she is.

    Difficulty: *Easy*
    Objective: *Essay*

16. Student should note that "MK" begins when the narrator is an adult on a beach in Maine. Next, she is a girl in Wuhan. From Wuhan she travels with her mother to Shanghai, where she first stays with the Barretts and then attends the Shanghai American School as a boarding student. Sometime later, she travels with her family to San Francisco and from there crosses the country by train, ending up with her relatives in Pittsburgh. Later, she attends high school and college. At the end of the selection, she is an adult again. Students might say that the story is told out of order so that the narrator can attract the reader's attention or so that the writer can show the event in her adult life that caused her to start thinking about her childhood.

    Difficulty: *Average*
    Objective: *Essay*

17. Students may say the author found her first truths about America in books that she read as a child living in China. She developed her own ideas of what life in America would be like. When she finally got to America, however, reality and her "truths" did not match. At first, the new truth disappointed her. As she got older, she realized that she could combine the truths of her storybook heroes and the world she saw around her.

    Difficulty: *Average*
    Objective: *Essay*

Selection Test B, p. 66

Critical Reading

1. ANS: C	DIF: Average	OBJ: Comprehension
2. ANS: D	DIF: Average	OBJ: Reading
3. ANS: C	DIF: Challenging	OBJ: Reading
4. ANS: A	DIF: Challenging	OBJ: Interpretation
5. ANS: C	DIF: Average	OBJ: Comprehension
6. ANS: A	DIF: Average	OBJ: Interpretation
7. ANS: C	DIF: Average	OBJ: Reading
8. ANS: D	DIF: Challenging	OBJ: Interpretation

9. ANS: B	DIF: Challenging	OBJ: Interpretation
10. ANS: D	DIF: Average	OBJ: Comprehension
11. ANS: C	DIF: Average	OBJ: Interpretation
12. ANS: A	DIF: Challenging	OBJ: Literary Analysis
13. ANS: D	DIF: Challenging	OBJ: Literary Analysis

Vocabulary and Grammar

14. ANS: C	DIF: Average	OBJ: Vocabulary
15. ANS: A	DIF: Average	OBJ: Vocabulary
16. ANS: A	DIF: Average	OBJ: Grammar
17. ANS: D	DIF: Challenging	OBJ: Grammar

Essay

18. Students should note that "MK" begins when the narrator is an adult on a beach in Maine. Next, she is a girl in Wuhan. From Wuhan she travels with her mother to Shanghai, where she first stays with the Barretts and then attends the Shanghai American School as a boarding student. Sometime later, she travels with her family to San Francisco and from there crosses the country by train, ending up with her relatives in Pittsburgh. Later, she attends high school and college. At the end of the selection, she appears to be an adult again. They might point out that the beginning serves to attract the reader's attention or allows the narrator to describe the event that set off the memories of her childhood and allowed her to reach an understanding of the course of her life.

    Difficulty: *Average*
    Objective: *Essay*

19. From "MK," the reader learns that Priscilla Alden is a character in *The Courtship of Miles Standish*, a book about the Pilgrims, who were among the first European settlers in America. Jean, the narrator of "MK," identifies with Alden because Alden came to America from another country and Jean herself will be going to the United States after having lived in another country. The two are different in that they lived at different times. Students with some knowledge of the Pilgrims may also point out that Alden came from England, whereas Jean is coming from China. It seems that for Jean, Alden represents America, and she imagines that Alden can give her advice about becoming American. Students may also say that Alden is important to Jean because she is a character in a book that Jean's father read with her.

    Difficulty: *Challenging*
    Objective: *Essay*

20. Students may say the author found her first truths about America in books that she read as a child living in China. She developed her own ideas of what life in America would be like and what it meant to be an American. When she finally got to America, however, reality and her "truths" did not match. At first, the new truth did nothing but disappoint her, but as she got older she realized that she could combine the truths of her storybook heroes and the world she saw around her.

Difficulty: *Average*
Objective: *Essay*

from An American Childhood
by Annie Dillard

Vocabulary Warm-up Exercises, p. 70

A. 1. considered
2. immense
3. seldom
4. flung
5. bordered
6. compare
7. strategy
8. glory

B. Sample Answers

1. No, it would not be easy to answer because a complex question is a question that is hard to understand.

2. No, the jury would not believe the witness because they would have no doubt that he could not be trusted.

3. Yes, the horse would almost certainly win the race because it was faster than anyone believed was possible.

4. No, if you are precisely on time, you are exactly on time, not a minute early or late.

5. Yes, someone who is able to play the piano perfectly is a very skilled musician.

6. Yes, if my teacher approved the topic, she thought it was good or acceptable, so I would do my project on that topic.

7. No, I would not be allowed to join because I am not grown up.

8. No, childhood is the early part of life, before you go to work and have a career.

Reading Warm-up A, p. 71

Words that students are to circle appear in parentheses.

Sample Answers

1. They were too safe and familiar. I disagree because I consider my back yard a lot of fun.

2. (bushes); *Bordered* means "surrounded."

3. You could roast a whole cow in that barbeque. No, a barbeque might be big, but not that big.

4. When we wanted adventure; They are both plots of land.

5. First we pulled up our socks to protect our legs. Then, very carefully, we would walk in a circle, around and around, until we had tramped down the space.
A strategy is a smart plan for getting something done.

6. (trash); Something that has been flung has been tossed forcefully.

7. They did not mind because it was the hunt that mattered. *Seldom* means "rarely."

8. They had a moment of glory when they found something unexpected. I had a moment of glory when I won a spelling bee.

Reading Warm-up B, p. 72

Words that students are to circle appear in parentheses.

Sample Answers

1. Kevin spent his early childhood with his mother. My mother spent every summer of her childhood at the beach.

2. His mother approved because she thought a young boy needed his father. *Approved* means "thought it was acceptable or good."

3. Building contractors all over the city admired his work and gave him plenty of jobs. I am skilled at playing the drums.

4. (Work); I think algebra is complex.

5. When you are a grown-up, you will understand.

6. Mom has been too sick to keep it up. *Apparently* means "obviously or clearly."

7. The house looked *exactly* as it had before Kevin went away.

8. It means that it is hard to believe that Kevin enjoyed the work. "Unbelievably" is a synonym for *incredibly*.

Writing About the Big Question, p. 73

A. 1. believable
2. truth
3. awareness

B. Sample Answers

1. As I walked home from school on that chilly December afternoon, my fingers felt numb beneath my woolen mittens. I shivered. I was cold.

2. As I walked home on that warm day in July, suddenly, I saw snowflakes fall from the sky. It was happening again. I had wished it would be December and here it was, December. I shivered. I was cold.

C. Sample Answer

the reader relate the story to his or her own experiences.

I hit the snooze button and snuggled under my cozy warm covers. I did not want to go to school today. I drifted into a peaceful sleep. That is, until I heard the clunk clunk of my mother's high heels on the stairs. She was coming for me, and she was going to be angry that I didn't get up for school. I had to think quick. As she opened the door I faked a cough. It sounded pretty good.

Reading: Reread and Read Ahead to Confirm Meaning, p. 74

Sample Answers

1. Clue: "started"; Meaning: began

2. Clues: "lose ourselves," "except Mikey Fahey, who was just rounding the corner"; Meaning: suddenly disappeared from view

3. Clues: "point yourself, forget yourself, aim, dive";
   Meaning: throw with force
4. Clues: "wet," "full of snow"; Meaning: thoroughly wet

Literary Analysis: Point of View, p. 75

Sample Answers

1. Pronouns: me, I; What I learned: The boys welcome Dillard to their baseball games because she is a good pitcher.
2. Pronouns: us, we, I, us, we; What I learned: Dillard is surprised to find that the man is still chasing them, and she realizes that they are running as if to save their lives.
3. Pronouns: us, I, I, we; What I learned: The man chases Dillard and Mikey until the two children are out of breath and she supposes he is too, but he does not give up.

Vocabulary Builder, p. 76

Sample Answers

A. 1. Yes, they had a plan. I know because a *strategy* is a set of plans.
2. No, she did not have a choice. I know because *compelled* means "forced."
3. No, they had not planned an escape route. I know because *improvising* means "making up on the spur of the moment."
4. No, they did not hold unique meaning. I know because *perfunctorily* means "to do in a routine manner."
5. Yes, he believed he was correct to be angry with the kids. I know because *righteous* means "considered to be correct or justifiable."
6. Yes, you could see light through it. I know because *translucent* means "allowing light to pass through."

Sample Answers

1. My new school would need to have records moved over to know my history.
2. I would need someone to help me understand the foreign language.

Enrichment: Documentary Films, p. 77

Sample Answers

1. **Photographs:** houses and cars covered in snow in winter of 1952
2. **Interviews:** football coach talking about how to make a tackle
3. **Film/video:** Pittsburgh neighborhood after a snowstorm
4. **Newspaper clipping:** article about Annie Dillard

Open-Book Test, p. 78

Short Answer

1. Dillard appreciates football because it takes concentration and courage; she says you have to "fling yourself wholeheartedly" into it. Later in the selection, the man chasing her and Mikey doesn't give up; he flings himself wholeheartedly into his pursuit.

Difficulty: *Average* **Objective:** *Interpretation*

2. A *strategy* is a plan. Without a plan, the players would not be able to play well as a team.
Difficulty: *Easy* **Objective:** *Vocabulary*

3. Students should select and underline any sentence that uses *I, we, us,* etc.
Difficulty: *Easy* **Objective:** *Literary Analysis*

4. He chases them because they hit his car with snowballs as he drove by. He wants to teach them a lesson and maybe scare them a little, but he does not mean to hurt them or get them in trouble.
Difficulty: *Easy* **Objective:** *Interpretation*

5. The word *back* and the phrase *expected he would have quit* help explain the meaning of the word. When someone *glances,* they look quickly at something or someone. She was looking to see whether the man was still chasing them.
Difficulty: *Average* **Objective:** *Reading*

6. The words *half-blinded* and *coughing* suggest the meaning of the word *staggering.* "To stagger" means "to move unsteadily." They were staggering because they had all been running at top speed for quite a while.
Difficulty: *Average* **Objective:** *Reading*

7. The author admires him for the same reasons that she likes the game of football. She likes people who show determination and stay focused, and the driver does not give up. She says she was exhilarated by the chase, and that nothing else ever made her feel the same way.
Difficulty: *Challenging* **Objective:** *Interpretation*

8. The children *improvised* by "running a frantic course" and going through "backyard labyrinths." They made up their route as they went along.
Difficulty: *Average* **Objective:** *Vocabulary*

9. Sample answer: Annie and Mikey took one last gulp of air and began to walk home. The young man watched them walk off before he realized he had no idea how to get to his car.
Difficulty: *Challenging* **Objective:** *Literary Analysis*

10. Sample answer: Known: how she feels about football; how she feels about the chase; Unknown: how the driver feels; how Mikey feels.

Students may say they would prefer the third person because it would give more information. Others may say they prefer the first person because it provides detailed information about Annie.
Difficulty: *Average* **Objective:** *Literary Analysis*

Essay

11. The author likes football because it requires concentration and because it is physically challenging. She also says that "nothing girls did could compare with it," which shows that she likes doing things that girls don't usually do.
Difficulty: *Easy* **Objective:** *Essay*

12. The author says, "I wanted the glory to last forever." Her feelings of disappointment are based on the fact that she enjoyed the thrill of being chased so much that anything following the chase was bound to be a letdown. She doesn't seem scared about being scolded and calls it "beside the point." The point was the chase itself.

    Difficulty: *Average*   **Objective:** *Essay*

13. The author writes, "I don't know how he found his way back to his car." Annie and Mikey have led him all over the neighborhood and far away from his car. The young man is determined to catch them no matter how cold or tired or lost he becomes. He is wholeheartedly involved in the chase, just as Annie says you must be wholeheartedly involved in anything you are doing. Only at the end does Annie realize that the man must have been totally lost.

    Difficulty: *Challenging*   **Objective:** *Essay*

14. Sample answer: The driver's truth of the episode would probably be very different, in that he would express anger at having his windshield hit and having to chase kids all over a neighborhood. He might not see it as an experience filled with "glory," as the writer did. His truth is not any more or less real than Dillard's; it is different.

    Difficulty: *Average*   **Objective:** *Essay*

Oral Response

15. Students' answers will vary but should show adequate preparation and be well supported by appropriate examples from the selections.

    Difficulty: *Average*   **Objective:** *Oral Interpretation*

Selection Test A, p. 81

Critical Reading

1. ANS: C	DIF: Easy	OBJ: Comprehension
2. ANS: D	DIF: Easy	OBJ: Comprehension
3. ANS: B	DIF: Easy	OBJ: Reading
4. ANS: B	DIF: Easy	OBJ: Reading
5. ANS: C	DIF: Easy	OBJ: Interpretation
6. ANS: D	DIF: Easy	OBJ: Interpretation
7. ANS: B	DIF: Easy	OBJ: Literary Analysis
8. ANS: A	DIF: Easy	OBJ: Literary Analysis
9. ANS: C	DIF: Easy	OBJ: Interpretation
10. ANS: B	DIF: Easy	OBJ: Comprehension
11. ANS: B	DIF: Easy	OBJ: Interpretation

Vocabulary and Grammar

12. ANS: A	DIF: Easy	OBJ: Vocabulary
13. ANS: B	DIF: Easy	OBJ: Grammar
14. ANS: D	DIF: Easy	OBJ: Grammar

Essay

15. Students may say that Dillard chose to write in the first person in order to be true to herself, in order to reveal all of her own feelings without having to make up the thoughts and feelings of other characters, and in order to communicate her thoughts and experiences directly, without filtering them through a fictional character. Students should recognize that the same information conveyed by a third-person narrator would not have used the pronoun *I* and might have included the thoughts and experiences of other characters as well.

    Difficulty: *Easy*

    Objective: *Essay*

16. Students should recognize Dillard's toughness and passion and cite details from the selection to support their descriptions. Some students may say they like her because she is passionate about things she does (playing football, running from the man in the black Buick) and because she appears to play with the boys as an equal (tackling players in football, throwing with "a boy's arm" in baseball). Others may say they dislike her because she appears to be conceited (for example, about her acceptance by the boys) and perhaps ignores other girls.

    Difficulty: *Easy*

    Objective: *Essay*

17. Sample answer: The driver's truth of the episode would probably be very different because he would express anger at having his windshield hit and having to chase kids all over a neighborhood. He might not see it as an experience filled with "glory," as the writer did. So the truth he sees in this situation might be very different from Dillard's.

    Difficulty: Average

    Objective: *Essay*

Selection Test B, p. 84

Critical Reading

1. ANS: C	DIF: Average	OBJ: Interpretation
2. ANS: D	DIF: Challenging	OBJ: Reading
3. ANS: B	DIF: Average	OBJ: Interpretation
4. ANS: D	DIF: Average	OBJ: Comprehension
5. ANS: B	DIF: Challenging	OBJ: Reading
6. ANS: B	DIF: Average	OBJ: Comprehension
7. ANS: B	DIF: Average	OBJ: Reading
8. ANS: D	DIF: Average	OBJ: Interpretation
9. ANS: B	DIF: Average	OBJ: Reading
10. ANS: B	DIF: Challenging	OBJ: Interpretation
11. ANS: B	DIF: Challenging	OBJ: Interpretation
12. ANS: B	DIF: Average	OBJ: Interpretation
13. ANS: B	DIF: Average	OBJ: Literary Analysis
14. ANS: C	DIF: Challenging	OBJ: Literary Analysis

Vocabulary and Grammar

15. ANS: D	DIF: Average	OBJ: Vocabulary
16. ANS: B	DIF: Average	OBJ: Grammar

Essay

17. Students may recognize that Dillard tells the story of the snowball and the chase to illustrate a point that is important to her: it is essential in life to act with passion. Students may point to any of a number of other reasons—for example, to describe what she was like as a child or to show the kinds of activities she enjoyed.

    Difficulty: *Average*

    Objective: *Essay*

18. Students should point out that Dillard, writing from the first-person point of view, gives no information about the man beyond describing his appearance. Students should demonstrate that they understand that if the story were told from the man's point of view, his motives, feelings, and thoughts could be revealed.

    Difficulty: *Challenging*

    Objective: *Essay*

19. Sample answer: The driver's truth of the episode would probably be very different in that he would express anger at having his windshield hit and having to chase kids all over a neighborhood. He might not see it as an experience filled with "glory," as the writer did. His truth is not any more or less real than Dillard's; it is different.

    Difficulty: Average

    Objective: *Essay*

"The Luckiest Time of All" by Lucille Clifton

Vocabulary Warm-up Exercises, p. 88

A.
1. shined
2. cutest
3. hind
4. luck
5. reminds
6. exactly
7. noticed
8. pennies

B. Sample Answers
1. False. If an object is well hidden, no one would see it easily.
2. False. If you are acquainted with someone, you do not know him or her well.
3. False. A granddaughter is the daughter of someone's son or daughter.
4. False. The length of a snake is measured from its head to the tip of its tail.
5. False. Blooms are flowers, and they grow on stems above ground.
6. True. A porch is attached to the outside of a house.
7. True. Twine is made up of several strands of string.
8. True. When you twirl, you spin like a top, and that makes you dizzy.

Reading Warm-up A, p. 89

Words that students are to circle appear in parentheses.

Sample Answers
1. (People waited for the circus to come to town.) One summer at the beach the sun shined so brightly I got a headache.
2. (a troop of acrobats, a high-wire act, and maybe a magic show); Today you can buy a piece of candy for a few pennies.
3. He put one foot exactly in front of the other. He had to walk precisely along the wire so that he would not fall off.
4. (animals); The animals' tricks were the cutest because animals are attractive when they jump through hoops and dance on their hind legs.
5. (danced); A bear can stand on its hind legs.
6. (a two-headed chicken, a bearded lady, and a tattooed man); What people saw was a matter of luck because every side show had something different.
7. (the amazing Gonzo); I do not believe the announcer's brother-in-law looked like Gonzo because no human is half-man and half-beast.
8. (the "beast" half was a fake); They probably noticed that because the "beast" half was just a costume.

Reading Warm-up B, p. 90

Words that students are to circle appear in parentheses.

Sample Answers
1. (outside the house); A porch is a roofed structure attached to the outside of a house.
2. I think it's time we got to know each other.
3. (bouquet of daisy); Black-eyed Susans are my favorite wildflower blooms.
4. Olivia is Bill's granddaughter, and her mother is Bill's daughter.
5. (a white box); I might tie up a bundle of magazines with twine.
6. I would measure a length of twine with a measuring tape.
7. Olivia spied a music box in the box. I spied a deer in the field across the street.
8. Olivia began to twirl around when the music box played the waltz. I might see someone twirl at a skating rink or on a dance floor.

Writing About the Big Question, p. 91

A.
1. evaluate
2. conclude
3. reality

B. Sample Answers
1. found penny (good luck);   broken mirror (bad luck)

2. No, I do not think an object can bring good or bad luck. I think that it is the belief in the object, not the object itself, that persuades someone to think it brings luck.

C. Sample Answer

be consistent in order to be believable.

When a character in a work of fiction acts in a consistent way, that character is believable. For example, if a character is afraid of dogs and will not go into her friend's house because there is a dog there, I believe in that character. She is realistic. I then want to read more of the story. On the other hand, if she is suddenly volunteering at the dog pound, I do not believe in that character and I lose interest in the story.

Reading: Reread and Read Ahead to Confirm Meaning, p. 92

Sample Answers

1. Clues: music and wonders as we never had seen! They had everything there; Meaning: everything good that you could imagine, a whole world of exciting things
2. Clues: hit that dancing dog right on the nose! I flew! Round and round the Silas Greene we run; Meaning: chased, ran
3. Clues: picked up, talkin to him soft and sweet; Meaning: holding gently, as a baby is held by a cradle
4. Clues: helped me find my stone, searched and searched; Meaning: spotted, caught sight of, found

Literary Analysis: Point of View, p. 93

Sample Answers

1. Pronoun: her; What I learned: Elzie shook her head and laughed.
2. Pronoun: they; What I learned: Elzie and Tee rocked in their rocking chairs and smiled.
3. Pronouns: her, she, their; What I learned: Lucille Clifton learned to appreciate books and poetry from the example set by her parents.

Vocabulary Builder, p. 94

Sample Answers

A. 1. No, mountain climbers would not use twine to secure themselves because it is not strong enough.
2. Yes, if I am acquainted with someone, I likely know where he or she lives because when I get to know people, I usually find out such information.
3. Yes, women are more likely to have plaited hair because more women wear braids in their hair.
4. No, it is likely that you approached the animal from behind because the hind legs are in the back.
5. No, it is not likely that it would be boring to see one of the Seven Wonders because a *wonder* is meant to be sensational.
6. Yes, if I spied an old friend, I would be seeing him or her in person because to spy something means "to see in plain view."

Sample Answers

1. The word *access* relates to moving into or getting near something.
2. The word *adhere* relates to sticking to or being close or near to.

Enrichment: Hyperbole, p. 95

1. Literal
2. Hyperbole
3. Hyperbole
4. Literal
5. Literal
6. Literal
7. Hyperbole
8. Hyperbole
9. Hyperbole
10. Literal

from **An American Childhood** by Annie Dillard "The Luckiest Time of All" by Lucille Clifton

Integrated Language Skills: Grammar, p. 96

A. 1. boys', girls'
2. snowball's, car's
3. boy's, neighbors'
4. women's, girl's
B. 1. woman's, dog's
2. boys', cars'
3. man's, pants'

"The Luckiest Time of All" by Lucille Clifton

Open-Book Test, p. 99

Short Answer

1. She receives a bunch of dogwood blossoms. Dogwoods bloom in the spring, which is the time of year when she met her husband. The story she tells is about how they met.

   Difficulty: *Average* **Objective:** *Interpretation*

2. The switch occurs after the first paragraph, when Mrs. Pickens becomes the first-person narrator. She uses the pronouns *I, me,* and *we* to tell her story.

   Difficulty: *Easy* **Objective:** *Literary Analysis*

3. Elzie says there was "such music and wonders as we never had seen!" It seemed to her as though there was "everything" at Silas Greene. *The world* conveys her sense of excitement at seeing this new place full of activities and people she had never experienced before.

   Difficulty: *Challenging* **Objective:** *Reading*

4. Elzie realized that she should not have thrown away her lucky stone. She says, "Soon as it left my hand it seemed like I reached back out for to take it back."

   Difficulty: *Easy* **Objective:** *Interpretation*

5. "Grinnin fit to bust" means Amos has a huge smile across his face. If it were any bigger, his face would "bust," or break.
   Difficulty: *Average*   **Objective:** *Reading*

6. Mr. Pickens uses the *twine*, which is strong cord, as a lasso to loop around the dog's leg and stop it from chasing Elzie. It is a good choice because it makes a long, flexible loop to snag the dog.
   Difficulty: *Easy*   **Objective:** *Vocabulary*

7. The author lets Elzie tell most of the story in first person because it is a story she knows and remembers. Her voice makes the telling more powerful. However, the author switches effectively back to third person in order to let Tee ask questions that the reader wants to know the answers to.
   Difficulty: *Challenging*   **Objective:** *Literary Analysis*

8. The word *acquainted* means "familiar." She was just getting to know Mr. Pickens at the Silas Greene show, so Elzie is describing the beginning of their relationship. She also mentions that he is the person "who was gonna be your Great-granddaddy," which lets the reader know she had just met him.
   Difficulty: *Average*   **Objective:** *Vocabulary*

9. Character: Tee; Observations: 1. Tee noticed smile on Mrs. Pickens's face; 2. Tee says the stone wasn't so lucky. Knowing Tee helps me learn that Mrs. Pickens thinks that was the luckiest time of all—when she met her future husband.
   Difficulty: *Average*   **Objective:** *Literary Analysis*

10. Elzie thinks the time of the story was the luckiest time of all because it was when she met Mr. Pickens. She says their meeting was "luckier for me than for anybody."
    Difficulty: *Average*   **Objective:** *Interpretation*

Essay

11. The character readers learn most about is Elzie. She is old enough to be a great-grandmother. She cares most about her husband and sees him as kind and gentle. She also cares about passing along the story of her love to her great-granddaughter.
    Difficulty: *Easy*   **Objective:** *Essay*

12. Tee can see that her great-grandmother really loves her great-grandfather, not only because he saved her from the dog, but because he took the time to make sure the dog was not hurt. She could tell that he had a warm, gentle side that would be important in a husband. Tee can learn that such a person would make a good mate for her as she grows up.
    Difficulty: *Average*   **Objective:** *Essay*

13. Even though Elzie did not end up going off to join the Silas Greene show, she clearly has had a fulfilling life with Mr. Pickens. Although she may have intended to have a life of adventure, she ended up getting a long-lasting love that was probably of more value to her.
    Difficulty: *Challenging*   **Objective:** *Essay*

14. Elzie does not seem to have been lucky in terms of material success—the way that she speaks seems to indicate that she has not had much world experience and that her life has been pretty simple. However, she does seem to have been lucky with respect to finding love in her life, along with an appreciation for things that matter, such as close relationships with her family members. She would certainly say that she was lucky.
    Difficulty: *Average*   **Objective:** *Essay*

Oral Response

15. Oral responses should be clear, well organized, and well supported by appropriate examples from the selection.
    Difficulty: *Average*   **Objective:** *Oral Interpretation*

"The Luckiest Time of All" by Lucille Clifton

Selection Test A, p. 102

Critical Reading

1. ANS: B	DIF: Easy	OBJ: Literary Analysis
2. ANS: C	DIF: Easy	OBJ: Comprehension
3. ANS: B	DIF: Easy	OBJ: Reading
4. ANS: C	DIF: Easy	OBJ: Interpretation
5. ANS: A	DIF: Easy	OBJ: Reading
6. ANS: C	DIF: Easy	OBJ: Interpretation
7. ANS: C	DIF: Easy	OBJ: Comprehension
8. ANS: D	DIF: Easy	OBJ: Comprehension
9. ANS: B	DIF: Easy	OBJ: Reading
10. ANS: C	DIF: Easy	OBJ: Comprehension
11. ANS: B	DIF: Easy	OBJ: Literary Analysis
12. ANS: D	DIF: Easy	OBJ: Literary Analysis
13. ANS: C	DIF: Easy	OBJ: Interpretation

Vocabulary and Grammar

14. ANS: C	DIF: Easy	OBJ: Vocabulary
15. ANS: A	DIF: Easy	OBJ: Grammar

Essay

16. Students should recognize the few characteristics about Elzie that the narrator reveals: She is old enough to be a great-grandmother and to remember a time when traveling shows were an exciting event in a child's life; she lives (or lived) in the South; she loves her husband dearly and has always valued his kindness and gentleness. Students might say that she appears to have lived a simple life, and they might note that she speaks in a dialect that suggests a rural setting.
    Difficulty: *Easy*
    Objective: *Essay*

17. Students should draw a connection between an event in the story and a lesson that might be learned from it. They might say, for example, that sometimes a seemingly glamorous place or event, such as the traveling

show, on closer inspection loses its glamour, or they might say that a simple gesture by a stranger, such as Mr. Pickens's checking to see if the dog is hurt, can be indicative of his or her character.

Difficulty: *Easy*

Objective: *Essay*

18. Elzie does not seem to have had luck in having material things. Her way of speaking shows that she has not had much experience in the world and that her life has been pretty simple. However, she has had luck in finding love in her life. She is also lucky because she appreciates things that matter, such as close family relations. She would probably say that she was lucky.

Difficulty: *Average*

Objective: *Essay*

Selection Test B, p. 105

Critical Reading

1. ANS: C	DIF: Average	OBJ: Literary Analysis
2. ANS: B	DIF: Average	OBJ: Literary Analysis
3. ANS: D	DIF: Average	OBJ: Literary Analysis
4. ANS: D	DIF: Average	OBJ: Comprehension
5. ANS: B	DIF: Challenging	OBJ: Reading
6. ANS: B	DIF: Average	OBJ: Interpretation
7. ANS: C	DIF: Challenging	OBJ: Reading
8. ANS: C	DIF: Average	OBJ: Comprehension
9. ANS: A	DIF: Average	OBJ: Comprehension
10. ANS: C	DIF: Average	OBJ: Reading
11. ANS: B	DIF: Challenging	OBJ: Interpretation
12. ANS: B	DIF: Challenging	OBJ: Comprehension
13. ANS: A	DIF: Challenging	OBJ: Interpretation
14. ANS: C	DIF: Challenging	OBJ: Literary Analysis
15. ANS: B	DIF: Challenging	OBJ: Literary Analysis

Vocabulary and Grammar

16. ANS: A	DIF: Average	OBJ: Vocabulary
17. ANS: A	DIF: Average	OBJ: Grammar

Essay

18. Students will most likely make the case that Elzie has been happy and has enjoyed her life with her husband. The fact that she tells Tee the story of her first meeting with Mr. Pickens is evidence that this is a happy memory. Elzie also expresses herself in an upbeat way, another indication that she has a positive view of her life. In addition, according to the narrator, Elzie laughs or smiles during her storytelling. Students may conclude that a successful marriage to a kind, gentle man made up for any disappointments Elzie might have had about not joining the traveling show.

Difficulty: *Average*

Objective: *Essay*

19. Students should realize that the narrator has a small role in the story. The narrator simply reveals two characters, Elzie and Tee, and the setting, a porch with a rocking chair on a spring afternoon. All of the other information—about Elzie herself, about Ovella Wilson, about the Silas Greene show, and about Mr. Pickens—is revealed by Elzie in the form of dialogue. Students may realize that the extensive use of dialogue diminishes the narrator's role and allows Elzie to come alive for the reader.

Difficulty: *Challenging*

Objective: *Essay*

20. Elzie does not seem to have been lucky in terms of material success—the way that she speaks seems to indicate that she has not had much world experience and that her life has been pretty simple. However, she does seem to have been lucky with respect to finding love in her life, along with an appreciation for things that matter, such as close relationships with her family members. She would certainly say that she was lucky.

Difficulty: *Average*

Objective: *Essay*

from **Barrio Boy** by Ernesto Galarza
"A Day's Wait" by Ernest Hemingway

Vocabulary Warm-up Exercises, p. 109

A. 1. native
2. foreign
3. various
4. instructions
5. secure
6. miserable
7. condition
8. progress

B. Sample Answers

1. value; The discovery has great value because it will save lives.
2. often; I often go to the park after school, so everyone there knows me.
3. defeat; Our team will defeat the champions and win the tournament this year.
4. threat; Hurricanes are a threat to many communities on the coast.
5. needless; Dad says that a new car would be a needless expense because the car we have is in good condition.
6. definitely; I am completely in favor of the class trip, so I will definitely go.
7. alike; My eyes and my mother's eyes are alike.
8. virus; I was sick for a week with the virus that is going around.

Reading Warm-up A, p. 110

Words that students are to circle appear in parentheses.

Sample Answers

1. the language of their country; My native state is Montana; that is where I was born.

2. Many things may seem strange. You may be confused and afraid of making mistakes. You may feel shy; I do not agree because I think I would love the adventure of being in a new place.

3. you do not know the language. The words on the chalkboard and in the books look like gibberish; A teacher might demonstrate how to follow the instructions or ask another student to translate the instructions.

4. (good); When I am in excellent condition, I feel full of energy.

5. The words on the chalkboard and in the books look like gibberish. You cannot understand the teacher's instructions. Classmates, who do not know your language, cannot speak to you; if classmates are friendly and helpful, a student from another country might feel less miserable.

6. After several months, many students still need coaching or the help of an interpreter; Someone might feel secure when he or she knew what to expect.

7. Learning the various subjects in a new language is difficult because it involves learning more than basic vocabulary. The various subjects I study include math, English, science, and social studies.

8. Many graduate with honors; I am making progress in math.

Reading Warm-up B, p. 111

Words that students are to circle appear in parentheses.

Sample Answers

1. A "touch" of influenza; A moose is similar to an elk.

2. (A mild case of the flu); A nuisance is a bother, but a menace is a serious threat.

3. (disease); Another name for influenza is the flu.

4. chills, sudden high fever, headache, and aching muscles; When people get the flu, they frequently stay in bed for a few days.

5. A vaccine that could control influenza was a discovery of major importance. It was of importance because the flu can be a deadly disease.

6. research revealed that there are three types of flu viruses; At school a student might overcome the problem of learning to read.

7. Most doctors believe it is unnecessary to vaccinate everyone against the flu.

8. Everyone should absolutely talk to his or her doctor about getting vaccinated against the flu.

Writing About the Big Question, p. 112

A. 1. reality
2. evaluate
3. explain
4. evidence

B. Sample Answers

1. I used to be frightened to talk on the phone to strangers, so I would never answer the phone when it rang.

2. I thought about my problem and **concluded** that a voice on the phone could not harm me. I **convinced** myself that it was okay to answer the phone. Still, it was difficult for me to do it the first few times. But after a while I got used to it.

C. Sample Answer

you can imagine yourself.

I saw a movie two kids got lost and ended up in a haunted house. The part that was realistic was that it is easy for kids to get lost when they go out for a walk in the woods, and when they get lost, they could meet dangerous people. What was unrealistic was the presence of ghosts and goblins in the house.

Literary Analysis: Comparing Fiction and Nonfiction, p. 113

Sample Answers

1. Ernesto / the boy's father

2. Ernesto, his mother, and Miss Ryan / the boy and his father

3. There is no dialogue. / The boy asks when he will die; the father wonders why he thinks he will die; the boy tells him what the boys at his school in France said; his father explains that he has confused the Celsius and Fahrenheit thermometers.

4. Ernesto's mother goes with him on his first day of school in the United States. The principal takes Ernesto to his class. Ernesto begins to feel comfortable. His teacher, Miss Ryan, helps and encourages him and tutors him privately. He learns to speak English. / The father sees that the boy is ill, sends him to bed, and calls for a doctor. The doctor announces the boy's temperature and leaves some medicine. Throughout the day the boy appears to be bothered by something.

5. Ernesto and his mother speak no English and feel nervous in the American school. Ernesto also feels nervous because the principal and his teacher are tall. He feels reassured by their kindness and by his teacher's patience and private lessons. / The boy is apparently scared because he is sure he is going to die at any minute. He may also wonder why no one around him seems concerned about his fatal condition.

6. All of the foreign students learn to speak English. Because of Miss Hopley and Miss Ryan, Ernesto understands that he can be a proud American without feeling ashamed of being Mexican. / The boy explains his concern to his father, and his father explains the difference between the Celsius and Fahrenheit scales. The next day, the boy shows that he feels relieved.

Vocabulary Builder, p. 114

Sample Answers

A. 1. Infected people are kept away from healthy people so that infectious disease does not spread.

2. A formidable school project might be a 25-page research paper on the principles of molecular biology.

3. Someone might call a typewriter a contraption because it seems old-fashioned and strange.

4. Elizabeth is evidently healthy if signs of her health can be observed. She might look muscular and have a good complexion, for example.

5. A reassuring gesture might be a hug or a pat on the back.

6. The dog has forced the birds to fly out of the bushes.

B. 1. B; 2. C; 3. D

Open-Book Test, p. 116

Short Answer

1. Sample answers: sensitive, enthusiastic, skillful. She builds her students' self-esteem and values their differences while skillfully teaching them English.
Difficulty: *Average* **Objective:** *Interpretation*

2. "Becoming a proud American" means learning English and embracing American values while still being proud of being a Mexican. He says the school and the teacher do a good job of not "scrubbing away what made us originally foreign."
Difficulty: *Challenging* **Objective:** *Interpretation*

3. *Evidently* means "clearly or obviously." The details about how the dog flushes out quail and how the father is able to shoot two birds show that Hemingway clearly knew about hunting.
Difficulty: *Average* **Objective:** *Vocabulary*

4. The father is understanding about his son's concern. He calmly explains the difference in the two temperature scales and sympathetically calls his son "Poor old Shatz."
Difficulty: *Easy* **Objective:** *Interpretation*

5. The boy is waiting to die, while the father is waiting for his son's condition to improve.
Difficulty: *Average* **Objective:** *Interpretation*

6. *Reassuring* means "having the effect of restoring confidence." The father tells his son that on the thermometer the doctor used ninety-eight is normal, not thirty-seven. The effect of these words is that the boy relaxes because he no longer believes that he is going to die.
Difficulty: *Challenging* **Objective:** *Vocabulary*

7. The narrator of *Barrio Boy* is the author, Ernesto Galarza, who is also a character in the narrative. The narrator of "A Day's Wait" is the father in the story. Both narrators use the first-person pronouns *I* and *me*.
Difficulty: *Easy* **Objective:** *Literary Analysis*

8. *Barrio Boy* recounts events in the lives of real people, a characteristic of nonfiction. "A Day's Wait" tells about imaginary characters and events, a characteristic of fiction.
Difficulty: *Average* **Objective:** *Literary Analysis*

9. Ernesto describes his emotions as he speaks directly to the reader, such as when he talks about his fears of attending the new school. The sick boy's emotions are revealed through his actions and speech, such as when he stares at the foot of his bed, looking very strangely.
Difficulty: *Challenging* **Objective:** *Literary Analysis*

10. Although he is afraid of attending school in America, Ernest never says so and tries to do his best. The boy in the story fears he will die, but he doesn't voice these fears to his father and even tells his father to stay away so he will not catch the disease.
Difficulty: *Average* **Objective:** *Literary Analysis*

Essay

11. Students may note that both boys feel fear. Ernesto is scared because he is attending a new school, while the sick boy is scared because he believes he is dying. Both boys overcome their obstacles through trust and communication. Ernesto overcomes his fears by trusting in the kindness of his teacher and speaking English even when he mispronounces words. After a day of silence, the sick boy trusts his father enough to tell the man what is bothering him. Both boys have adults in their lives who help them. Ernesto has Miss Hopley and Miss Ryan; the sick boy has his father.
Difficulty: *Easy* **Objective:** *Essay*

12. Students should observe that Ernesto trusts Miss Ryan and thrives under her kind tutelage. He correctly pronounces *butterfly* and soon progresses to reading sentences, for which he is highly praised by his teacher. He likes and respects her to the point of admitting that he loves her. She, in turn, is considerate and supportive of him. The boy in "A Day's Wait" cares about his father. When he believes he has a fatal contagious disease, he tells his father to stay away from him. He resists drawing close to his father, however, until at last he confides in him. In turn, the father is very caring toward his son and concerned about his welfare. When the boy finally tells him what is bothering him, the father is very understanding.
Difficulty: *Average* **Objective:** *Essay*

13. Students should point out that, as fiction, Barrio Boy would include imaginary characters and events. As a result, it might include more dialogue and the plot might have more suspense and drama. On the other hand, as nonfiction "A Day's Wait" would have to tell about real people and events, so it would be restricted by what actually occurred. There might be less dialogue, since the exact words of real people might be difficult to remember. It would also most likely include more facts and details about the boy's situation. The two would remain the same in that they are both narratives and must contain a narrator, characters, dialogue, and story events.
Difficulty: *Challenging* **Objective:** *Essay*

14. Students should indicate that, in Barrio Boy, the experiences Ernesto has at Lincoln School prove that the school is a nurturing place. The principal is warm and welcoming to the frightened boy. His teacher, Miss

Ryan, goes out of her way to make the students feel comfortable. At the school, the teachers call the students as their parents do. Children are not punished for speaking their native tongue on the playground. All of this proves that the school wishes to make proud Americans by having students show pride in their heritage as they embrace their new life in America.

Students should note that because the boy in "A Day's Wait" refuses to discuss his fear of dying, he does not tell anyone about his misconception. The boy is so convinced that his temperature will be fatal that he does not note his father's lack of concern. The fact that his father goes hunting shows that he does not feel his son's illness is so severe. It is only when his father takes the boy's temperature near the end of the story that his son's fears are exposed. Once the father knows what is bothering his son, he reassures him that a temperature of one hundred and two is not fatal on the thermometer they are using.

Difficulty: *Average* **Objective:** *Essay*

Oral Response

15. Oral responses should be clear, well organized, and well supported by appropriate examples from the literary works.

Difficulty: *Average* **Objective:** *Oral Interpretation*

Selection Test A, p. 119

Critical Reading

1. ANS: C	DIF: Easy	OBJ: Interpretation
2. ANS: D	DIF: Easy	OBJ: Interpretation
3. ANS: A	DIF: Easy	OBJ: Interpretation
4. ANS: C	DIF: Easy	OBJ: Comprehension
5. ANS: B	DIF: Easy	OBJ: Literary Analysis
6. ANS: B	DIF: Easy	OBJ: Comprehension
7. ANS: A	DIF: Easy	OBJ: Comprehension
8. ANS: D	DIF: Easy	OBJ: Interpretation
9. ANS: D	DIF: Easy	OBJ: Literary Analysis
10. ANS: A	DIF: Easy	OBJ: Literary Analysis
11. ANS: A	DIF: Easy	OBJ: Literary Analysis
12. ANS: B	DIF: Easy	OBJ: Literary Analysis

Vocabulary

13. ANS: A	DIF: Easy	OBJ: Vocabulary
14. ANS: B	DIF: Easy	OBJ: Vocabulary
15. ANS: C	DIF: Easy	OBJ: Vocabulary

Essay

16. Students may observe that both boys feel fear and anxiety. The boy in "A Day's Wait" is scared because he believes he is dying. Ernesto is scared because he is attending a new school where all communication is in a language he does not understand. Both boys overcome their obstacles through trust and communication. After a day of silence, the boy in "A Day's Wait" trusts his father enough to tell him what is bothering him—and learns that his fear is based on a misunderstanding. Ernesto overcomes his fear by trusting in the kindness of his teacher and speaking English even when he mispronounces words. Both boys have adults in their lives who help them. The boy in "A Day's Wait" has his father; Ernesto has his mother, Miss Hopley, and Miss Ryan.

Difficulty: *Easy*

Objective: *Essay*

17. Students should demonstrate an understanding of fiction as a work about imagined characters and events and nonfiction as a work about actual characters and events. They should identify *Barrio Boy* as a work of nonfiction and "A Day's Wait" as a work of fiction. They should identify the narrator of *Barrio Boy* as the writer himself as he remembers his childhood and the narrator of "A Day's Wait" as the boy's father. Finally, they should realize that both selections are told from the first-person point of view.

Difficulty: *Easy*

Objective: *Essay*

18. Ernesto is expecting school to be unpleasant. He later finds out that Lincoln School is a good place. The principal is warm and welcoming to the frightened boy. His teacher, Miss Ryan, goes out of her way to make the students feel comfortable. Students should note that the boy in "A Day's Wait" refuses to discuss his fear of dying, so no one knows about his fear. The boy is so convinced that he is going to die that he does not note his father's lack of concern. The fact that his father goes hunting shows that he does not feel his son's illness is so bad. Once the father knows what is bothering his son, he reassures him that a temperature of one hundred and two is not so bad on the thermometer they are using.

Difficulty: *Average*

Objective: *Essay*

Selection Test B, p. 122

Critical Reading

1. ANS: D	DIF: Average	OBJ: Interpretation
2. ANS: A	DIF: Average	OBJ: Comprehension
3. ANS: B	DIF: Challenging	OBJ: Interpretation
4. ANS: A	DIF: Average	OBJ: Interpretation
5. ANS: B	DIF: Average	OBJ: Comprehension
6. ANS: B	DIF: Average	OBJ: Literary Analysis
7. ANS: C	DIF: Challenging	OBJ: Literary Analysis
8. ANS: D	DIF: Challenging	OBJ: Literary Analysis
9. ANS: A	DIF: Average	OBJ: Literary Analysis
10. ANS: B	DIF: Challenging	OBJ: Literary Analysis
11. ANS: B	DIF: Challenging	OBJ: Literary Analysis
12. ANS: D	DIF: Average	OBJ: Literary Analysis

Vocabulary

Essay

16. Students should observe that the boy in "A Day's Wait" quietly disobeys his father, not going to bed when his father tells him to. When he believes that he has a fatal contagious disease, he shows that he cares about his father—and the other members of the household—by telling them to stay away from him. He resists drawing close to his father, however, until at last he confides in him. Unlike the boy in "A Day's Wait," Ernesto never resists Miss Ryan. He likes her right away and quickly comes to respect her. He admits to loving her, though it is not the love of a boy for a parent.

    Difficulty: *Average*

    Objective: *Essay*

17. Students should correctly identify the genre, narrator, and point of view of each work. They should recognize that dialogue is incidental to the excerpt from *Barrio Boy*, whereas "A Day's Wait" relies heavily on dialogue to reveal the action, and they should make reasoned comparisons of the main characters.

    Difficulty: *Challenging*

    Objective: *Essay*

18. • Students should indicate that the experiences Ernesto has at Lincoln School prove that the school is a nurturing place. The principal is warm and welcoming to the frightened boy. His teacher, Miss Ryan, goes out of her way to make the students feel comfortable. At the school, the teachers call the students as their parents do. Children are not punished for speaking their native tongue on the playground. All of this proves that the school wishes to make proud Americans by having students show pride in their heritage as they embrace their new life in America.

    • Students should note that because the boy refuses to discuss his fear of dying, he does not tell anyone about his misconception. The boy is so convinced that his temperature will be fatal that he does not note his father's lack of concern. The fact that his father goes hunting shows that he does not feel his son's illness is so severe. It is only when his father takes the boy's temperature near the end of the story that his son's fears are exposed. Once the father knows what is bothering his son, he reassures him that a temperature of one hundred and two is not fatal on the thermometer they are using.

    Difficulty: *Average*

    Objective: *Essay*

Writing Workshop

Descriptive Essay: Integrating Grammar Skills, p. 126

A. 1. alumni
    2. children
    3. curricula

B. 1. Four men went hunting for deer.
    2. The dates in parentheses show when we received the data.
    3. The two women sheared more than a dozen sheep.

Benchmark Test 1, p. 127

MULTIPLE CHOICE

1. ANS: B
2. ANS: B
3. ANS: D
4. ANS: C
5. ANS: B
6. ANS: C
7. ANS: A
8. ANS: C
9. ANS: D
10. ANS: A
11. ANS: C
12. ANS: B
13. ANS: C
14. ANS: D
15. ANS: B
16. ANS: D
17. ANS: A
18. ANS: A
19. ANS: D
20. ANS: C
21. ANS: B
22. ANS: A
23. ANS: B
24. ANS: B
25. ANS: C
26. ANS: A
27. ANS: D
28. ANS: B
29. ANS: B
30. ANS: D

WRITING

31. Students' descriptions of an object in nature should contain exaggerations for effect.

32. Students should be evaluated on their use of textual evidence to compare and contrast. They should show an understanding of setting or characterization. Students should submit a thought-out paragraph and not simply a list of similarities and differences.

33. Students' descriptions should contain vivid sensory language that helps the reader picture the setting.

"All Summer in a Day" by Ray Bradbury

Vocabulary Warm-up Exercises, p. 135

A. 1. blessed
2. frail
3. fumbling
4. pleading
5. muffled
6. immense
7. gush
8. crushed

B. Sample Answers

1. picture; Amber took lifelike pictures with her digital camera.
2. soaked; Bobby's shoes were soaked, and they squished as he walked.
3. enormous; The enormous sandwich fed all ten people.
4. put; Brian put an extra paragraph in his letter to make his message clear.
5. foretell; Did the fortune teller's crystal ball foretell the future?
6. memory; Madeline's memory of her grandfather was vague because she had hardly known him.
7. stopped; Flights out of Boston's airport were stopped until the fog cleared.
8. culture; In certain ways the culture of the ancient Romans was like ours.

Reading Warm-up A, p. 136

Words that students are to circle appear in parentheses.

Sample Answers

1. cool water against his hot skin; how refreshing that was; *Blessed* means "bringing comfort or joy."
2. The sun was weaker then; *Frail* means "weak; not strong."
3. (walked through them [the piles of raked leaves]); The fumbling player never caught the ball.
4. (giants); *Immense* means "extremely large."
5. (the weaker creatures); An aluminum can might be crushed.
6. after a thick snowfall blanketed the streets; *Muffled* means "covered to prevent sound from being heard."
7. (begging); *Pleading* means "begging or making a sincere appeal."

8. the melting snow; A gush of rain caused the gutters to overflow.

Reading Warm-up B, p. 137

Words that students are to circle appear in parentheses.

Sample Answers

1. plants and animals might be found there; *Predict* means "to foretell."
2. (human); Civilization is the culture or way of life of a people.
3. tiny; *Gigantic* means "very big; huge."
4. a gigantic, dense cloud covers most of Venus's surface; My photograph of the Grand Canyon helps me remember my vacation in Arizona.
5. (the heat); The heat is trapped, making the planet's surface very hot.
6. (lava flows); *Drenched* means "soaked with liquid."
7. (those formations); As a remembrance of the time they spent together, Brooke's cousin sent Brooke a picture of the two of them.
8. (probes); The editor inserted a comma into the compound sentence.

Writing About the Big Question, p. 138

A. 1. factual
2. debate
3. factual

B. Sample Answers

1. My dog;   My computer
2. The two things I picked are **evidence** of how I spend most of my time. The **reality** of my life is that I come home from school and immediately take my dog for a walk. I love spending time playing catch with my dog or just cuddling with her and petting her. I also **revealed** that my other favorite thing is my computer which helps me research all kinds of interesting information.

C. Sample Answer

my sister, my dog, pizza

The feelings of the girl and what she missed were true and believable. The fact that she was living on Venus was fiction.

Reading: Recognize Details That Indicate the Author's Purpose, p. 139

1. to entertain and/or to create a mood
2. to inform
3. to entertain and/or to create a mood
4. to entertain, to inform, and/or to create a mood

Literary Analysis: Setting, p. 140

Sample Answers

1. The setting is a shower in the underground school. Margot had become terrified of the water, which she seems to associate with the constant rain of Venus.

2. The setting is the underground school, a gloomy or frightening place. Margot is terrified or perhaps very angry about being kept from seeing the sun.

3. The setting is Venus during the brief time when the rain stops. It seems to be a safe, comforting place, and the children react to it with joy.

Vocabulary Builder, p. 141

A. Sample answers to items 2–4 and 6:

1. Correct

2. It is said that water is vital to life; you cannot live without it.

3. During the storm, the wind blew tumultuously.

4. Because Margot was not resilient, she could not get used to conditions on Venus.

5. Correct

6. During the holiday season, we always savored the sweet smell of pumpkin pie as it came out of the oven.

B. Sample Answer

As we drove along the road, we felt nothing but the pure vitality of our youth. Little did we know that soon we would have an accident in which one of us would survive and the other would not revive after emergency treatment.

Enrichment: Figurative Language, p. 142

A. 1. metaphor, metaphor; "Margot," "an old photograph" and "her voice," "a ghost"

2. simile; "the sun on their cheeks," "a warm iron"

3. metaphor; "the jungle," "a nest of octopi"

4. simile; "animals escaped from their caves," "the children"

B. Students' similes or metaphors should demonstrate their understanding of these concepts.

Open-Book Test, p. 143

Short Answer

1. The children live on Venus, where it has been raining for seven years. The children have been told that the rain will stop and they will see the sun.
   Difficulty: *Easy*   **Objective:** *Literary Analysis*

2. Sample answer: Margot has been on Venus for only four years. The other children have always lived there. They do not remember the sun, but Margot does. The author's purpose in making Margot different is to emphasize the strangeness of life on Venus.
   Difficulty: *Challenging*   **Objective:** *Reading*

3. The word *slackening* means "easing." The children are waiting for the rain to stop and for the sun to come out, which the scientists have told them will happen.
   Difficulty: *Easy*   **Objective:** *Vocabulary*

4. The author describes Margot as "frail" and washed-out looking. She is almost a "ghost" in her appearance, suggesting that her feelings are also very delicate. It is as if she is fading and dying without the sun.

Difficulty: *Average*   **Objective:** *Interpretation*

5. Margot and the other children share the circumstance of suffering from constant rain and a lack of sun. Because she has seen the sun more recently than the others, they are jealous and distrustful of her. They do not believe what she says about the sun and accuse her of lying.
   Difficulty: *Easy*   **Objective:** *Interpretation*

6. The author uses the word *crime* to emphasize how strongly the other children feel about Margot. They hate her for remembering the sun and treat her as though she had committed some illegal act.
   Difficulty: *Average*   **Objective:** *Reading*

7. Example 1: Clutches her hands to ears; Example 2: Screams that water must not touch her head. Her reaction is intense because it magnifies how she feels about the rain. The shower is like rain inside. She feels trapped by being "rained on" both inside and outside.
   Difficulty: *Average*   **Objective:** *Literary Analysis*

8. Resilient means "springing back into shape." The children are *resilient* because, like the weeds, they are able to bounce back on a daily basis without letting the rain discourage them.
   Difficulty: *Average*   **Objective:** *Vocabulary*

9. The children become excited at seeing the sun, running around and turning their faces to the sky. They look around them and enjoy sounds and colors they have not experienced in years, behaving as though they have been shut in cages. When the rain begins again, one of them starts to cry, and they all become sad.
   Difficulty: *Easy*   **Objective:** *Literary Analysis*

10. Sample answer: The children feel guilty. One of them lets out a cry and they cannot meet one another's glances. They are "solemn and pale." However, they are slow to let Margot out, because they are afraid of her reaction or of getting in trouble.
    Difficulty: *Challenging*   **Objective:** *Interpretation*

Essay

11. Phrases such as "thousands and thousands of days" and "the drum and gush of water" give a strong sense of how constant the rain is, so the reader gets a sense of the characters being trapped in the constant rain. When the sun comes out, the change is so strong that all sound seems to stop, causing the children to feel shocked. The mood changes a bit when the sun comes out, but the overall mood of the story is sad and angry.
    Difficulty: *Easy*   **Objective:** *Essay*

12. Sample answer: The author uses very strong visual images of the rain coming in "tidal waves" that "crushed" the forests repeatedly. In addition, he describes the warmth of the sun through Margot's eyes as a flower, a coin, and a fire, to give readers a sense of the power of the sun and her relationship to it.
    Difficulty: *Average*   **Objective:** *Essay*

13. Sample answer: Margot's experience could be compared to that of a child moving to a new school or, more likely, moving from one country or culture to another. Her experience was in sharp contrast to that of the children around her. They didn't understand her reality or believe her. Being challenged in this way could be very difficult for anyone moving to a new place.
    Difficulty: *Challenging* **Objective:** *Essay*

14. Students may say that Margot found the truth about the sun by experiencing it. But because her truth did not match their own experience, the other children refused to believe her and treated her cruelly. When the children found that Margot was telling the truth—when they experienced that truth for themselves—they realized that their treatment of Margot was wrong. Both Margot and the children relied on their experience to find the truth. However, the children refused to believe anything but their own experience, which limited their understanding.
    Difficulty: *Average* **Objective:** *Essay*

Oral Response

15. Oral responses should be clear, well organized, and well supported by appropriate examples from the selections.
    Difficulty: *Average* **Objective:** *Oral Interpretation*

Selection Test A, p. 146

Critical Reading

1. ANS: C	DIF: Easy	OBJ: Comprehension
2. ANS: B	DIF: Easy	OBJ: Reading
3. ANS: B	DIF: Easy	OBJ: Literary Analysis
4. ANS: A	DIF: Easy	OBJ: Reading
5. ANS: B	DIF: Easy	OBJ: Comprehension
6. ANS: D	DIF: Easy	OBJ: Interpretation
7. ANS: A	DIF: Easy	OBJ: Interpretation
8. ANS: C	DIF: Easy	OBJ: Comprehension
9. ANS: D	DIF: Easy	OBJ: Interpretation
10. ANS: B	DIF: Easy	OBJ: Literary Analysis

Vocabulary and Grammar

11. ANS: A	DIF: Easy	OBJ: Vocabulary
12. ANS: B	DIF: Easy	OBJ: Grammar
13. ANS: C	DIF: Easy	OBJ: Grammar

Essay

14. Students should state that the setting is the planet Venus, where it rains incessantly for years on end, with the sun shining for only a couple of hours every seven years. They might mention the forests, the underground city, and the constant noise of the rainfall. In describing the mood, they will likely describe a gloominess. Finally, students should recognize that the setting in effect creates the mood of the story.
    Difficulty: *Easy*
    Objective: *Essay*

15. Students should point to Margot's pale skin and the washed-out colors of her eyes, lips, and hair. They might also mention her ghostlike voice. Margot is also weak-willed—she allows herself to be shoved by one of the boys in her class. In addition, she does not like to play, she shuns the others' games, and she comes alive only when talking about, writing about, or looking forward to seeing the sun.
    Difficulty: *Easy*
    Objective: *Essay*

16. Students may say that Margot found the truth about the sun by experiencing it. But the other children refused to believe her and treated her cruelly because their experience was different. When the children found that Margot was telling the truth—when they experienced that truth for themselves—they realized that their treatment of Margot was wrong.
    Difficulty: *Average*
    Objective: *Essay*

Selection Test B, p. 149

Critical Reading

1. ANS: D	DIF: Average	OBJ: Comprehension
2. ANS: A	DIF: Average	OBJ: Interpretation
3. ANS: B	DIF: Average	OBJ: Comprehension
4. ANS: B	DIF: Average	OBJ: Literary Analysis
5. ANS: D	DIF: Average	OBJ: Comprehension
6. ANS: C	DIF: Average	OBJ: Interpretation
7. ANS: B	DIF: Challenging	OBJ: Literary Analysis
8. ANS: C	DIF: Challenging	OBJ: Reading
9. ANS: C	DIF: Challenging	OBJ: Literary Analysis
10. ANS: B	DIF: Average	OBJ: Reading
11. ANS: C	DIF: Average	OBJ: Reading
12. ANS: C	DIF: Average	OBJ: Literary Analysis

Vocabulary and Grammar

13. ANS: A	DIF: Average	OBJ: Vocabulary
14. ANS: C	DIF: Challenging	OBJ: Vocabulary
15. ANS: A	DIF: Average	OBJ: Grammar
16. ANS: C	DIF: Challenging	OBJ: Grammar

Essay

17. Students should refer to some of these differences: Margot has lived on Earth, while they have lived on Venus all their lives; she remembers what the sun looks and feels like, while they cannot recall it; she does not want to play their games because she misses the sun so much; she is pale and silent and thin. They resent her for setting herself apart from them; they resent that she knows what the sun is like; they resent that her parents will take her back to Earth while they must remain on Venus.
    Difficulty: *Average*
    Objective: *Essay*

18. Expect students to refer to images but not to use direct quotations from the story. Students should include in their essays a statement relating the images to their experience of the setting. Some images (including direct quotations) are presented here:

For sight, they might refer to gold, "a yellow crayon or a coin large enough to buy the world with," Margot's washed-out appearance, the trembling closet door, the sun "very large" and "the color of flaming bronze," the sky "a blazing blue tile color," the jungle "a nest of octopi, clustering up great arms of fleshlike weed, wavering," "the color of rubber and ash," "the color of stones and white cheeses and ink," "the color of the moon," the jungle as a "mattress," the children standing "like so many stakes," and the "blue and terrible" lightning.

For sound, they might remember the children stirring at night, "the tatting drum, the endless shaking down of clear bead necklaces upon the roof," and so on, Margot's ghostlike voice, her screams in the shower rooms, her "muffled cries" from behind the closet door, the absence of sound when the rain stops, the children's laughter, the "sigh and squeak" of the jungle vegetation, the "boom of thunder," "the gigantic sound of the rain falling in tons and avalanches," the silence behind the closet door.

For touch, they might refer to "a warmness, like a blushing in the face," "the sun on their cheeks like a warm iron," the cold drops of rain on their noses, cheeks, and mouths, and so on.

Difficulty: *Challenging*

Objective: *Essay*

19. Students may say that Margot found the truth about the sun by experiencing it. But because her truth did not match their own experience, the other children refused to believe her and treated her cruelly. When the children found that Margot was telling the truth—when they experienced that truth for themselves—they realized that their treatment of Margot was wrong. Both Margot and the children relied on their experience to find the truth. However, the children refused to believe anything but their own experience, which limited their understanding.

Difficulty: *Average*

Objective: *Essay*

"Suzy and Leah" by Jane Yolen

Vocabulary Warm-up Exercises, p. 153

A. 1. diary
2. trim
3. prickly
4. porcupine
5. pecked
6. furious
7. fever
8. shrank

B. Sample Answers

1. No; *assigned* means "appointed to carry out a duty," so if you have been assigned to do something, you have not volunteered to do it.

2. Yes, there is danger, because barbed wire has sharp, pointed spears that can hurt you.

3. Yes, he or she is lying, because a false answer is one that is untrue.

4. No; a grouch is an unpleasant, ill-tempered person.

5. No; a rickety house is poorly built, so it would not be permanent or last for a long time.

6. No, it would not be pleasant to take a breath of stale air because something that is stale is not fresh.

Reading Warm-up A, p. 154

Words that students are to circle appear in parentheses.

Sample Answers

1. her family endured constant hunger. There was much sickness and fever due to poor nutrition and unclean conditions. Anne Frank's diary tells how two Jewish families in Amsterdam hid from the Nazis.

2. (due to poor nutrition and unclean conditions); A fever is an abnormally high body temperature that often accompanies an illness.

3. (barbed wire like a horrible prickly porcupine); Trim is the edging around something.

4. the fence, with its trim of barbed wire; Barbed wire has pointed spears that look like the quills of a porcupine.

5. The soldier probably sounded angry and threatening. The wind during a hurricane sounds furious.

6. The woman and her brother shrank in fear. The child, afraid of the storm, shrank into a corner of the room.

7. the butt of his rifle; The hungry chicken pecked at the grain.

Reading Warm-up B, p. 155

Words that students are to circle appear in parentheses.

Sample Answers

1. His face was fixed in a permanent frown. A grouch is an ill-tempered, unpleasant person.

2. (fence); *Rickety* means "unstable or poorly made."

3. A permanent frown is one that never goes away. The scar from the appendectomy was likely to be permanent.

4. Sean thinks Mr. Mulligan should put up barbed wire because he does not seem to like people coming into his yard. Barbed wire might be used to keep cattle in an enclosed area.

5. Sean was assigned the job of bringing cookies to Mr. Mulligan; *Assigned* means "appointed to do a job."

6. (old); Cereal, rolls, crackers, and cake can get stale.

7. *False* means "fake" or "not true or real."

8. Mr. Mulligan's appendix was infected. (his neighbor was doubled up in pain), (Mr. Mulligan groaned), (He had appendicitis.)

Writing About the Big Question, p. 156

A. 1. fiction/truth
2. convince
3. awareness
4. evaluate

B. Sample Answers

1. clothing worn; common foods eaten; prices of clothing and food
2. To write a novel that takes place in the future, the author would have to have an **awareness** of what inventions are possible in the future. Even so, the novel would be all **fiction** as opposed to a historical novel, which is partly fact. There can be no **factual** information about the future because it hasn't taken place yet.

C. Sample Answer

the Salem Witch Hunts

The fact that the hunts took place and that people were executed on the suspicion of being a witch would be factual. I would make up a fictional character—a thirteen-year-old girl whose mother is accused of being a witch.

Reading: Recognize Details That Indicate the Author's Purpose, p. 157

1. to inform
2. to inform and/or to create a mood
3. to entertain
4. to inform and/or to create a mood
5. to entertain

Literary Analysis: Setting, p. 158

Sample Answers

1. Suzy is describing the refugee camp. She thinks it is awful and cannot imagine anyone living there.
2. Leah is talking about the American refugee camp and the German concentration camp. She feels unsafe in the refugee camp.
3. Leah is writing about the American school. She finds it odd that Americans call a room a bathroom when it contains no bath.
4. Suzy is describing the German concentration camps. She is horrified and can hardly believe what her mother has told her.

Vocabulary Builder, p. 159

A. Sample answers to items 2 through 5:

1. Correct.
2. The porridge made a wonderful breakfast.
3. The permanent frown on Leah's face remained even when Suzy offered candy.
4. The teacher was wrong when she falsely accused Sam of cheating.
5. It is common to keep items like dishes in the kitchen cupboard.
6. Correct.

B. Sample answers to items 2 and 3:

1. Correct
2. The porridge made a wonderful breakfast.

3. The permanent frown on Leah's face remained even when Suzy offered candy.

C. 1. The word *manual* relates to work done with the hands instead of machines.
2. The word *manual* relates to being able to control the camera using human knowledge.
3. The word *manual* relates to the extreme skill in the artist's hands.

Enrichment: Communication Skills, p. 160

Students will have completed the assignment successfully if they and their partners complete the chart and effectively discuss the similarities and differences in their ideas.

"All Summer in a Day" by Ray Bradbury
"Suzy and Leah" by Jane Yolen

Integrated Language Skills: Grammar, p. 161

A. 1. I, she, I; circle *her*
2. They, I; circle *them*
3. She; circle *him*
4. They, she; circle *her*
5. He, she; circle *her, him*
6. They; circle *them, her*

B. 1. They wanted to see the sun, so she let them go outside.
2. She hoped to see the sun, but they locked her in the closet.
3. He said she was a liar, but she stuck to her story.
4. She refuses Suzy's candy because she doesn't want to look like an animal.

"Suzy and Leah" by Jane Yolen

Open-Book Test, p. 164

Short Answer

1. *Refugees* are people who have to leave their country because it is unsafe. Leah and the others have fled Germany and the Nazi concentration camps.
   Difficulty: *Easy* **Objective:** *Vocabulary*
2. Leah is in a refugee camp that has "rickety wooden buildings" surrounded by a high fence with barbed wire. It is not fancy, but it is better than a concentration camp. Suzy thinks it is awful because she has nothing but her comfortable home to compare it to.
   Difficulty: *Average* **Objective:** *Literary Analysis*
3. Avi has stopped speaking. His grandmother hid him from the Nazis in a cupboard. When they took her away, he stayed in the cupboard for three days "without food, without water, without words."
   Difficulty: *Easy* **Objective:** *Interpretation*
4. The author is emphasizing how foreign and new everything is to the refugee children. They still behave as if each treat is their last. Suzy laughs at them, which shows how little she understands about them (although

she then helps them). Leah refuses to take anything from Suzy because she laughed, which broadens the gap between them.

Difficulty: *Challenging*   **Objective:** *Reading*

5. Leah does not feel safe. The Americans say the refugees are safe, but she heard the same from the Germans, so she does not believe it. She does not trust the Americans in any way.

Difficulty: *Average*   **Objective:** *Interpretation*

6. Suzy has lived a comfortable life and so has no understanding of why Leah is so sensitive and serious. She helps the children by bringing treats, but she also laughs at them and resents their wearing her old clothes. All she recognizes is that they are different from her.

Difficulty: *Challenging*   **Objective:** *Interpretation*

7. Leah thinks school is strange: the Americans call the toilets the bathroom, and she is in school with boys for the first time. She says she does not care about being placed in a low grade, but she probably does. She is also scared about the name tags because they remind her of being labeled as a Jew in Germany.

Difficulty: *Challenging*   **Objective:** *Literary Analysis*

8. The word *permanent* means "lasting for a long time." Suzy is annoyed that Leah does not seem to appreciate people being nice to her. She does not expect Leah to change, but she seems to want her to.

Difficulty: *Average*   **Objective:** *Vocabulary*

9. Sample answer: Before: doesn't want to give Leah her green dress; doesn't understand why Leah dislikes her so much. After: asks her mother questions about Leah's experiences; gives Leah her own diary.

Difficulty: *Average*   **Objective:** *Reading*

10. Leah explains that in the German camp, people who were sick were killed because they could not work. She was afraid to tell anyone that she was sick. It makes a lot of sense.

Difficulty: *Easy*   **Objective:** *Interpretation*

Essay

11. The similarities are that they both have places to sleep and eat, and they are both in safe places. However, Leah's shelter is not a home, and she feels trapped there rather than protected. Suzy's house seems comfortable, based on the description of the things she owns and how her mother looks.

Difficulty: *Easy*   **Objective:** *Essay*

12. Leah seems to be trying to maintain a connection with the good part of her past, which includes her dead mother and brother. In fact, she worries about liking Suzy's mother, because she is afraid that she might forget her own mother as she tries to adjust to life in a new place.

Difficulty: *Average*   **Objective:** *Essay*

13. Sample answer: Leah seems more sensitive than some of the other refugees. She does not rush to the fence to receive sweets. She is wary of Suzy and the other Americans. She seems not to trust anyone still. She is also concerned about the other refugees whose English is not as good as hers, and she has a special concern for Avi. She also refuses to wear a name tag, because she fears that it is like wearing a yellow star.

Difficulty: *Challenging*   **Objective:** *Essay*

14. Students should say that Suzy finds the truth by reading Leah's diary. Some may say this was not the best way to find out because she did it without Leah's knowledge. Leah may feel as if she cannot trust Suzy and they will never really be friends. Others may say it was the best way because otherwise she would not have found out the truth. Leah would not have told her. With the truth out in the open, the path is cleared for the girls to have a true friendship.

Difficulty: *Average*   **Objective:** *Essay*

Oral Response

15. Oral responses should be clear, well organized, and well supported by appropriate examples from the selection.

Difficulty: *Average*   **Objective:** *Oral Interpretation*

"Suzy and Leah" by Jane Yolen

Selection Test A, p. 167

Critical Reading

1. ANS: A	DIF: Easy	OBJ: Literary Analysis
2. ANS: D	DIF: Easy	OBJ: Literary Analysis
3. ANS: B	DIF: Easy	OBJ: Interpretation
4. ANS: C	DIF: Easy	OBJ: Comprehension
5. ANS: C	DIF: Easy	OBJ: Interpretation
6. ANS: C	DIF: Easy	OBJ: Interpretation
7. ANS: B	DIF: Easy	OBJ: Interpretation
8. ANS: C	DIF: Easy	OBJ: Comprehension
9. ANS: C	DIF: Easy	OBJ: Reading
10. ANS: D	DIF: Easy	OBJ: Comprehension
11. ANS: B	DIF: Easy	OBJ: Interpretation

Vocabulary and Grammar

12. ANS: C	DIF: Easy	OBJ: Vocabulary
13. ANS: D	DIF: Easy	OBJ: Grammar
14. ANS: D	DIF: Easy	OBJ: Grammar

Essay

15. Students may suggest that Leah's experiences as a Jew in Nazi Germany taught her that a government may abuse and murder its citizens. Leah has evidently been imprisoned in a Nazi concentration camp, where her mother and brother died. Now, in the United States, she is again in a camp, and she wonders whether Americans will turn out to be as cruel to the Jews as the Germans

were. She keeps her thoughts and feelings to herself so as not to call attention to herself or to the little boy named Avi. She resents Suzy's attempts to give her things because she thinks that Suzy does not see her for who she is.

In contrast, Suzy seems to have experienced no hardship and to know little about the events that have been taking place in the world as she has been growing up. She has nice clothes, plenty of food, and a caring mother. She wishes to share some of her possessions with others, and she does not understand why one child, Leah, is unfriendly and ungrateful. Only after she reads Leah's diary and asks her mother to explain the parts she does not understand does Suzy realize the terrible experience Leah has undergone as a Jew in Nazi Europe. This knowledge makes her more determined to be a better friend to Leah.

Difficulty: *Easy*

Objective: *Essay*

16. Students who choose one of the settings in the United States should discuss how it brings Suzy and Leah together and allows each character to reveal her background and her thoughts about the other character. At the refugee camp, the school, and Suzy's home, the conflict between Suzy and Leah is established; at the hospital, it is resolved. Students who choose to write about the Nazi concentration camp might discuss Leah's conflict with herself as she struggles to make sense of her new surroundings in terms of the experiences she has had.

Difficulty: *Easy*

Objective: *Essay*

17. Students should say that Suzy finds the truth by reading Leah's diary. Some may say this was not the best way to find out because she did it without Leah's knowledge. Leah may feel as though she cannot trust Suzy and they will never really be friends. Others may say it was the best way because otherwise she would not have found out the truth. Leah would not have told her.

Difficulty: *Average*

Objective: *Essay*

Selection Test B, p. 170

Critical Reading

1. ANS: C	DIF: Challenging	OBJ: Literary Analysis
2. ANS: B	DIF: Average	OBJ: Literary Analysis
3. ANS: B	DIF: Challenging	OBJ: Interpretation
4. ANS: D	DIF: Challenging	OBJ: Comprehension
5. ANS: A	DIF: Challenging	OBJ: Interpretation
6. ANS: A	DIF: Average	OBJ: Reading
7. ANS: C	DIF: Challenging	OBJ: Interpretation
8. ANS: C	DIF: Challenging	OBJ: Interpretation
9. ANS: B	DIF: Average	OBJ: Interpretation
10. ANS: B	DIF: Average	OBJ: Reading
11. ANS: C	DIF: Average	OBJ: Interpretation

12. ANS: A	DIF: Average	OBJ: Interpretation
13. ANS: D	DIF: Average	OBJ: Literary Analysis
14. ANS: C	DIF: Average	OBJ: Comprehension

Vocabulary and Grammar

15. ANS: C	DIF: Average	OBJ: Vocabulary
16. ANS: A	DIF: Average	OBJ: Vocabulary
17. ANS: A	DIF: Average	OBJ: Grammar
18. ANS: C	DIF: Average	OBJ: Grammar

Essay

19. Students might realize that in effect "Suzy and Leah" has two first-person narrators. Students should at least realize that the reader learns about the characters from their own words in their diary entries. The author has each character tell about herself and reflect on the other character. In that way, the reader sees Leah from her own point of view and from Suzy's, and the reader similarly sees Suzy from her point of view and from Leah's.

Difficulty: *Average*

Objective: *Essay*

20. Students should recognize that the central setting—the refugee camp—brings together the two main characters, Leah and Suzy, and creates the circumstances for their conflict. Leah, a resident of the camp, has been traumatized by her experiences in Nazi Germany, while Suzy, a resident of the town in which the camp is located, apparently knows nothing of the Nazis' treatment of Europe's Jews. Suzy visits the camp to offer candy to the residents and naively wonders why one girl, Leah, remains aloof. The conflict is intensified at Suzy's school and is resolved at the hospital. Leah fears she will be killed if her illness is discovered. Instead, her life is saved, and she begins to understand that she is safe. And finally, at the hospital, she and Suzy reach an understanding.

Difficulty: *Challenging*

Objective: *Essay*

21. Students should say that Suzy finds the truth by reading Leah's diary. Some may say this was not the best way to find out because she did it without Leah's knowledge. Leah may feel as though she cannot trust Suzy and they will never really be friends. Others may say it was the best way because otherwise she would not have found out the truth. Leah would not have told her. With the truth out in the open, the path is cleared for the girls to have a true friendship.

Difficulty: *Average*

Objective: *Essay*

"My First Free Summer" by Julia Alvarez

Vocabulary Warm-up Exercises, p. 174

A. 1. scheduled
2. connections

3. activities
4. documents
5. reviews
6. accompanied
7. terminal
8. runway

B. **Sample Answers**

1. F; If you are attending something, you will be at the place or the event.
2. T; An attitude is a feeling, or mind-set, in relation to something.
3. F; *Bliss* means "joy," so it is the opposite of *sorrow*.
4. F; In a democracy the government is ruled by all the people, not one person.
5. T; *Endured* means "put up with something" such as a long lecture.
6. F; *Escorting* means "bringing someone somewhere," so if someone is escorting you, he or she is going along with you, not following you.
7. F; Prospects are the chances for success, so if a team's prospects are good, the chances are the team will win.
8. T; *Summoned* means "called together for a meeting," so if a principal summoned students, she wanted to meet with them.

Reading Warm-up A, p. 175

Words that students are to circle appear in parentheses.

Sample Answers

1. (a bustling airline terminal); A terminal is a transportation station.
2. Flights are scheduled. Computers are programmed to display arrivals and departures. Baggage is tagged and inspected. Security guards check passports and other documents before passengers board the planes. Meanwhile, a ticket agent reviews seat assignments. Outside mechanics check the aircraft. They ready each runway before a plane lands or takes off; Before traveling, I pack my bags and make sure I have my ticket and identification.
3. (flights); *Scheduled* means "planned for a certain time."
4. (passports and other documents); Personal documents, such as birth certificates, should be kept in a safe place.
5. If an agent reviews two tickets with the same assignment, he or she must find a different seat for one of the passengers. *Reviews* means "examines" or "inspects."
6. a plane lands or takes off; A runway is a strip of pavement where planes take off and land.
7. (contacts); A movie star might have connections with producers and directors.
8. an increase in air travel; The changing color of the leaves *accompanied* the cool fall weather.

Reading Warm-up B, p. 176

Words that students are to circle appear in parentheses.

Sample Answers

1. (for earning a living); Prospects are expected chances for success.
2. (harsh treatment); We endured high temperatures in the desert.
3. (more freedom); A democracy is a government ruled by the people or their elected officials.
4. (positive); Yes, their positive attitude would have helped the immigrants endure the hardships of their situation.
5. (great joy); I experience bliss when I listen to my favorite music.
6. The officials were escorting the immigrants from station to station in the huge complex of buildings on Ellis Island. *Escorting* means "bringing someone somewhere."
7. They did not have the luxury of attending information sessions. I like attending ballgames.
8. The immigrants were summoned to meet with a series of officials. The bell summoned us to class.

Writing About the Big Question, p. 177

A. 1. reveal
2. insight
3. debate

B. **Sample Answers**

1. The other day, I borrowed my sister's dictionary from her desk and left it in my room accidentally. She thought I intentionally took it from her to annoy her.
2. I might be able to **convince** my sister that my intent was not to annoy her. I would have to sit down with her and sincerely apologize and tell her the **truth**. She may not believe me, though, because I cannot prove that my intent was good.

C. **Sample Answer**

sometimes lets you see the events differently from how you originally saw them.

When I was four years old, my parents moved here from Mexico. I do not remember the move. I was too young. But I could use the fact that we moved and some of the stories my parents tell to create a fictional work. For example, they had a lot of trouble learning English, and there are some funny stories about how I, as a four-year-old, helped them to get around because I learned the language more quickly.

Reading: Use Background Information to Determine the Author's Purpose, p. 178

1. to inform or to inform and create a mood
2. to entertain or to entertain and inform
3. to inform

Literary Analysis: Historical Context, p. 179

Sample Answers

1. Because Alvarez does not know the seriousness of the political situation, she is able to live a carefree existence.

2. Now the reality of the political situation affects Alvarez's life: She is lonely, and her family is fearful.

3. The family is apparently at such risk that they must flee the country in a hurry. Politics has totally disrupted Alvarez's life.

4. The political situation has placed the family at the mercy of the U.S. immigration officials, and Alvarez, sensing her parents' fear, has become fearful herself.

Vocabulary Builder, p. 180

A. 1. Before her first free summer, Julia vowed to pass all her subjects.

2. The mission of the diplomats was to negotiate the terms of the treaty.

3. When Julia's mother summoned her daughters, they came to her.

4. The *repressive* government banned freedom of speech and religion for all of its citizens.

5. The judge argued against a harsh sentence because of all the *extenuating* circumstances of the crime.

6. When all the witnesses offered a *contradiction* to the defendant's testimony, it was obvious that the defendant was lying.

B. 1. F; A prediction tells what will happen in the future.

2. T; This is an accurate summary of the function of a dictionary.

3. F; A dictator rules by force and is seldom put into office by a democratic election.

Enrichment: Life and Literature, p. 181

1. She had difficulty telling where one word ended and the next word began.

2. He realized just how brutal the Trujillo dictatorship was.

3. Because she survived the Trujillo dictatorship, she felt a responsibility to tell the story of these three women who did not survive to tell their story themselves.

4. A genre is a category of something, such as literature.

5. Alvarez has shown her commitment to the Dominican Republic by writing the story of the Mirabel sisters, founding an organic farm there, and writing children's books for people on the farm who are learning to read.

Open-Book Test, p. 182

Short Answer

1. Alvarez spent her summers in summer school because she had trouble mastering many of her American school subjects, especially English.
   Difficulty: *Easy* **Objective:** *Interpretation*

2. The word *vowed* means "promised." You can assume that because she promised to become a better student, it would happen.
   Difficulty: *Easy* **Objective:** *Vocabulary*

3. Her description shows that the holidays were all related to the dictator who controlled the Dominican Republic. It shows the power and absolute control of the dictator.
   Difficulty: *Average* **Objective:** *Literary Analysis*

4. The author was learning English and American history and geography. The information sets the historical context by showing what Alvarez's parents hoped would happen. She was being taught these subjects to learn about "the nation that would soon be liberating" them from the dictatorship.
   Difficulty: *Average* **Objective:** *Literary Analysis*

5. Her grandfather had donated the land on which the school was built, and her grandmother had encouraged the person who founded the school. The author was one of very few Dominicans who were allowed to attend.
   Difficulty: *Easy* **Objective:** *Interpretation*

6. A diplomat works with another nation. Therefore, it makes sense that he or she would speak at least two languages.
   Difficulty: *Average* **Objective:** *Vocabulary*

7. That summer, the antigovernment plot her father had been a part of "unraveled." People were leaving the country as quickly as they could to avoid arrest, so many of her friends and cousins were already gone. It had become unsafe for them, and for the author's family, to stay.
   Difficulty: *Challenging* **Objective:** *Literary Analysis*

8. The author is demonstrating that trying to leave the country was not necessarily safe or easy. She started to appreciate, at that point, the seriousness of her family's situation. The "cat-and-mouse game" played by the dictator was very real.
   Difficulty: *Average* **Objective:** *Reading*

9. She uses the phrase "Freedom and liberty and justice for all . . ." The phrase shows that she has finally made a connection between the American ideals she has been studying in school and the country to which they are going. Her family can only be free and safe in America, and they must go.
   Difficulty: *Challenging* **Objective:** *Reading*

10. **Beginning:** hates going to the American school
    Middle: "straightened out" in 5th grade but only to escape summer school
    End: tells the American official she is "ready for school"
    She goes from hating the American school to realizing that what she has already learned will help her in her new country.
    Difficulty: *Average* **Objective:** *Interpretation*

Essay

11. Sample answer: The author does not like going to the American school. It is different from and harder than the Dominican schools her friends attend. She does not understand why her mother insists she attend. She dislikes and resents having to learn "rocks-in-your-mouth" English and about pilgrims. She likens going to school with being "imprisoned."
    Difficulty: *Easy* **Objective:** *Essay*

12. The Dominican Republic was trapped under a brutal dictator before and during the author's childhood. The

author's parents were involved in antigovernment activities that eventually made it too dangerous for the family to remain in the Dominican Republic. When the plot was discovered, they were forced to flee with their children to the United States.

Difficulty: *Average*   **Objective:** *Essay*

13. At the beginning of "My First Free Summer," the young girl knows very little about what is happening politically. All she knows is that her friends gets lots of dictator-related holidays, and she is jealous. When her mother tells the children that they are leaving for the United States, she thinks they are going on a trip. Only after seeing her parents' fear and waiting for an airplane that does not appear does she realize that they are fleeing and in danger.

Difficulty: *Challenging*   **Objective:** *Essay*

14. Students may suggest that the best way to find the truth is to live it. The author knew she was missing something with every summer she was forced to go to summer school. The Dominican people knew they were living under the control of a brutal dictator who did not allow freedoms. Living without freedom made them appreciate the truth of freedom.

Difficulty: *Average*   **Objective:** *Essay*

Oral Response

15. Oral responses should be clear, well organized, and well supported by appropriate examples from the selection.

Difficulty: *Average*   **Objective:** *Oral Interpretation*

Selection Test A, p. 185

Critical Reading

1. ANS: B	DIF: Easy	OBJ: Literary Analysis
2. ANS: A	DIF: Easy	OBJ: Reading
3. ANS: D	DIF: Easy	OBJ: Comprehension
4. ANS: D	DIF: Easy	OBJ: Comprehension
5. ANS: D	DIF: Easy	OBJ: Interpretation
6. ANS: C	DIF: Easy	OBJ: Literary Analysis
7. ANS: B	DIF: Easy	OBJ: Reading
8. ANS: A	DIF: Easy	OBJ: Interpretation
9. ANS: A	DIF: Easy	OBJ: Reading
10. ANS: C	DIF: Easy	OBJ: Interpretation

Vocabulary and Grammar

11. ANS: A	DIF: Easy	OBJ: Vocabulary
12. ANS: A	DIF: Easy	OBJ: Grammar

Essay

13. Students will likely find more similarities than differences between Alvarez's attitudes and experiences and their own or those of their classmates. They may find the subjects she studies familiar—the Pilgrims; the geography of the states; the principles of freedom, liberty, and justice; and so on. They may share her ambivalence

about studying, and they may agree that learning a foreign language is the hardest thing of all. They might point out that unlike the Dominican Republic, the public schools in the United States are not dominated by a dictator who freely declares holidays.

Difficulty: *Easy*

Objective: *Essay*

14. Students should recognize that the ten-year-old Alvarez knew only that the dictator declared a great many school holidays and that during the summer of 1960 things changed: Her cousins had left for the United States, the U.S. embassy had closed and Americans were advised to leave the country, her parents were terrified, and a black Volkswagen that her sister said was driven by "secret police" blocked their driveway each night. At the airport, Alvarez realizes that the family's trip to the United States is not a vacation but an escape to freedom. The information the adult narrator fills in includes the fact that the country had been governed by a "bloody and repressive" dictatorship for the last thirty years and that her father had been involved in the antigovernment plot that was uncovered in 1960.

Difficulty: *Easy*

Objective: *Essay*

15. Students may suggest that the best way to know what it means to be free is to go through it themselves. The author knew she was missing something with every summer she was forced to go to summer school. The Dominican people knew they were living under the control of a dictator who did not allow freedoms. Living without freedom made them appreciate true freedom.

Difficulty: *Average*

Objective: *Essay*

Selection Test B, p. 188

Critical Reading

1. ANS: D	DIF: Average	OBJ: Interpretation
2. ANS: C	DIF: Challenging	OBJ: Literary Analysis
3. ANS: A	DIF: Average	OBJ: Reading
4. ANS: A	DIF: Average	OBJ: Interpretation
5. ANS: B	DIF: Challenging	OBJ: Interpretation
6. ANS: B	DIF: Average	OBJ: Interpretation
7. ANS: B	DIF: Average	OBJ: Reading
8. ANS: B	DIF: Average	OBJ: Comprehension
9. ANS: A	DIF: Average	OBJ: Interpretation
10. ANS: B	DIF: Challenging	OBJ: Reading
11. ANS: C	DIF: Average	OBJ: Reading
12. ANS: B	DIF: Challenging	OBJ: Literary Analysis

Vocabulary and Grammar

13. ANS: A	DIF: Average	OBJ: Vocabulary
14. ANS: B	DIF: Average	OBJ: Vocabulary

Essay

15. Students may name a number of purposes—to entertain, to inform, to reflect on events. Perhaps the best answer is that Alvarez's purpose is to reflect on the events of her tenth summer. Support for that point may be the ten-year-old Julia's realization that her family is escaping a dangerous political situation, that they are seeking "freedom and liberty and justice for all."

    Difficulty: *Average*

    Objective: *Essay*

16. Students should recognize that the ten-year-old Alvarez knew only that the dictator declared a great many school holidays and that during the summer of 1960 things changed: Her cousins left for the United States, the U.S. embassy closed, her parents were terrified, and her sister referred to "secret police" and the possibility of their being murdered. At the airport, Alvarez gains a wider perspective when she realizes that the family's trip to the United States is not a vacation but an escape to freedom. The information the adult narrator fills in includes the fact that the country had been governed by a "bloody and repressive" dictatorship and that her father had been involved in an antigovernment plot. Most students will probably agree that the story successfully integrates the two points of view. As evidence, they may point to the emotions the story elicits in readers as the family reaches its destination.

    Difficulty: *Challenging*

    Objective: *Essay*

17. Students may suggest that the best way to find the truth is to live it. The author knew she was missing something with every summer she was forced to go to summer school. The Dominican people knew they were living under the control of a brutal dictator who did not allow freedoms. Living without freedom made them appreciate the truth of freedom.

    Difficulty: *Average*

    Objective: *Essay*

"Angela's Ashes" by Frank McCourt

Vocabulary Warm-up Exercises, p. 192

A.
1. reciting
2. germs
3. apparatus
4. remarkable
5. parcel
6. stitches
7. ward
8. crisis

B. Sample Answers
1. A <u>torrent</u> means a fast-moving flood, so a torrent of words would not be spoken slowly.
2. Most likely you could not put a bandage on an <u>internal</u> injury because it is inside the body and could not be seen from the outside.

3. No, you could only accuse a person of <u>disobedience</u> if he does not follow the rules.
4. A plant suffering from <u>blight</u> has some sort of illness, so you could try to heal the plant by cleaning it, putting it in a new location, and perhaps spraying it with some plant medicine.
5. She does not expect him back in a week, because she gave him a <u>fortnight</u> off, which means two weeks.
6. If your friend <u>collapsed</u> suddenly on the sidewalk, you would try to make the friend comfortable and call 911 to seek medical help, if needed.
7. One reason people like to visit <u>foreign</u> countries is to see what life is like in countries outside of their home country.
8. If a person injured his leg or foot and could not walk easily, then that person's <u>circumstances</u> might require the use of crutches.

Reading Warm-up A, p. 193

Sample Answers

1. (small package); The *parcel* Jan received in the mail contained two books.
2. <u>group of patient rooms</u>: You would see beds, doctors, nurses, and medicines in a hospital *ward*.
3. <u>five kidney-shaped purple pillows, sewn together in a line</u>; Lulu could pretend her stomach was under her hat or up her sleeve and stuff the pillows in one of those places.
4. <u>some young patients were still very sick. They had not yet started to get better</u>; Jack's parents sat up with him all night until the swelling in his leg started to go down and they knew the crisis was over.
5. (his head had been sewn up after an operation); You can find stitches in clothing, in bed linens, in stuffed animals, in sails used on sailboats, and in the upholstery inside of cars.
6. (a silly poem); Jasmine loved the song so much that she memorized the words without realizing it and found herself <u>reciting</u> them to her friends the next day at lunch.
7. Erik's crown was *remarkable* because it was made of balloons, three feet long, and shaped like a boat; I once visited the Grand Canyon, which is so huge, beautiful, and unusual that it is <u>remarkable</u>.
8. <u>bacteria . . . dirty the royal crown!</u>; It would not be a good idea for a child who is already sick or weak from an operation to be exposed to *germs*, which can cause illness.

Reading Warm-up B, p. 194

Sample Answers

1. <u>It could take time for a body to show outward signs of a disease</u>: Jack fell down and got a scratch on his head, but the doctor determined he had no *internal* injuries.
2. <u>the whole crew was kept out of the city. The ship's cargo was burned</u>: A person who *collapsed* might have done so after running a long race or after suffering extreme fatigue.

Unit 1 Resources: Fiction and Nonfiction

3. (plague); The survivors of the hurricane were grateful for everyone's help, and their words of thanks burst from them like a *torrent* of water rushing over rocks.

4. A person could be fined, arrested, or even put to death: Obedience, following orders, compliance.

5. One person might be exposed to radioactive materials. Another person might have a virus that is hard to cure: The word *circumstances* is used to mean the situation a person finds himself in, or the events that have happened to put him in the place where he is now.

6. (or for twice as long as that—an entire month); There are twelve *fortnights* in six months.

7. plants, live animals; When he is at home in Mexico he likes to wear hats from his trips to *foreign* countries like China and Peru.

8. (Plant parasites and other plant diseases); The plant turned brown because it did not receive enough water, not because it was suffering from any *blight*.

Writing About the Big Question, p. 195

A. 1. explain
2. insight
3. evaluate, reveal

B. Sample Answers

1. I would write a memoir about transferring to a new school in the seventh grade and having to find friends. I would write about how kind some kids were to me so that readers would **conclude** that it is very important to welcome newcomers to their schools.

2. I would ask my grandfather to write a memoir about what life was like when he was growing up. The **reality** of life without computers and television would give me an **awareness** of how life has changed over the past seventy years.

C. Sample Answer

may later prove to be very important.

If the author cheated on a test and felt guilty for many years about it, she could then use that experience in writing a work of fiction. She could write a story about an older person who feels guilty, or she may use it in a story about a kid trying to decide whether to cheat on a test.

Reading: Use Background Information to Determine the Author's Purpose, p. 196

1. to inform the reader about Patricia's illness

2. to create a mood—to evoke the loneliness and desolate atmosphere of the hospital

3. to entertain with Patricia's mockery of the nurse's scolding

Literary Analysis: Historical Context, p. 197

1. This passage makes it clear that there is a war going on, that Francis's family is very poor, and that there are shortages of basic necessities like bread. It is possible

that the poverty of Francis's family is one reason that he got sick.

2. Seamus refers to the long history of Ireland's sufferings, which forms a cultural and historical background to the individual suffering of Francis and Patricia in the story.

3. The nurse refers to Irish people's resentment of the English, whom they have always regarded as their cruel masters—perhaps even responsible for the conditions of poverty and ill health that have led to Ireland's misfortunes of the past and present.

Vocabulary Builder, p. 198

A. Sample Responses:

1. To protect the health of the people, the town will ban trans fats in restaurant food.

2. After losing five games in a row, the basketball team was desperate for a win.

3. After running in the heat, I wanted to guzzle the whole glass of water.

4. This ticket line is so long that it will take a miracle for us to get into the show.

5. On Memorial Day, we sang patriotic songs to honor soldiers who had died in wars.

6. In the army, saluting an officer of higher rank is standard practice.

B. 1. F; A person who feels desperate on first seeing an exam probably does not know any answers and so does not expect to do well.

2. T; A person who is in despair is without hope and so is likely to have a negative outlook on life.

3. F; A time of prosperity is a time of wealth, so people would probably not be living in poverty.

Enrichment: Medical Science, p. 199

Typhoid Fever

Symptoms: high fever, sweating, digestive problems, rarely a rash

Cause: caused by the bacteria *Salmonella typhi*

How common in 1940: fairly rare—declined during first half of twentieth century because of vaccinations and better hygiene

How common now: extremely rare because of antibiotics

Diagnosis: tests of blood marrow and stool cultures, Widal test

Treatment: antibiotics

Diphtheria

Symptoms: sore throat, fever, chills, cough; membrane forms on tonsils, pharynx, and nasal cavity

Cause: caused by the bacteria *Corynebacterium diphtheriae*; spreads by physical contact, sneezing

How common in 1940: Common before 1940; In the 1920s about 100,000 to 200,000 cases of diphtheria per year in the United States, with about 13,000 to 15,000 deaths

How common now: Very rare—almost wiped out in advanced countries thanks to antibiotics available after World War II

Diagnosis: throat exam, throat culture

Treatment: antibiotics and injection of antitoxin

"My First Free Summer" by Julia Alvarez
"Angela's Ashes" by Frank McCourt

Integrated Language Skills: Grammar, p. 200

A. 1. her; 2. my, her; 3. their; 4. our; 5. his; 6. their
B. 1. her, her; 2. my, their; 3. her; 4. his; 5. their

"Angela's Ashes" by Frank McCourt

Open-Book Test, p. 203

Short Answer

1. The word *miracle* suggests that Frank's recovery is a remarkable event. The fact that Frank is a marvel for surviving typhoid suggests that the disease is often deadly.
   Difficulty: *Easy*   **Objective:** *Vocabulary*

2. Sample answers: "You won't be able to stop marching and saluting." "Say your rosary, Francis, and pray for your internal apparatus." These details show that Patricia was full of life and enjoyed having fun.
   Difficulty: *Average*   **Objective:** *Interpretation*

3. During a war there are likely to be shortages of basic products, such as flour. The flour mill therefore needs to produce more flour and will employ a lot of people in order to do so.
   Difficulty: *Challenging*   **Objective:** *Literary Analysis*

4. With so little to do and nobody to talk to, Frank and Patricia have a very great desire or need for companionship and diversion.
   Difficulty: *Average*   **Objective:** *Vocabulary*

5. Seamus is generous and sympathetic. Students should cite one of Seamus's generous acts. For example, he takes the children's side when they are scolded by the nurse. He talks kindly to them.
   Difficulty: *Easy*   **Objective:** *Interpretation*

6. They have a lot in common: They have suffered or are suffering from serious illnesses, and they are in a place that is unfriendly. They also share a love of reading.
   Difficulty: *Challenging*   **Objective:** *Interpretation*

7. Because of the conflict, the nurses disapprove of the book on English history that Frank reads and the English poem that Frank and Patricia enjoy.
   Difficulty: *Average*   **Objective:** *Literary Analysis*

8. The Kerry nurse and Sister Rita are supposed to be comforting the sick. Instead, they are unkind to the two

sick children and punish them. Their cruelty makes Patricia's death even more touching.
   Difficulty: *Challenging*   **Objective:** *Reading*

9. From the nurse's words and tone it is clear that the hatred of the Irish for the English is long-standing and deep.
   Difficulty: *Easy*   **Objective:** *Interpretation*

10. Patricia was a smart, beautiful girl with a wonderful attitude. Seamus thinks it is terrible that such a good person should have died alone in a bathroom.
    Difficulty: *Average*   **Objective:** *Interpretation*

Essay

11. Students should note that when children are recovering from an illness in a hospital, they need company, and they need to be involved in interesting activities. In the Fever Hospital, Frank and Patricia are not allowed to talk to each other. The only activity they are allowed is reading, but they may read only religious books, which are probably not very interesting. The children also probably want to be comforted, but instead the nurses only scold them and take away the few pleasures they have.
    Difficulty: *Easy*   **Objective:** *Essay*

12. Students might suggest that all of the humor in the excerpt shows that the young Frank recognized and appreciated humor. He also seemed to observe people's characteristics—for example, the Kerry nurse's accent and Seamus's concerns about his job. That observation of detail, along with his discovery of Shakespeare and his enjoyment of "The Highwayman," are indications that he might later become a writer. Students will likely also point out that Frank was lonely (he wants his father to visit) and sensitive (he feels like crying when he learns that Patricia will soon die).
    Difficulty: *Average*   **Objective:** *Essay*

13. Students should recognize that Patricia could write about only what she knows, so conversations between Frank and the other characters would be reported only if Patricia overheard them or was told about them. On the other hand, Patricia could reveal her thoughts and feelings. For example, the reader would learn whether she realizes she is going to die and, if she does, how she feels about dying so young. After Frank is taken upstairs, she would know about him only from Seamus's reports. In addition, the narrative would have to end differently—before her death.
    Difficulty: *Challenging*   **Objective:** *Essay*

14. In their essays, students should point to the references to English and Irish history as an indication that the bad feelings between the two peoples are rooted in history. They should recognize that McCourt (or anyone else) could best find the truth about the animosity by researching the history of Ireland's relationship to England.
    Difficulty: *Average*   **Objective:** *Essay*

Oral Response

15. Oral responses should be clear, well organized, and well supported by appropriate examples from the excerpt from McCourt's memoir.

    Difficulty: *Average*   **Objective:** *Oral Interpretation*

Selection Test A, p. 206

Critical Reading

1. ANS: C   DIF: Average   OBJ: Comprehension
2. ANS: A   DIF: Easy   OBJ: Interpretation
3. ANS: A   DIF: Easy   OBJ: Comprehension
4. ANS: B   DIF: Average   OBJ: Interpretation
5. ANS: D   DIF: Average   OBJ: Reading Skill
6. ANS: B   DIF: Challenging   OBJ: Literary Analysis
7. ANS: C   DIF: Average   OBJ: Literary Analysis
8. ANS: D   DIF: Easy   OBJ: Literary Analysis
9. ANS: C   DIF: Easy   OBJ: Literary Analysis
10. ANS: B   DIF: Average   OBJ: Reading Skill
11. ANS: C   DIF: Easy   OBJ: Interpretation
12. ANS: D   DIF: Easy   OBJ: Interpretation
13. ANS: D   DIF: Average   OBJ: Interpretation
14. ANS: A   DIF: Easy   OBJ: Comprehension

Vocabulary

15. ANS: B   DIF: Average   OBJ: Vocabulary
16. ANS: A   DIF: Easy   OBJ: Vocabulary
17. ANS: C   DIF: Easy   OBJ: Vocabulary
18. ANS: C   DIF: Average   OBJ: Vocabulary

Essay

19. Some students might prefer a private room because their roommate might not be as charming and engaging as Patricia is, and they might value privacy over companionship.. Others might prefer having a roommate, even at the risk of having someone who is not so charming, because being alone in a hospital bed can be very boring and lonely.

    Difficulty: *Easy*

    Objective: *Easay*

20. Seamus helps Francis and Patricia to become friends, even though the nurses disapprove. He helps them exchange books and messages, and helps them to communicate with each other. He is also friendly when other people around them are not.

    Difficulty: *Average*

    Objective: *Easay*

21. Students should note that the friendship between Francis and Patricia begins because both are confined in the hospital. When they start talking, they realize that they both have a sense of humor and that they dislike the strict nurses. Finally, they learn that they both love reading and literature, and they share their favorite passages from the books they are reading.

    Difficulty: *Easy*

    Objective: *Essay*

22. In their essays, students might suggest researching books, encyclopedias, Web sites that give information about English and Irish history. They might also suggest interviews with people who are familiar with the conflict.

    Difficulty: *Easy*

    Objective: *Essay*

Selection Test B, p. 209

Critical Reading

1. ANS: D   DIF: Average   OBJ: Comprehension
2. ANS: C   DIF: Easy   OBJ: Interpretation
3. ANS: B   DIF: Easy   OBJ: Literary Analysis
4. ANS: D   DIF: Average   OBJ: Interpretation
5. ANS: A   DIF: Challenging   OBJ: Literary Analysis
6. ANS: A   DIF: Challenging   OBJ: Literary Analysis
7. ANS: B   DIF: Average   OBJ: Reading Skill
8. ANS: D   DIF: Challenging   OBJ: Reading Skill
9. ANS: C   DIF: Challenging   OBJ: Comprehension
10. ANS: A   DIF: Easy   OBJ: Comprehension
11. ANS: C   DIF: Average   OBJ: Interpretation
12. ANS: D   DIF: Average   OBJ: Interpretation

Vocabulary

13. ANS: C   DIF: Average   OBJ: Vocabulary
14. ANS: D   DIF: Average   OBJ: Vocabulary
15. ANS: A   DIF: Average   OBJ: Vocabulary
16. ANS: A   DIF: Average   OBJ: Grammar
17. ANS: D   DIF: Average   OBJ: Grammar

Essay

18. Some students might write that a patient recovering from surgery or an illness might not be able to concentrate, so that reading might be difficult, and TV or Internet surfing might be better. Others might write that watching TV or surfing the Internet don't really stimulate the imagination as well as reading, so that books might be a better escape.

    Difficulty: *Easy*

    Objective: *Easay*

19. Students might note that the nurses stick by a strict set of rules.; for example, they are afraid that communication between the patients might spread germs, and they also believe that it is wrong for a boy and girl to become friends. Seamus is far more sympathetic to the patients' need for human contact and entertainment, and he helps them to communicate and to exchange books and messages. Some students might say that the nurses' approach is designed to protect the patients' well-being, Others might note that the nurses' are too strict and do not think about the real human needs, as Seamus does.

    Difficulty: *Average*

    Objective: *Essay*

20. Students might note that literature and books give Patricia and Francis a common interest on which to base their friendship. The literature and books that they share also make them feel better even though they are in a difficult, strict environment and have to deal with strict treatment by the nurses. Their love of literature becomes a way that they can rebel and that ties them closer together.

Difficulty: *Easy*

Objective: *Essay*

21. In their essays, students should refer to English and Irish history as a sign that the bad feelings between the two peoples have a long history. They should recog-nize that McCourt (or anyone else) could best find the truth about the bad feelings by researching the history of Ire-land's relationship to England.

Difficulty: *Easy*

Objective: *Essay*

"Stolen Day" by Sherwood Anderson
"The Night the Bed Fell" by James Thurber

Vocabulary Warm-up Exercises, p. 213

A. 1. formed
2. nervous
3. persuaded
4. confident
5. frantic
6. occasions
7. incidents
8. suspected

B. 1. Tom was very <u>solemn</u> and never laughed or told jokes.
2. Jane read a book, and <u>afterwards</u>, she fell asleep.
3. Lynn <u>detected</u> smoke, so she hung up with Gina and called 911.
4. Carl was <u>accustomed</u> to waking up early since he had done it many times before.
5. The empty box in Drake's room is <u>evidence</u> that he ate the cookies.
6. Mary's <u>apprehension</u> was so great that she refused to enter the cave.
7. The sun indicated that the rain was about to <u>cease</u>.

Reading Warm-up A, p. 214

Sample Answers

1. (guessed); Rita suspected that someone had been read-ing her diary.
2. <u>morning assembly</u>; Occasions are times or events.
3. <u>when the class formed a line to go outside, when they walked through the halls to the library, and when they traded homework papers to grade</u>; Several incidents with my friend Karen got me in trouble.
4. (a line); I formed a language club at school.

5. <u>He had spent nearly the entire morning near his class-mate</u>; certain.
6. (panicked); We were frantic as we searched for the miss-ing ring.
7. (worry); I was nervous before my piano recital.
8. <u>But you'll have to stay home from school for a while</u>; convinced.

Reading Warm-up B, p. 215

Sample Answers

1. (stop); Mr. Jones demanded that the class cease talking immediately.
2. <u>the monster that had lived for years in the hall closet</u>; proof.
3. (expression); serious.
4. <u>that the sound was coming from within her parents' room</u>; The animals detected that a storm was about to hit the forest.
5. (turn back); The soldiers marched <u>onward</u> for two days before reaching the fortress.
6. <u>The growls grew fiercer and Sally became more fright-ened.</u>; Someone may have apprehension about getting a bad grade.
7. <u>Sally was sure she could never get used to such an obnoxious noise.</u>; I am accustomed to eating an early dinner.
8. (she fell asleep); *Afterwards* means later.

Writing About the Big Question, p. 216

A. 1. reality/truth
2. perceive
3. believable

B. Sample Answers

1. what to eat for dinner;   what time to go to bed
2. I would **explain** my side of the story and give as much **factual evidence** as I could. I would tell the whole **truth** and hope to be believed.

C. Sample Answer

they may each have a different perception of what happened.

On my birthday, my brother forgot to say happy birthday to me. He did not say it until our mother reminded him. He was being self-centered.

I didn't say happy birthday to my brother because I woke up with a terrible headache and couldn't think clearly. When it finally got better, I said happy birthday to him but he was already angry.

Literary Analysis: Comparing Characters, p. 217

Sample Answers

[Character: Briggs Beall in "The Night the Bed Fell"]

[Words that describe the character directly] nervous, has his crotchets

[What the character says and does] He wakes up every hour to ensure he's still breathing.

[How other characters talk about or act toward the character] The narrator deceives him by telling him that if Briggs stops breathing, he'll wake up and save him.

[Character: The mother in "The Night the Bed Fell"]

[Words that describe the character directly] hysterical, frantic

[What the character says and does] When she hears a bed fall, she believes that the father is dying from the bed falling on him in the attic.

[How other characters talk about or act toward the character] They try to reassure her that they are all right and that she is all right.

[Character: Narrator in "Stolen Day"]

[Words that describe the character directly: "It must be that all children are actors"; "I got tired of sitting and was lying on the porch."]

[What the character says and does: "'I ache all over,' I said"; "I never ran so hard in my life."]

[How other characters talk about or act toward the character: She [Mother] was pretty busy that day and hadn't paid much attention to me"; "It made me sick to hear them, the way they all laughed."]

Vocabulary Builder, p. 218

Sample Answers to items 1, 3, 6, and 7

A.
1. The girl's smile was *ominous* as she pulled the tail of her new puppy.
2. Correct
3. The boy was *solemn* after he heard the bad news.
4. Correct
5. Correct
6. The smells from the cheese counter were *pungent*.
7. The man with a criminal record was considered the most likely *culprit* of the robbery.

B.
1. C
2. D
3. A
4. B
5. C
6. A
7. D

Open-Book Test, p. 220

Short Answer

1. The boy begins to think he has Walter's illness because that disease prevents Walter from having to attend school but still allows him to get around and go fishing.
   Difficulty: *Average*   **Objective:** *Interpretation*

2. This scary flashback supports his feeling that his mother does not pay attention to him but would be very upset if he were found dead.
   Difficulty: *Challenging*   **Objective:** *Interpretation*

3. Sample examples: "He had been able to walk down there all right."; "I kept on crying and it worked all right." Reveals jealousy of Walter; ability to get what he wants even if he lies.

   The narrator is pretty self-centered. He wants the attention and freedom and doesn't care what he does to get them.
   Difficulty: *Average*   **Objective:** *Interpretation*

4. Solemn means "serious." The family bursts into laughter when the narrator announces he has inflammatory rheumatism. Their reaction is the opposite of solemn.
   Difficulty: *Challenging*   **Objective:** *Vocabulary*

5. They are unusual. Each member has definite ideas that contribute to a more and more ridiculous situation.
   Difficulty: *Easy*   **Objective:** *Interpretation*

6. Since *ominous* means "threatening," you would feel fearful if you heard ominous sounds.
   Difficulty: *Average*   **Objective:** *Vocabulary*

7. The family in "Stolen Day" is presented more realistically. They go to school and to work. The mother cares for the family. The family in "The Night the Bed Fell" is almost unreal because they are all so ridiculous. Each one is more absurd than the next.
   Difficulty: *Easy*   **Objective:** *Literary Analysis*

8. Anderson portrays the mother as a straightforward and busy woman. She cares for her son and is responsible. In contrast, Thurber portrays his mother as excitable and silly. With little proof, she insists that the bed fell on her husband and causes an uproar.
   Difficulty: *Average*   **Objective:** *Literary Analysis*

9. The boy relates more of his feelings so the reader can feel more for his situation. For example, we know that he is embarrassed when his family laughs at him and that he is hurt when his mother ignores him. Thurber does not take things as seriously.
   Difficulty: *Average*   **Objective:** *Literary Analysis*

10. Thurber is more successful. He recognizes that family members are eccentric and does not allow it to bother him. On the other hand, the boy in "Stolen Day" bears the brunt of his family's laughter. Rather than playing this down, he lets it bother him and winds up in tears.
    Difficulty: *Challenging*   **Objective:** *Literary Analysis*

Essay

11. Students will probably find the narrator from "Stolen Day" to be ridiculous. Just because he admires Walter's freedom, he decides he has inflammatory rheumatism. When his family laughs at him, he doesn't see the humor in his situation and just cries. Students could choose almost any character from "The Night the Bed Fell" as being ridiculous. For example, they might choose the mother. She is so excitable that she immediately panics when she hears the crash, assuming that the bed has fallen on her husband. Rather than getting the facts, she turns the entire household into an uproar

Unit 1 Resources: Fiction and Nonfiction

over the event. The fact that these characters are ridiculous adds humor to both selections.

Difficulty: *Easy* **Objective:** *Essay*

12. Most students will feel that the boy in "Stolen Day" learns the most. The story ends with him in tears because his family laughs at him for believing he has inflammatory rheumatism. This incident might teach him that it does not pay to try to be something you are not. Also, the joy in being physically able to reel in the fish might teach him to be thankful that he is a healthy boy. Most students will probably say that Thurber learns the least in "The Night the Bed Fell." He is very aware at the beginning of the essay that his family is eccentric and he has come to terms with this fact. One further incident showing their eccentricity probably does not have much of an effect on him one way or the other.

Difficulty: *Average* **Objective:** *Essay*

13. Students might note that the boys would talk about difficulties with family members. They would agree that families present challenges. On the other hand, they might disagree in how seriously to take these difficulties. Thurber would probably suggest that the young boy takes things too seriously and that he should not have taken offense when the others laughed. The young boy might suggest that Thurber should take time to think through situations before reacting to them, such as when he is sure he is in danger.

Difficulty: *Challenging* **Objective:** *Essay*

14. Students who choose "Stolen Day" might say that the story shows that thinking things through will eventually lead to the truth. The narrator tries to convince himself that he has inflammatory rheumatism and that his mother does not care about him. The truth, of course, is the exact opposite, which he realizes by the end of the day. Students choosing Thurber's essay probably will point out that almost nobody in his family seems to recognize the truth. They all deal with reality through their own eccentricities. However, the truth of the situation is eventually found simply because everyone keeps going until the mess is sorted out.

Difficulty: *Average* **Objective:** *Essay*

Oral Response

15. Oral responses should be clear, well organized, and well supported by appropriate examples from the selections.

Difficulty: *Average* **Objective:** *Oral Interpretation*

Selection Test A, p. 223

Critical Reading

1. ANS: C	DIF: Easy	OBJ: Comprehension
2. ANS: B	DIF: Easy	OBJ: Comprehension
3. ANS: D	DIF: Easy	OBJ: Interpretation
4. ANS: A	DIF: Easy	OBJ: Interpretation
5. ANS: D	DIF: Average	OBJ: Literary Analysis
6. ANS: A	DIF: Average	OBJ: Comprehension
7. ANS: C	DIF: Average	OBJ: Literary Analysis

8. ANS: D	DIF: Average	OBJ: Interpretation
9. ANS: C	DIF: Easy	OBJ: Comprehension
10. ANS: D	DIF: Average	OBJ: Interpretation
11. ANS: B	DIF: Easy	OBJ: Comprehension
12. ANS: B	DIF: Average	OBJ: Literary Analysis
13. ANS: C	DIF: Average	OBJ: Interpretation
14. ANS: D	DIF: Average	OBJ: Interpretation
15. ANS: A	DIF: Average	OBJ: Interpretation
16. ANS: B	DIF: Average	OBJ: Literary Analysis

Vocabulary

17. ANS: C	DIF: Average	OBJ: Vocabulary
18. ANS: C	DIF: Average	OBJ: Vocabulary
19. ANS: B	DIF: Average	OBJ: Vocabulary

Essay

20. When students write about "Stolen Day," they will most likely write about the mother. When they write about "The Night the Bed Fell," they may write about any number of colorful characters portrayed in the story. The key to the analysis is that the students' essays focus on one character from each story and that they adequately describe the character. A successful essay will include specific ways that each writer developed the character in the story and the narrator's relationship to the character.

Difficulty: *Average*

Objective: *Literary Analysis*

21. The narrator of "Stolen Day" is a boy who is seeking attention within his family. They ridicule him regularly, and he has several siblings and a busy mother. The boy tells his teacher and mother that he aches, but this did not get him much sympathy or attention. After he goes fishing, he does become a big hero in the family. This then is quickly deflated by his family ridiculing him for telling them that he has inflammatory rheumatism. The boy in "The Night the Bed Fell" is much more comfortable with his place in his family. They all have eccentric ways, and he seems amused by them but not bothered. We see a clear picture of him by how he handles Briggs Beall's unreasonable thought that he will suffocate in his sleep. The boy assures him that he will monitor his breathing as they sleep and will be there to wake him. It's as if he is the pillar of sanity within his family.

Difficulty: *Average*

Objective: *Literary Analysis*

22. Students who choose "Stolen Day" might say that the story shows that thinking through things will lead to the truth. The narrator tries to convince himself that he has inflammatory rheumatism and that his mother does not care about him. The truth, of course, is the exact opposite, which he realizes by the end of the day. Students choosing "The Night the Bed Fell" might note that nearly everyone in this family has trouble seeing the truth. They all deal with reality in a peculiar way. However,

they eventually do find the truth because everyone keeps going until the mess is sorted out.

Difficulty: *Average*

Objective: *Essay*

Selection Test B, p. 226

Critical Reading

1. ANS: D	DIF: Average	OBJ: Interpretation
2. ANS: C	DIF: Average	OBJ: Comprehension
3. ANS: A	DIF: Challenging	OBJ: Interpretation
4. ANS: A	DIF: Average	OBJ: Comprehension
5. ANS: B	DIF: Average	OBJ: Interpretation
6. ANS: C	DIF: Average	OBJ: Interpretation
7. ANS: C	DIF: Average	OBJ: Literary Analysis
8. ANS: D	DIF: Average	OBJ: Literary Analysis
9. ANS: A	DIF: Average	OBJ: Literary Analysis
10. ANS: D	DIF: Average	OBJ: Literary Analysis
11. ANS: A	DIF: Challenging	OBJ: Literary Analysis
12. ANS: C	DIF: Challenging	OBJ: Literary Analysis
13. ANS: B	DIF: Challenging	OBJ: Literary Analysis
14. ANS: A	DIF: Average	OBJ: Interpretation
15. ANS: A	DIF: Average	OBJ: Interpretation

Vocabulary

16. ANS: B	DIF: Average	OBJ: Vocabulary
17. ANS: A	DIF: Average	OBJ: Vocabulary
18. ANS: A	DIF: Average	OBJ: Vocabulary
19. ANS: B	DIF: Average	OBJ: Vocabulary

Essay

20. When students write about "Stolen Day," they will most likely write about the mother. When they write about "The Night the Bed Fell," they may write about any number of colorful characters portrayed in the story. The key to the analysis is that the students' essays focus on one character from each story. A successful essay will cite specifics from each text that demonstrate how each writer developed the character in the story through the character's words and actions. Students must compare the two characters, citing similarities to or differences from the text.

Difficulty: *Challenging*

Objective: *Literary Analysis*

21. The narrator of "Stolen Day" is a boy who is seeking attention within his family. They ridicule him regularly, and he has several siblings and a busy mother. The boy in "The Night the Bed Fell" is much more comfortable with his place in his family. His family members have eccentric ways, and he seems amused by them, not bothered. Successful essays will cite specific details from each text where the boys' thoughts, words, and actions reveal

key elements to the boys' characters. A key scene in "Stolen Day" occurs when the narrator's mother does not pay him much attention after he tells her he aches, he gets angry, and goes fishing. A key scene in "The Night the Bed Fell" occurs when the narrator reassures Briggs Beall that he will keep watch over him as he sleeps and not let him suffocate. One boy is deflated by his family, the other is seemingly the pillar of sanity within his family.

Difficulty: *Average*

Objective: *Essay*

22. Students who choose "Stolen Day" might say that the story shows that thinking through things will eventually lead to the truth. The narrator tries to convince himself that he has inflammatory rheumatism and that his mother does not care about him. The truth, of course, is the exact opposite, which he realizes by the end of the day. Students choosing Thurber's essay probably will point out that almost nobody in his family seems to recognize the truth. They all deal with reality through their own eccentricities. However, the truth of the situation is eventually found simply because everyone keeps going until the mess is sorted out.

Difficulty: *Average*

Objective: *Essay*

Writing Workshop

Autobiographical Narrative: Integrating Grammar Skills, p. 230

A. 1. <u>Everyone</u> needed to study **his or her** notes for the test.

2. <u>Most</u> of the students wrote **their** notes in spiral notebooks.

3. A <u>few</u> of my friends copied **their** notes onto a computer.

4. Neither <u>Jack</u> nor <u>Leon</u> could find **his** notes.

B. 1. Most of the students enjoyed **their** art classes.

2. Carlos was learning the skills that **he** needed to become a sculptor.

3. Everyone in the pottery class had **his or her** chance to use the potter's wheel.

4. Either Sonya or Penny had two of **her** fashion designs made into dresses.

Vocabulary Workshop—1, pp. 231–232

Sample Answers

A. Some answers may vary, based on the dictionary used. Possible responses are shown.

1. 4 syllables

2. noun

3. Latin, Middle English

4. 3 definitions

5. round, rounded, plump

B. Synonyms and sentences will vary. Possible responses are shown.

1. noun
2. a method for sending things or mail rapidly
3. chuckle, giggle, snicker
4. Samples: raced, zoomed, sprinted
5. Samples: shouted, whispered, whined

Benchmark Test 2, p. 234

MULTIPLE CHOICE

1. ANS: C
2. ANS: D
3. ANS: A
4. ANS: B
5. ANS: C
6. ANS: D
7. ANS: B
8. ANS: D
9. ANS: A
10. ANS: C
11. ANS: A
12. ANS: D
13. ANS: B
14. ANS: D
15. ANS: B
16. ANS: C
17. ANS: A
18. ANS: C
19. ANS: A
20. ANS: B
21. ANS: B
22. ANS: C
23. ANS: A
24. ANS: B
25. ANS: A
26. ANS: C
27. ANS: A
28. ANS: C
29. ANS: A
30. ANS: C

WRITING

31. Students' paragraphs should adequately answer the six questions in four or fewer sentences.
32. Students' letters should clearly state the topic of their proposed article, a brief summary of the article, and persuasive reasons why the magazine should publish the article. Each letter should also include a date, greeting, closing, and signature.
33. Students' timelines should show at least three details related to an autobiographical narrative about a humorous event. The details should be in chronological order and should be written in complete sentences.

Vocabulary in Context, p. 240

MULTIPLE CHOICE

1. ANS: A
2. ANS: B
3. ANS: A
4. ANS: C
5. ANS: C
6. ANS: D
7. ANS: C
8. ANS: A
9. ANS: A
10. ANS: C
11. ANS: B
12. ANS: D
13. ANS: B
14. ANS: A
15. ANS: D
16. ANS: D
17. ANS: D
18. ANS: C
19. ANS: C
20. ANS: B